THE RIGHT TO BE FORGOTTEN ON THE INTERNET

GOOGLE *v* SPAIN

ARTEMI RALLO

Electronic Privacy Information Center
1718 Connecticut Ave. NW
Suite 200

Visit the EPIC Bookstore
http://www.epic.org/bookstore

SUMMARY

INTRODUCTION TO THE ENGLISH EDITION

CHAPTER I.- THE RIGHT TO BE FORGOTTEN: A SUCCESSFUL YET EQUIVOCAL EMERGING CONCEPT

1.- OBLIVION AS A POTENTIAL ALL-ENCOMPASSING RIGHT: ITS NECESSARY NARROWING TO THE VIRTUAL WORLD OF THE INTERNET

2.- RECOGNITION OF THE RIGHT TO BE FORGOTTEN IN THE EUROPEAN UNION

2.1.- BACKGROUND (2009): THE RIGHT TO BE FORGOTTEN AS DATA PORTABILITY AND ERASURE ON THE INTERNET

2.2.- THE EUROPEAN COMMISSION'S COMMUNICATION *A COMPREHENSIVE APPROACH ON PERSONAL DATA PROTECTION IN THE EUROPEAN UNION* (2010): THE RIGHT TO BE FORGOTTEN AS ERASURE OF PERSONAL DATA

2.3.- THE DRAFT EUROPEAN REGULATION ON DATA PROTECTION (2012): THE RIGHT TO BE FORGOTTEN AS A RIGHT TO "NOTIFY" THIRD PARTIES OF REQUESTS FOR DELETION

2.4.- THE LONG EUROPEAN DEBATE AND THE PRESSURES OF MULTINATIONAL TECHNOLOGY CORPORATIONS AGAINST THE RIGHT TO BE FORGOTTEN (2012-2016)

2.5.- RECOGNITION OF THE RIGHT TO BE FORGOTTEN IN THE GENERAL DATA PROTECTION REGULATION (2016)

CHAPTER II.- THE RIGHT TO BE FORGOTTEN IN SPAIN (I): THE OBJECTION/ERASURE OF DATA INDEXED BY SEARCH ENGINES ON THE INTERNET

1.- THE SINGULARITY OF A *GENUINELY* SPANISH PROBLEM: INDEXATION OF OFFICIAL GAZETTES

1.1.- The "first case" regarding the right to be forgotten: notice of an administrative penalty published in the Official Gazette

1.2.- The indexation of Constitutional Court (*Tribunal Constitucional,*

3

2.8.- Specific criteria for two distinct domains: online media and digital versions of official gazettes

CHAPTER IV.- THE RIGHT TO BE FORGOTTEN IN EUROPE

1.- EUROPEAN AND AMERICAN COMPARATIVE LAW

2.- JUDICIAL PRECEDENTS

2.1.- Deletion of personal data (and its impact on the Internet) in the case law of the European Court of Human Rights (ECtHR)

2.2.- The Court of Justice of the European Union (CJEU) as a driving force for data protection on the Internet

3.- QUESTION REFERRED BY THE SPANISH NATIONAL HIGH COURT TO THE CJEU FOR A PRELIMINARY RULING (C-131/12)

3.1.- The case of an administrative announcement of an auction resulting from a seizure published in *La Vanguardia*: ¿a bad *leading case*?

3.2.- The questions referred by the Spanish National High Court (*Audiencia Nacional*): Decision of 27 February 2013

4.- THE OPINION OF THE ADVOCATE GENERAL OF THE CJEU (25.6.13): *REJECTION OF THE RIGHT TO BE FORGOTTEN IN THE CURRENT EU LEGAL SYSTEM*

4.1.- A *preliminary assumption*: the development of the Internet requires reducing the scope of protection of the right to data protection

4.2.- Application of national legislation to search engines with establishments involved in selling targeted advertising to inhabitants of that Member State

4.3.- The search engine "processes" personal data, but it is not the "controller" due to its *unawareness* of their nature as personal data

4.4.- The Directive does not provide for a general right to be forgotten based on *subjective preferences*

5.- THE JUDGMENT OF THE CJEU (*CASE C-131/12*, 13 MAY 2014, *GOOGLE SPAIN v. AEPD*): THE UNQUESTIONABLE EFFECTIVE PROTECTION OF THE RIGHT TO BE FORGOTTEN AGAINST

INTERNET SEARCH ENGINES

5.1.- The *constitutional* protection of the right to data protection as a general principle of EU law enshrined in the Charter of Fundamental Rights of the European Union (CFREU)

5.2.- An impeccable understanding of the function of Internet search engines in today's information society and of their impact on privacy

5.3.- The activity of search engines constitutes "processing" of "personal data"

5.4.- National subsidiaries intended to sell advertising space offered by the search engine are "establishments" subject to national legislation

5.5.- Internet search engines have a primary "responsibility," separate and different from that of webmasters

5.6.- The right to data protection prevails over the "mere economic interest" of search engines, which are not covered by the "journalistic exemption"

5.7.- The individual right to data protection prevails over a general "interest of Internet users"

5.8.- The rights to erasure and to object as a balanced tool to require the search engines to remove the data even if they were lawfully published and even if the webmaster has not erased them

5.9.- The "course of time" justifies the right to be forgotten without "harm or prejudice" being required

5.10.- Limits of the right to be forgotten: data concerning "public figures" or "information of public interest"

CHAPTER V.- THE IMPLEMENTATION OF THE CJEU JUDGMENT (*CASE* GOOGLE V. SPAIN)

1.- GOOGLE COMPLIES WITH THE CJEU JUDGMENT: AN UNNECESSARY ADVISORY COUNCIL

2.- THE EFFECTIVENESS OF THE ARTICLE 29 WORKING PARTY GUIDELINES ON THE IMPLEMENTATION OF THE CJEU'S JUDGMENT

INTRODUCTION TO THE ENGLISH EDITION

The Spanish edition of this book (Madrid, 2014) was undertaken by the Center for Political and Constitutional Studies (*Centro de Estudios Políticos y Constitucionales*). I really want to thank this prestigious Spanish public body for their audacity in publishing a book about these emerging issues, as well as for their generosity in authorizing an English edition by the Electronic Privacy Information Center.

The publication of this book by EPIC is a personal honor, and it also provides an invaluable opportunity for English-speaking readers to gain first-hand knowledge on the background of *Google v. Spain*.[1] Marc Rotenberg is the person who should be credited for achieving this goal. His worldwide leadership in the protection of privacy never falters and knows no boundaries. Indeed, his insistence and focus on making this work available to the public in the United States can only be compared to my deepest acknowledgment and appreciation.

The *right to be forgotten* has been widely covered by the media and legal scholars over the last decade. It has come hand in hand with the tremendous omnipresence of the Internet in our lives, although no legal system had acknowledged this right until it was recently enshrined in the European Data Protection Regulation (GDPR).

---

[1] Fortunately, English-speaking scholars have shown their interest in the Case *Google v. Spain* in recent works: ALLEN, A. & ROTENBERG, M.: *Privacy Law and Society* 1517-1552, West Academic, St. Paul, 2016; EPIC: "The Right to Be Forgotten (Google v. Spain)" (https://epic.org/privacy/right-to-be-forgotten/); MARC ROTENBERG: "The Right to Privacy is Global," *US News and World Report*, Dec. 5, 2014 (https://www.usnews.com/debate-club/should-there-be-a-right-to-be-forgotten-on-the-internet/the-right-to-privacy-is-global); GEORGE BROCK: THE RIGHT TO BE FORGOTTEN: PRIVACY AND THE MEDIA IN THE DIGITAL AGE, I.B. Tauris & Reuters Institute for the Study of Journalism, University of Oxford, London-New York, 2016; DAVID HOFFMAN, PAULA BRUENING & SOPHIA CARTER: "The right to obscurity: how we can implement the Google Spain", *North Carolina Journal of Law & Technology*, volume 17, Issue 3, march, 2016, pp. 437-482; ROBERT POST: *Google Spain, the Right to Be Forgotten, and Personal Data*, draft 2, Yale Law School, 2016 (manuscript); BRENDAN VAN ALSENOY & MARIEKE KOEKKOEK: *Internet and jurisdiction after Google Spain: the extraterritorial reach of the EU's "right to be forgotten"*, Working Paper No. 152, Leuven Centre for Global Governance Studies, March 2015; HERKE KRANENBORG: "Google and the Right to Be Forgotten (Case C-131/12, Google Spain)", *European Data Protection Law Review*, vol. 1-1, 2015, pp. 70-79.

The initial craving for Internet presence -and particularly for search engine visibility (mainly in Google), the desire to *become someone* in the modern world, has given way to an intense demand for erasure of personal data online. This shift was triggered by the fear that those personal data could undermine the image, privacy and reputation of individuals.

As the best scholars have already pointed out,[2] historically, society's general principle has been to forget, and it has only remembered by default. However, technology has brought a paradigm shift, and currently *remembrance prevails as the general principle*, whereas *oblivion only comes by default*. This explains the pressing and constant demand for removing personal information from the Internet under the *right to be forgotten*.

Nevertheless, it is very difficult to consolidate this right, as this book tries to illustrate. These difficulties stem from the *historical and dogmatic weakness* inherent to a *brand new* social and legal environment. The Internet, as the cornerstone of our everyday life for two decades now, has cast aside a myriad of previous legal concepts and categories which are hardly applicable to the Internet world. *New rights*, such as data protection, are meant to contain this hurricane of risks and threats, but due to their short existence they have yet to become well-established from a legal standpoint.

The foregoing suggests that the quest for immediate acknowledgement of the right to be forgotten will not be very successful. This is why the *great legal win* marked by the Court of Justice of the European Union (CJEU) Judgment in *Google v. Spain* has had such a major impact.

In this legal version of "David versus Goliath," the CJEU neither *panicked* -as the large Internet multinationals did when they saw a threat to their business model based on the massive processing of personal information- nor was intimidated by the alleged risks (which were groundless) for the future technological development of modern society. There were no reasons to panic, and in any event any fears would have been insensitive to a legitimate social demand for protection of individual rights. Furthermore, the 2007 Treaty of Lisbon entails a *constitutional decision* that should not be disregarded; this Treaty conferred legal value on the Charter of Fundamental Rights of the European Union and, in particular, it granted a new fundamental right to data protection to all EU citizens.

---

[2] VICTOR MAYER-SCHÖNBERGER: *The Virtue of Forgetting in the Digital Age,* Princeton University Press, Oxford, 2009.

It was most certainly going to be hard *to stem the tide*, and to deny the need to protect the right to be forgotten, in the light of social needs and the unstoppable public demand for erasure and objection to personal data processing on the Internet.

This book seeks to illustrate the validity and reasonableness of the legal arguments underlying this claim. This work addresses the legal analysis of the cases heard by the Spanish Data Protection Agency since 2007 regarding the right to be forgotten and, particularly, *Google v. Spain*.

Needless to say, this is not an exclusively national issue. Therefore, we have broadened the scope of the study to comprise other European and American cases, European scholarly and legislative works, as well as very significant case law precedents of the CJEU and the European Court of Human Rights (ECtHR). Finally, this new edition has updated the effects of the CJEU's ruling and the issues attached to its implementation.

This book is mainly a set of *case studies*, since the case-by-case analysis makes it possible to fully show the issues that arise when fundamental rights collide. Furthermore, this methodology benefits from the author's practical experience in a legal and regulatory context where the legal categories are somewhat blurred and the facts to which they apply are often dismissed as trivial or immaterial.

This is not the scholarly work of a constitutional law professor sitting in his college office. The author has first-hand experience of what is recorded in this book, since he has been the Director of the Spanish Data Protection Agency (AEPD) during the time period under consideration (2007-2011).

I cannot help but mention how useful it was for me to have a close cooperation with Privacy Commissioners from many countries, such as the Vice-Chairman of the EU Group of Data Protection Authorities (Article 29 Working Party) and the Chairman of the Ibero-American Data Protection Network. During my tenure as AEPD Director, I had to attend a wide array of conferences and international meetings in which there was barely any reference to the right to be forgotten on the Internet: Montreal, Washington, Tel Aviv, Strasbourg, Cambridge, Brussels, London, Mexico, Bogota, Uruguay, Jerusalem, Panama, Berlin, Paris, Casablanca, Zagreb, etc.

For the preparation of this book, the invitations from Professor David Erdos to lecture on the *right to be forgotten* at the Center for Socio-Legal Studies (Oxford University) and at the Faculty of Law of the University of Cambridge were extremely useful, as well as the invitations from Professor George Brock to the Reuters Institute for the Study of Journalism of the University of Oxford, from Professor Olivia Tambou to Université Paris-Dauphine, from Commissioner Jennifer Stoddart to the Privacy Commissioner Office in Canada, from the Faculty of Law in Grenoble, from the Croatian Data Protection Authority, from the Computers, Privacy & Data Protection International Conference in Brussels, etc. I was even invited to the *Google Legal Summit!* held in Los Angeles.

This book is not an isolated study, since it falls within the context of the line of research promoted by the Universidad Jaume I on *"La reforma del sistema europeo de protección de datos"* ("The reform of the European Data Protection System") financed by the Spanish Ministry of Economy and Competitiveness (DER2012-34764 and DER2015-63635-R) including researchers from European (Oxford, Paris-Dauphine, Brussels and Roma Tré) and Spanish (Alcalá, Miguel Hernández, Oberta de Catalunya, Valencia and Jaume I) universities.

Last but not least, I wish to express my appreciation for the highly qualified members of the AEPD and for the college colleagues who have contributed to the preparation and dissemination of this book. I would also like to extend my gratitude to Pablo García Molina, who has made a huge effort in making the challenging translation of this book possible, thus making it accessible to English-speaking readers.

Castellón (Spain), 1 January 2018

ARTEMI RALLO

Constitutional Law Full Professor
University Jaume I at Castellón (Spain)
Former Director of the Spanish Data Protection Agency

CHAPTER I

THE RIGHT TO BE FORGOTTEN: A SUCCESSFUL YET EQUIVOCAL EMERGING CONCEPT

1.- OBLIVION AS A POTENTIAL ALL-ENCOMPASSING RIGHT: ITS NECESSARY NARROWING TO THE VIRTUAL WORLD OF THE INTERNET

Today, the *right to be forgotten* is a reality. However, until its recognition by the European General Regulation on Data Protection in April 2016, no other provision had enshrined it because there was no common definition for such legal concept. It was hard for any legal system to regulate, recognize or protect something that also lacked a clear definition in social reality. In other words, how to guarantee a right with undetermined boundaries and scope?

Certainly, the law attaches legal consequences –both constitutive (positive) and abrogative (negative)– to the *passage of time*. Without any individual actions required, time produces by itself positive legal effects (for instance, usucaption or acquisitive prescription in Civil Law systems) or negative legal effects (statutes of limitations for criminal offenses). Comparative law provides many examples –not to be mentioned here– where the expiration of certain deadlines entails termination, revocation or oblivion of the legal effects stemming from punitive provisions. Sometimes, even the existence or the acknowledgement of such effects is eliminated, as with the deletion of criminal records.

In spite of the undeniable tensions surrounding the conflict between *oblivion* and *memory* (affecting, particularly, the prosecution of crimes against humanity), there is still today a social conviction that in certain realms –especially in criminal matters– *forgetting* is intrinsic to the protection of human dignity. Therefore, far from conceptualizing and regulating an autonomous right to be forgotten, society has just adopted specific provisions for diverse situations where the passage of time leads to termination or oblivion of their legal effects.

Hence, even in the absence of a free-standing right to be forgotten, what accounts for the flood of scientific works referring to the 'the right to be forgotten' or 'the right to oblivion'?[3] The answer lies in two words: the Internet.

The Internet *galaxy*[4] has changed contemporary societies' life in every dimension. As splendidly illustrated by Viktor Mayer-Schönberger's pioneering and essential book *Delete: The Virtue of Forgetting in the Digital Age*,[5] the Internet has marked a real *shift* in the meaning we used to give to memory and oblivion, as well as in the potential impact on human dignity of disseminating personal information. The boundaries inherent to off-line reality (limited space and time) have been swept away by an on-line reality summarized in two explosive features: universality and eternity. The global and constant flow[6] of personal information in almost three decades of the Internet's existence[7] offers a glimpse of the extraordinary risks and threats[8] facing the future of human dignity: since the Internet cannot be *stopped*,[9] we need preventive responses to tackle the emergence of the *right to be forgotten on the Internet*.

---

[3] However, a good example of the erratic, profuse, and vague use of the term 'right to be forgotten' or 'right to oblivion' is the work of JEREMY WARNER ("The Right to Oblivion: Data Retention from Canada to Europe in Three Backward Steps," *University of Ottawa Law & Technology Journal*, vol. 2-1, pp. 75-104). In spite of the title, it only deals with a comparative analysis of Canadian and European Union legislation on data retention –mainly focusing on their implementation in the field of public security– without mentioning their impact on the Internet. Also, among others, the study by FRANZ WERRO ("The Right to Inform v the Right to be Forgotten: A Transatlantic Crash," *Liability in the Third Millennium, Liber Amicorum Gert Brüggemeier*, Baden-Baden, 2009, pp. 285-300) basically addressing the Swiss and US legal systems on the 'right to be forgotten' with respect to criminal records.

[4] I borrow this famous expression from MANUEL CASTELLS: *La galaxia Internet*, Areté, Barcelona, 2011.

[5] Princeton University Press, Oxford, 2009.

[6] For a very interesting study on the "life cycle" of personal data on the Internet, the changing nature of personal information over time, and a questioning of the conventional wisdom that "permanence" on the Internet, see MEG LETA AMBROSE: "It's About Time: Privacy, Information Life Cycles, and the Right to be Forgotten," *Stanford Technology Law Review*, vol. 16-2, 2013, pp. 101-154.

[7] For an early warning on the dynamic relationship between law and technology, see JOEL REIDEMBERG: *Lex Informatica: The Formulation of Information Policy Rules Through Technology*, *Texas Law Review*, vol. 76-3, 1998, pp. 553-593.

[8] Former CNIL and Article 29 Working Party Chairman, ALEX TÜRK, presents a general overview of this reality in his book *La vie privée en péril*, Odile Jacob, Paris, 2011. Particularly interesting are his reflections on *le droit à l'oubli* (p. 155).

[9] JONATHAN ZITTRAIN: *The future of the Internet and how to stop it*, Yale University Press, New Haven, 2008.

The right to be forgotten on the Internet has nothing to do with the end of memory, obliterating the past,[10] distorting history,[11] or an alleged establishment of universal censorship on the right to information.

Only biased readings[12] can try to mislead those who engage in this debate in good faith, taking advantage of how difficult it is to grasp the Internet's impact on the surrounding reality. Neither individual memory nor collective history is –or can be– at stake as a

---

[10] Outside the debate on the right to be forgotten on the Internet, an interesting work refuting the argument that individuals and nations have the right to forget, see GREGORY W. STREICH: "Is There a Right to Forget? Historical, Injustices, Race, Memory, and Identity," *New Political Science*, vol. 24-4, 2002, pp. 525-542.

[11] Drawing from Orwell's work, this fear leads PIERRE TRUDEL to state that *le droit à l'oublie* should be *un droit à oublier:* "Le «droit à l'oubli» tel que préconisé par l'Union européenne est présenté comme un antidote contre la «société de surveillance» décrite par Orwell dans son roman 1984. Mais dans ce roman, l'on décrit une autre dérive, aussi dangereuse que la surveillance généralisée contre laquelle il est essentiel de se prémunir. Dans 1984, des scribes à la solde du ministère de la vérité réécrivaient l'histoire, effaçant ce qui ne convenait plus et réécrivant au gré des besoins et des fantasmes du dictateur. Le droit à l'oubli tel que mis de l'avant dans les projets de l'Union européenne n'est pas très loin de cela : il procède d'une conception qui tient pour insignifiantes les exigences de la vie collective. Il témoigne d'une vision qui place le droit à la vie privée des individus –du moins ceux qui ont les moyens de le faire valoir– au-dessus des exigences de transparence à l'égard de ce qui concerne l'espace public. En somme, c'est un droit à oublier !" [« La menace du 'droit à l'oublie'," 5 October 2013 (http://blogues.journaldemontreal.com/pierretrudel/droit/la-menace-du-droit-a-loubli/)].

[12] A prototypical example of the vested interests behind such arguments is the set of posts by PETER FLEISCHER, Google's Global Privacy Counsel, on his personal blog and, particularly, those of 9 March 2011 ("Foggy Thinking about the Right to Oblivion," (http://peterfleischer.blogspot.com/2011/03/foggy-thinking-about-right-to-oblivion.html), 5 September 2011 ("'The Right to be Forgotten', seen from Spain," 5 September 2011, http://peterfleischer.blogspot.com/2011/09/right-to-be-forgotten-seen-from-spain.html) and 29 January 2012 ("The right to be forgotten, or how to edit your history," 29 January 2012, (http://peterfleischer.blogspot.co.uk/2012/01/right-to-be-forgotten-or-how-to-edit.html). The 17 February 2013 text is very revealing: "Don Quixote. Re-read Don Quixote as you follow the debate about revising Europe's privacy laws. Is it more noble to pursue the glory of fantasy over the indignities of the real world? ... Don Quixote is defending privacy against the American-mega-corporate-privacy-slayers. Don Quixote is defending the Right to be Forgotten. Sadly, things don't end well for the noble knight, unsettling and unsaid...American companies will come out big winners, compared to their European rivals" (http://peterfleischer.blogspot.com.es/2013/02/dox-quixote.html).

result of the Internet's cleansing certain personal data about individuals who are not (and do not intend to be) of public interest.

Use of the Internet is not and cannot be made conditional upon universal publicity of any personal data entered into it. A person's memory of one's own information is an individual (subjective) right, but recollection of anonymous citizens' data can never be conceived as a right to preserve historical integrity. The right to know and to be informed covers all matters of general interest, but not every personal data provided deliberately or otherwise by individuals in the framework of their personal and social relations. The Internet is the great contemporary tool used by society to enhance its information and knowledge capabilities. It cannot turn into an oppressive space preventing individuals from reviewing their own actions, updating their own history or reaffirming their own identity[13] over time.

On the contrary, the debate on the right to be forgotten[14] has everything to do with the future risks of the Internet for reputation, privacy, liberty, and human dignity, as pointed out by Solove.[15]

In view of the massive flow of personal data on the Internet, the threats to individuals must not be trivialized. The fundamental right to data

---

[13] On the anchoring of "the right to be forgotten" in the "right to identity," see NORBERTO NUNO GOMES DE ANDRADE: "El olvido: El derecho a ser diferente... de uno mismo. Una reconsideración del derecho a ser olvidado," *IDP Revista de Derecho, Internet y Política*, vol. 13, 2012, pp. 67-83. For an Italian perspective, see GIUSELLA FINOCCHIARO: "La memoria della rete e il diritto all´oblio," *Il diritto dell'informazione e dell'informatica*, vol. 3, 2010, pp. 391-404. Also on the link between identity and anonymity, see SERGIO NIGER: "Il diritto all'oblio," *Diritto all'anonimato: anonimato, nome e identità personale*, G. Finocchiaro (ed.), Cedam, Padua, 2008, pp. 59-73.
[14] For a philosophical approach, see ANTOINETTE ROUVROY: "Réinventer l'art d'oublier et de se faire oublier dans la société de l'information," April 2008 (http://works.bepress.com/antoinette_rouvroy/5). For a moral assessment, see IVAN SZEKELY: "The Right to Forget, the Right to be Forgotten. Personal Reflections on the Fate of Personal Data in the Information Society," S. Gutwirth et al. (eds.), *European Data Protection: In Good Health?*, Springer, 2012, pp. 347-363.
[15] DANIEL J. SOLOVE: *The future of reputation: gossip, rumor, and privacy on the Internet*, New Haven and London, Yale University Press, 2007.

protection should be strengthened.[16] Most of this personal information may be considered irrelevant and non-privacy intrusive in the strict sense of the term. Surely the paradigm shift in the current understanding of the right to privacy –the tension[17] between considering privacy as a *right* or a mere *expectation*[18]– has much to do with the public's willingness to share personal information perceived as harmless for the development of their personality.

However, temporary accumulation of such an enormous mass of personal data inevitably makes profiling an easy task. These profiles may not only jeopardize privacy but may also threaten the reputation of individuals, and hence their own liberty and dignity. Do individuals not have the right in the online world to "leave the past behind," to a "clean slate"? Human dignity calls for an affirmative answer.[19]

Individuals' inability to review, update, rectify or challenge personal information available online necessarily implies a restriction of individual freedom, which basically translates into self-censorship rather than digital *withdrawal*.[20] Unwanted universal access to personal data on the Internet

---

[16] See MARIA DEL CARMEN GUERRERO PICO: *El impacto de Internet en el Derecho Fundamental a la Protección de Datos de Carácter Personal*, Thomson-Civitas, Pamplona, 2006. Regarding the Internet's impact on the fundamental rights system in general and/or, in particular, the conflicts arising from its clash with the freedom of expression and information, see PALOMA LLANEZA GONZÁLEZ, P.: *Internet y comunicaciones digitales: régimen legal de las tecnologías de la información y de la comunicación*, Bosh, Barcelona, 2000; PABLO GARCÍA MEXIA (dir.): *Principios de Derecho de Internet*, Tirant lo Blanch, Valencia, 2005.

[17] For an interesting revisionist analysis, see AMITAI ETZIONI: *Los límites de la privacidad*, Editorial B de F, Montevideo-Buenos Aires, 2012 (in particular, pp. 5-23 and 285-338).

[18] Worth mentioning is the study on the privacy expectations of online social network users analyzing the results of a joint survey by the Universities of Miami (USA) and Ryerson (Canada): AVNER LEVIN & PATRICIA SANCHEZ ABRIL: "Two Notions of Privacy Online," *Vanderbilt Journal of Entertainment & Technology Law*, vol. 11-4, 2009, pp. 1001-1051.

[19] That is the approach taken by LUIZ COSTA & YVES POULLET: "But forgetfulness is larger. It is one dimension of how people deal with their own history, being related not only to leaving the past behind but also to leaving in the present without the threat of a kind of 'Miranda warning,' where whatever you say can be used against you in the future. In this sense the right to be forgotten is closely related to entitlements of dignity and self-development. Once again, privacy appears as the pre-requisite of our liberties" ("Privacy and the Regulation of 2012," *Computer Law and Security Review*, 28-3, June, 2012, p. 257).

[20] VICTOR MAYER-SCHÖNBERGER: *Delete: The Virtue of Forgetting in the Digital Age…*, pp. 128-134.

(detrimental to the social recognition deserved by everyone) jeopardizes individuals' reputation and implies self-limitation of their freedom.

As Google's then-CEO Eric Schmidt predicted, time on the Internet plays against individuals: "Young people may one day have to change their names in order to escape their previous online activity."[21] Internet multinational corporations have not hesitated to declare the death of online privacy on the premise that *if you have something that you don't want anyone to know, maybe you shouldn't be doing it in the first place*, since "we know roughly who you are, roughly what you care about, roughly who your friends are."[22]

Far from an exaggerated allegory, this Orwellian scenario is already a reality. Its manifestations will multiply in the future[23] unless society finds mechanisms to limit such interference in the private sphere, thus reversing the tendency governed by the nefarious principle "*if you have nothing to hide,*[24] *then you have nothing to worry.*" The right to be forgotten is the essential counterpoint to the path taken by the Internet, as bluntly stated by Viviane Reding, former Justice Commissioner and European Commission Vice-President: "God forgives and forgets but the Web never does!".[25]

Delimiting the scope of such alleged right to be forgotten on the Internet

---

[21] *The Wall Street Journal*, 23 September de 2010.

[22] Presentation by Eric Schmidt in Berlin, 7-9-2010 (http://techcrunch.com/2010/09/07/eric-schmidt-ifa). For further comments on Google's CEO's outburst, see the excellent study by OMER TENE: "What Google knows: privacy and Internet search engines," *Utah Law Review*, vol. 4, 2008, pp. 1433-1492.

[23] OMER TENE: "Privacy: The new generations," *International Data Privacy Law*, 2011, vol. 1-1, pp. 15-27.

[24] DANIEL J. SOLOVE warns about the need to rethink privacy's legitimizing principles to block the way to the *I have nothing to hide* principle regarding the use of the Internet: "The argument that no privacy problem exists if a person has nothing to hide is frequently made in connection with many privacy issues ... In order to respond to the nothing to hide argument, it is imperative that we have a theory about what privacy is and why it is valuable. At its core, the nothing to hide argument emerges from a conception of privacy and its value. What exactly is "privacy"? How valuable is privacy and how do we assess its value? How do we weigh privacy against countervailing values? These questions have long plagued those seeking to develop a theory of privacy and justifications for its legal protection" ("I've Got Nothing to Hide," *San Diego Law Review*, vol. 44, 2007, pp. 745-772).

[25] VIVIANE REDING: "Why the EU needs new personal data protection rules?," *The European Data Protection and Privacy Conference*, Brussels, 30 November 2010 (http://europa.eu/rapid/press-release_SPEECH-10-700_en.htm).

is, however, a much more complex task.[26]

Currently, the only non-controversial aspect of the right to be forgotten is probably its identification with the erasure of online content, that is, the deletion of personal data on the Internet. The existing international legal texts,[27] either regional or national, have only established one deletion modality based exclusively on individuals' right to request erasure when their data are no longer necessary to fulfill the purpose for which they were processed or stored. In practice, this subjective manifestation of data erasure as an individual right does not meet the ever more demanding requirements of society.[28] Also, the erasure of such data is not effective, given the unclear scope and meaning of the required condition (them no longer being necessary for the purpose for which they were collected). Thus, in practice, individual attempts to request erasure on the Internet fail.

---

[26] On the difficulties of subjecting Internet to the "old law," see PABLO GARCÍA MEXIA, P.: *Derecho Europeo de Internet*, Netbiblo, La Coruña, 2009.
[27] The OECD *Privacy Guidelines* adopted on 11 July 2013 (amending the original 1980 version) merely establish that: "Individuals should have the right... d) to challenge data relating to them and, if the challenge is successful, to have the data erased..." (Art. 13). Before that, the *International Standards on the Protection of Personal Data and Privacy* adopted by the International Conference of Data Protection and Privacy Commissioners held in Madrid on 5 November 2009, provided that: "The data subject has the right to request from the responsible person the deletion or rectification of personal data (...)" (Art. 17(1)) and that "The data subject may object to the processing of personal data where there is a legitimate reason related to his/her specific personal situation" (Art. 18(1)).
[28] It is worth referring to an interesting proposal by CHRIS CONLEY to enshrine a specific "right to delete" instead of the generic "right to privacy": "We propose that the best way to address this concern is to create a right to delete that gives individuals the ability to control their own history and thus escape it. This right comes from the idea that records are not just about a person; in our modern world, they are functionally part of our digital persona, and thus should be under our control whether we create them or not. By establishing a right to delete, and balancing that right with other concerns, we believe that we can reap the benefits of our ever-expanding technological capacities without leaving privacy behind. We envision this right as a combination of technical tools, legal regulation, and social norms and market pressure that will work in combination with other laws and technologies to promote individual control of personal information" ("The Right to Delete," AAAI Spring Symposium Series, North America, 2010, p. 58, http://www.aaai.org/ocs/index.php/SSS/SSS10/paper/view/1158/1482).

In view of the increasing volume of undesired personal data stored on Internet servers and services, it is not illusory to envisage a *global data deletion principle* incorporating new measures to ensure effective *privacy by deletion.*[29] This could be achieved through preventive mechanisms[30] (for instance, the *right to anonymity,*[31] *pseudonymity,*[32] or *default*

---

[29] BENJAMIN J. KEELE: "Privacy by deletion: the need for a global data deletion principle," *Indiana Journal of Global Legal Studies,* winter, 16-1, 2009, pp. 363-384.

[30] As pointed out by JEF AUSLOOS, "to really solve the issue, it is necessary to strike at the root. Many solutions have been proposed over the years. Worth mentioning in this context are: awareness-raising, transparency, clearer privacy notices, data-minimisation, stricter control on the purpose limitation principle, 'anonymisation', transparency, encryption, etc. The goal of each of these measures is to prevent (potentially harmful) information to be shared in the first place. But, in an ever-increasing social Internet, where many features depend on disclosing personal data, ex post measures are needed as well. Enabling a more effective control by the individual, the introduction of a (well-defined) 'right to be forgotten', therefore, seems appropriate at first sight" ("The 'Right to be Forgotten' - Worth remembering?," *Computer Law & Security Review,* vol. 28, 2012, p. 147).

[31] FRANK LA RUE warns about the inadequate protection of privacy on the Internet and the (only) relative anonymity of online users. In his opinion, States should guarantee that their citizens "can express themselves anonymously online and to refrain from adopting real-name registration systems" (*Report of the Special Rapporteur on the promotion and protection of the right to freedom of opinion and expression,* United Nations General Assembly, 16 May 2011, p. 22).

[32] On the advantages and disadvantages of this proposal, see KUMAYAMA, K.D.: "A right to pseudonymity," *Arizona Law Review,* summer, vol. 51, 2009, pp. 427-464. Interestingly, JISUK WOO points out that anonymity is better protected in the real world than in the virtual one ("The right not to be identified: privacy and anonymity in the interactive media environment," *New Media Society,* vol. 8-6, 2006, pp. 949-967 (http://nms.sagepub.com/content/8/6/949).

deletion[33]) and responsive mechanisms (*contextualizing* the information through *labels*[34] or bringing in mandatory online reputation insurance[35]).

To date, only two means have been put forward to materialize the right to be forgotten on the Internet: a) the establishment of expiration dates[36] for

---

[33] This proposal was first put forward by VICTOR MAYER-SCHÖNBERGER in the following simple and practical terms: "I propose that we shift the default when storing personal information back to where it has been for millennia, from remembering forever to forgetting over time. I suggest that we achieve this reversal with a combination of law and software. The primary role of law in my proposal is to mandate that those who create software that collects and stores data build into their code not only the ability to forget with time, but make such forgetting the default. The technical principle is similarly simple: Data is associated with meta-data that defines how long the underlying personal information ought to be stored. Once data has reached its expiry date, it will be deleted automatically by software, by Lessig's West Coast Code" ["Useful Void: The Art of Forgetting in the Age of Ubiquitous Computing," Harvard University, April 2007, p. 17 (http://www.vmsweb.net/attachments/pdf/Useful_Void.pdf)]. PAUL A. BERNAL has also embraced this approach: "A right to delete?," *European Journal of Law and Technology*, 2-2, 2011, pp. 1-18. In support of this proposal, CÉCILE DE TERWANGE considers that: "A technical response like that could contribute to tipping the balance in favor of the data subjects since the latter would benefit from protection without taking any initiative. This is particularly important in a such an opaque context as the Internet. Data subjects are often unaware of the processing of data. Granting a right that people would never think of exercising seems a misleading way of protecting them" ("Privacidad en Internet y el derecho a ser olvidado/derecho al olvido," *IDP Revista de Derecho, Internet y Política*, vol. 13, 2012, p. 61) (own translation).
[34] Contextualization would imply that users fight the information with more information, adding additional information to the online existing data to counter de-contextualization and to "put into context" any personal data (CARLOS CORTÉS: "Derecho al olvido: entre la protección de datos, la memoria y la vida personal en la era digital," p. 26 http://www.palermo.edu/cele/pdf/DerechoalolvidoiLEI.pdf).
[35] A singular proposal by MOROZOV, E.: "¿Un seguro para Internet?," *El País*, 15 March 2012, pp. 27 and 28.
[36] ENISA's study shows that technologies already exist (Vanish, X-pire, EpfCOM) that make it possible to erase personal information (pictures, etc.) when users set an expiration date [ENISA (Network and Information Security Agency): *The right to be forgotten – between expectations and practice*, European, 20 November 2012, p. 12 (http://www.enisa.europa.eu/activities/identity-and-trust/library/deliverables/the-right-to-be-forgotten)]. VICTOR MAYER-SCHÖNBERGER supports the applicability of this modality of the right to be forgotten in Internet search engines: "Google and other search engines may have to change their practices as well. No longer would they be able to store search queries forever. They would have to be deleted – forgotten – over time" ("Useful Void: The Art of Forgetting in the Age of Ubiquitous Computing," p. 18).

information, as advocated by Mayer-Schönberger[37]; and b) the exercise of the right to protection of personal data[38] and, in particular, its two specific practical dimensions: erasure and objection. The latter mechanism – followed by the Spanish Data Protection Agency (AEPD) and by the European legislature in the General Data Protection Regulation (GDPR)– has been hampered by the doubts and shortcomings affecting the right to data protection, a *new right* which is in itself difficult to apprehend and which still has unclear and unconsolidated legal boundaries.[39]

2.- RECOGNITION OF THE RIGHT TO BE FORGOTTEN IN THE EUROPEAN UNION

2.1.- BACKGROUND (2009): THE RIGHT TO BE FORGOTTEN AS DATA PORTABILITY AND ERASURE ON THE INTERNET

The *1995 Data Protection Directive* (95/46/EC)[40] was a milestone in the history of personal data protection in the European Union and, to a large extent, in the rest of the world.[41] Two decades after its adoption, it must be observed that globalization and the rapid technological change pose enormous challenges, especially with respect to the risks for privacy and personal data protection stemming from online activities.[42]

---

[37] VICTOR MAYER-SCHÖNBERGER: *Delete: The Virtue of Forgetting in the Digital Age…*, p. 171. JONATHAN ZITTRAIN argues for revising online reputation and for deleting Internet personal history every ten years (*The future of the Internet and how to stop it…*, p. 229). Examining the "practicability" of the right to be forgotten following Lessig's four principal 'regulators' (norms, market, code and law), JEF AUSLOOS raises doubts as to the viability of an "expiry date" as a manifestation of the right to be forgotten
("The 'Right to be Forgotten'-Worth remembering?," *Computer Law & Security Review…*, pp. 148-149).
[38] ARTEMI RALLO: *El derecho al olvido en Internet. Google v España*, CEPC, Madrid, 2014; PERE SIMON: *El régimen constitucional del derecho al olvido digital*, Tirant lo Blanch, Valencia, 2012.
[39] RICARD MARTINEZ: *Una aproximación crítica a la autodeterminación informativa*, Civitas, Pamplona, 2004.
[40] Directive 95/46/EC of the European Parliament and of the Council of 24 October 1995 on the protection of individuals with regard to the processing of personal data and on the free movement of such data (OFFICIAL JOURNAL L 281, 23/11/1995).
[41] CHRISTOPHER KUNER: *European Data Protection Law. Corporate Compliance and Regulation*, Oxford University Press, Oxford, 2007.
[42] See ARTEMI RALLO & ROSARIO GARCÍA (eds.): *Hacia un nuevo derecho europeo de protección de datos. Towards a new European Data Protection Regime*, Tirant lo Blanch, Valencia, 2015, a collective work on the European debate regarding the adoption of the GDPR.

In order to respond to these challenges, in 2009 the European Commission launched a review of the European legal framework. It considered that the implementation of data protection principles required clarification and refinement due to the impact of new technologies. This was all the more important considering the *constitutional status* given to real and effective protection of personal data after the 2007 Lisbon Treaty had made the *Charter of Fundamental Rights of the European Union* (CFREU) legally binding. Indeed, its Article 8 recognizes, enshrines and guarantees the *right to protection of personal data.*[43]

It should be noted that nothing in the public debate on the reform of European data protection law originally suggested that a specific provision on the right to be forgotten would be adopted.

The *Summary of replies to the public consultation about the future legal framework for protecting personal data* contains no mention in this regard.[44] Remarkably enough, also the European Data Protection Authorities (Article 29 Working Party) failed to mention this "new right" in their Joint Statement of 1 December 2009 (WP168): *The Future of Privacy. Joint contribution to the Consultation of the European Commission on the legal framework for the fundamental right to protection of personal data.*[45] This Joint Statement simply recalled that, as a result of the increasing use of the Internet (in particular, social networks), Directive 95/46/EC was not applicable to individuals who uploaded data "in the course of a household activity" or to Internet providers that received such data. The resulting lack of guarantees required a new legal framework so that Internet users and third parties could assert their rights.[46]

It was not until Commissioner Viviane Reding's first public statements that the European institutions showed their interest in recognizing and guaranteeing the right to be forgotten: "Internet users must have effective control of what they put online and be able to correct, withdraw or delete

---

[43] "1. Everyone has the right to the protection of personal data concerning him or her. 2. Such data must be processed fairly for specified purposes and on the basis of the consent of the person concerned or some other legitimate basis laid down by law. Everyone has the right of access to data which has been collected concerning him or her, and the right to have it rectified. 3. Compliance with these rules shall be subject to control by an independent authority."

[44] http://ec.europa.eu/justice/data-protection/review/actions/index_en.htm

[45] See a brief introduction to this Joint Statement of Article 29 Working Party in REBECCA WONG: "Data Protection: The future of privacy," *Computer Law and Security Review*, 27, 2011, p. 53.

[46] http://ec.europa.eu/justice/policies/privacy/docs/wpdocs/2009/wp168_en.pdf, pp. 1-28.

it at will. In the recent public consultation on the review of the data protection rules, we were told that there should be "a right to be forgotten." We need to look more closely at this idea. More control also means being able to move your data from one place to another, and to have it properly removed from the first location in the process. If I have my precious photos stored somewhere in the cloud, what happens if I want to change to another provider?"[47]

However, the European Commission tended to confuse the right to be forgotten with data portability when it first approached this concept. As a response to societal concerns about the restrictions imposed on users' control of their own data in social networks[48] (sometimes by preventing them from closing their accounts or erasing their data, and others by hampering the transfer of accounts or profiles from one online platform to another), the European authorities resolved to grant them control on the basis of the right to be forgotten (final erasure of data in an online account) / portability (transfer to another online account or platform).

2.2.- THE EUROPEAN COMMISSION'S COMMUNICATION *A COMPREHENSIVE APPROACH ON PERSONAL DATA PROTECTION IN THE EUROPEAN UNION* (2010): THE RIGHT TO BE FORGOTTEN AS ERASURE OF PERSONAL DATA

On 4 November 2010, the European Commission published its *Communication from the Commission to the European Parliament, the Council, the Economic and Social Committee and the Committee of the Regions "A comprehensive approach on personal data protection in the European Union."*[49] It was the first time that an official document issued by the European institutions made express reference to the *right to be forgotten.*[50]

---

[47] "Building Trust in Europe's Online Single Market," Speech at the American Chamber of Commerce to the EU, Brussels, 22 June 2010 (http://europa.eu/rapid/press-release_SPEECH-10-327_en.htm?locale=en).
[48] For further Information on this, see ARTEMI RALLO & RICARD MARTINEZ (eds.): *Derecho y redes sociales*, Civitas-Thomson Reuters, Pamplona, 2013.
[49] http://eur-lex.europa.eu/LexUriServ/LexUriServ.do?uri=CELEX:52012DC0009:en:NOT
[50] Viviane Reding's first public statements are very revealing of the importance of this original proposal: "Even though we have the best data protection laws in the world, the rapid pace of technology change has prompted new questions and challenges. Privacy nowadays has become a moving target: new risks need better legal remedies. These risks are related to how we live today. Personal data can easily be stored and then even more easily multiplied on the Web. But it is not easy to wipe it out. As somebody once said: "God forgives and forgets but the

According to this Communication, the *essential purpose* of such global approach to data protection was strengthening *individuals' rights* and *effective control over one's own data*. The European legal framework (Directive 95/46/EC and Article 8(2) CFREU –"Everyone has the right of access to data which has been collected concerning him or her, and the right to have it rectified"–) already recognized and protected the right to access, rectify, block or erase the data, except on legitimate grounds provided by law. Nevertheless, the Commission observed that the exercise of these rights was particularly challenging in the online world, "where data are often retained without the person concerned being informed and/or having given his or her agreement to it." The example of *social networking* was considered particularly enlightening, since it presented significant obstacles to the individuals' effective control over their data.

The European Commission undertook to study the means and regulatory reforms necessary to enhance control over personal data in the online world on the basis of the following axes:[51] 1) strengthening the principle of data minimization; 2) improving the conditions for the exercise of the rights of access, rectification, erasure or blocking of data; 3) ensuring "data portability" (granting individuals the explicit right to withdraw their pictures or lists of friends from an application or service, so that the withdrawn data may be transferred into another application or service, as far as technically possible, without hindrance from the data controllers); 4) and, finally, "clarifying the so-called 'right to be forgotten', i.e. the right of individuals to have their data no longer processed and deleted when they are no longer needed for legitimate purposes. This is the case,

---

Web never does!" This is why the "right to be forgotten" is so important for me. With more and more private data floating around the Web – especially on social networking site – people should have the right to have their data completely removed ... I believe individuals' need to be able to maintain control over their data ...I want to introduce the "right to be forgotten." Social network sites are a great way to stay in touch with friends and share information. But if people no longer want to use a service, they should have no problem wiping out their profiles. The right to be forgotten is particularly relevant to personal data that is no longer needed for the purposes for which it was collected. This right should also apply when a storage period, which the user agreed to, has expired," in "Why the EU needs new personal data protection rules?," *The European Data Protection and Privacy Conference,* Brussels, 30 November 2010 (http://europa.eu/rapid/press-release_SPEECH-10-700_en.htm).
[51] OMER TENE: "Reforming data protection in Europe and beyond: a critical assessment of the second wave of global privacy laws," *Hacia un nuevo derecho europeo de protección de datos. Towards a new European Data Protection Regime* (eds.) A. Rallo & R. García, Tirant lo Blanch, Valencia, 2015, pp. 143-206.

for example, when processing is based on the person's consent and when he or she withdraws consent or when the storage period has expired."[52]

The European Commission's Communication showed how the notion of the right to be forgotten as linked to the online environment –and, particularly, social networks– was gradually taking shape. At the same time, it reduced the initial confusion between the right to be forgotten and portability by giving a meaning of its own to the former, as "erasure of data."[53]

However, the Opinion of the European Data Protection Supervisor (EDPS) on the Commission's Communication highlights the link between both concepts. Data portability and the right to be forgotten are presented as two "connected" concepts "complementary" to the principles referred to in the existing Directive, providing a right to "object" to the further processing of personal data, and an obligation for the data controller to "delete" personal information when it is no longer necessary for the purposes for which it was collected: "These two new notions have mostly added value in an information society context, where more and more data are automatically stored and kept for indefinite periods of time. Practice shows that, even if data are uploaded by the data subject himself, the degree of control he effectively has on his personal data is in practice very limited. This is all the more true in view of the gigantic memory the Internet represents today."[54]

In the EDPS' view, these new rights could help shifting the balance in favor of citizens' rights. Data subjects would have more control over their personal information, and information would automatically disappear after a certain period of time, even if the user did not take any action or was not aware of the data storage.

---

[52] http://ec.europa.eu/justice/news/consulting_public/0006/com_2010_609_en.pdf
[53] Criticism of this proposal was quick in coming: "In the form proposed by the European Union, the right to be forgotten cannot easily render a substantial contribution to an improvement of data protection. The concept is probably too vague to be successful… a clearer picture of the actual objective of a new fundamental right is necessary. The proclamation of a right to be forgotten as such does not suffice. It recalls the myth of Pandora's box: Impelled by her natural curiosity, Pandora opened the box and all the evils contained in it escaped. Moreover, a concretization of the right to be forgotten might be achieved by more specific codes of conduct … encompassing practical commitments that could become the starting point for a future international memorandum or agreement" (ROLF H. WEBER: "The Right to Be Forgotten: More Than a Pandora's Box?," *Journal of Intellectual Property, Information Technology and E-Commerce Law,* vol. 2, 2011, p. 130 (http://www.jipitec.eu/issues/jipitec-2-2-2011/3084).
[54] http://www.edps.europa.eu/EDPSWEB/

It was certainly a bold approach which aimed at giving unambiguous content to the right to be forgotten, i.e., the deletion of the data after an "expiration date,"[55] as already provided for in specific national sectors such as court records or police and disciplinary files.

According to the EDPS,[56] this modality of the right to be forgotten would be governed by the following rules: a) deletion of personal data or the prohibition of further processing; b) after a certain expiration date; c) without any further action, effort or insistence required from the data subject to obtain the deletion of his/her data; d) deletion would take place in an objective and automated way (except where specific circumstances required a longer deadline); e) "privacy by default" would be ensured, since the burden of proof (obligation to automatically delete[57]) would be placed on the data controller, thus removing it from individuals and providing for the automatic deletion of data stored on mobile devices or computers after a fixed period of time; f) the right to be forgotten would be especially useful in the context of information society services (in the electronic environment), taking on its full meaning "in the media or the Internet, and notably in social networks."

For obvious reasons, the *Contribution of the Spanish Data Protection*

---

[55] VICTOR MAYER-SCHÖNBERGER summarizes the advantages of expiration dates in the following points: 1) they utilize already-existing technology; 2) legally, they reintroduce into the digital world forgetting by default, which is familiar and inherent to us, without establishing new rights or institutions; 3) they are a modest combination of legal and software mechanisms regulating human behavior; 4) they are politically less controversial; 5) they are intuitive for users. He also dismisses the arguments against this proposal: its alleged radicalism, the fact that it may jeopardize archives and libraries, potential conflicts with society's desire to remember, their lack of perfection, and the absence of alternative information power models (*Delete: The Virtue of Forgetting in the Digital Age...*, pp. 188-192).

[56] http://www.edps.europa.eu/EDPSWEB/

[57] Viviane Reding insisted on this after characterizing the right to be forgotten as the first "pillar" of citizens' rights: "The first is the right to be forgotten: a comprehensive set of existing and new rules to better cope with privacy risks online. When modernising the legislation, I want to explicitly clarify that people shall have the right – and not only the "possibility" – to withdraw their consent to data processing. The burden of proof should be on data controllers – those who process your personal data. They must prove that they need to keep the data rather than individuals having to prove that collecting their data is not necessary" (Viviane Reding: "Your data, your rights: Safeguarding your privacy in a connected world Privacy" Platform "The Review of the EU Data Protection Framework," Brussels, 16 March 2011, http://europa.eu/rapid/press-release_SPEECH-11-183_en.htm).

Agency (AEPD) to the Commission's Consultation on a comprehensive approach on personal data protection in the European Union is particularly relevant.[58] The AEPD agreed with the concerns expressed by the Commission on the need to clarify the "right to be forgotten" on the Internet. Many users faced work, social, and personal problems due to their presence in "search engines or social networks," and they would prefer that information not to be available on the Internet and their trace to be erased.

According to the AEPD, the mechanisms provided by the European legal framework on data protection –withdrawal of consent; prohibition to process excessive, inaccurate or incomplete data; right of rectification, erasure, blocking and objection– allowed for an effective exercise of the "right to be forgotten."

However, the AEPD focused on the need for European regulations to clarify and improve the exercise of the right to be forgotten. It suggested establishing simple mechanisms and adopting technologies to prevent indexation of personal data by search engines. It also suggested to ensure effective implementation in the short term. In the view of the Spanish Agency, the key for a genuine guarantee of the right to be forgotten on the Internet lied in the deletion of personal information on websites, the "prevention of indexation by search engines," and the prohibition of data retention and use by third parties.

The European Commission received many other comments, but few of them focused on the "right to be forgotten." Special mention must be made of the Contribution by the European Consumers' Association (AEC), which fully supported the proposal of the European Commission but with the caveat that freedom of expression, as a fundamental right, must be preserved: "The right to 'be forgotten': everything posted online may stay there for perpetuity, in some form or another –through Internet archives websites or search engines caches– even posts or pictures one thought no longer existed. This is even more relevant for young people; would they want appalling photos taken at parties 10 years earlier popping up on the Web to be seen by their future employer? We believe that a general right to 'be forgotten' on the Internet should be introduced similar to a right to 'the silence of the chips'/'to be left alone' which has been called for in the field of RFID/Internet of Things ... We ask the Commission to research how such right could be made effective in practice, keeping in mind that it is crucial to ensure that the fundamental

---

[58]http://www.agpd.es/portalwebAGPD/canaldocumentacion/textos interes/common/pdfs/aepd dpa es.pdf

right to freedom of expression is carefully safeguarded."[59]

2.3.- THE DRAFT EUROPEAN REGULATION ON DATA PROTECTION (2012): THE RIGHT TO BE FORGOTTEN AS A RIGHT TO "NOTIFY" THIRD PARTIES OF REQUESTS FOR DELETION

The Communication from the Commission "*A comprehensive approach on personal data protection in the European Union*" had raised great expectations[60] (and also concerns[61]) about the potential scope of the "right to be forgotten."

The European Parliament Resolution of 6 July 2011 on the Commission's Communication underlined the importance of "clarifying in detail and codifying the 'right to be forgotten' and of enabling data portability, while ensuring that full technical and organisational feasibility is developed and in place to allow for the exercise of those rights." It stressed that "individuals need sufficient control of their online data to enable them to use the internet responsibly" and that "there must be clear and precise identification of all the relevant elements underpinning this right."[62]

Feasibility and *regulatory status* were the two key questions confronting

---

[59] *EU General Data Protection Framework, BEUC, Answer to the consultation,* http://ec.europa.eu/justice/news/consulting_public/0003/contributions/organisations/beuc_en.pdf.

[60] For an analysis of opinion polls on data protection in Europe, see DARA HALLINAN, MICHAEL FRIEDEWALD & PAUL McCARTHY: "Citizens' perceptions of data protection and privacy in Europe," *Computer Law & Security Review*, vol. 28, 2012, pp. 263-272.

[61] A good example of these concerns is Peter Fleischer's 9 March 2011 post on his personal blog under the eloquent title "Foggy thinking about the Right to Oblivion": "In privacy circles, everybody's talking about the Right to be Forgotten. The European Commission has even proposed that the 'right to be forgotten' should be written into the up-coming revision of the Privacy Directive … But, what on earth is it? For most people, I think it's an attempt to give people the right to wash away digital muck, or delete the embarrassing stuff, or just start fresh. But unfortunately, it's more complicated than that … Next time you hear someone talk about the Right to be Oblivion, ask them what exactly they mean. Foggy thinking won't get us anywhere" (http://peterfleischer.blogspot.com.es/search?updated-max=2012-08-22T12:40:00%2B01:00&max-results=20).

[62] European Parliament Resolution of 6 July 2011 on a comprehensive approach on personal data protection in the European Union. (2011/2025(INI)) (http://www.europarl.europa.eu/sides/getDoc.do?pubRef=-//EP//NONSGML+TA+P7-TA-2011-0323+0+DOC+PDF+V0//EN).

a European legislature uncertain of whether the right to be forgotten on the Internet could be regulated and effectively guaranteed.

The European Commission's initiative received fresh impetus upon the publication in June 2011 of the results of the *Special Eurobarometer 359: Attitudes on Data Protection and Electronic Identity in the European Union*, specifically referred to the "right to be forgotten": "As regards the 'right to be forgotten,' a clear majority of Europeans (75 %) want to delete personal information on a website whenever they decide to do so; about reasons for deleting personal data, *3/4 of Internet users want to be able to delete their personal data whenever they decide to do so:* respondents who use the Internet were asked under what circumstances, if any, they would like personal information stored and collected through a website to be completely deleted; three-quarters of Internet users want to delete this information whenever they decide to do so (75%), while far fewer say they want to do so when they stop using the website (24%) or when they change their Internet provider (13%). Clearly, the majority of European Internet users would want to claim 'their right to be forgotten'. A country-by-country breakdown shows that in every single Member State a majority want to delete personal information *whenever they decide to*, with the highest proportions in Malta (83%) and the Czech Republic, Cyprus and Sweden (82%), and the lowest in the Netherlands (64%), Bulgaria (66%) and Italy (68%). In Spain was 81%."[63]

Finally, on 25 January 2012, the European Commission presented a *Proposal for a Regulation of the European Parliament and the Council on the protection of individuals with regard to the processing of personal data and on the free movement of such data*[64] (*General Data Protection Regulation–GDPR*[65]). Amid great public interest,[66] it seemed to dispel

---

[63] http://ec.europa.eu/public_opinion/archives/ebs/ebs_359_en.pdf.

[64] http://ec.europa.eu/justice/data-protection/document/review2012/com_2012_11_en.pdf

[65] For a general preliminary assessment, see ARTEMI RALLO: "Hacia un nuevo sistema europeo de protección de datos: las claves de la reforma," *Revista de Derecho Político*, vol. 85, September-December, 2012, pp. 13-56; PAUL DE HERT & VAGELIS PAPACONSTANTINOU: "The proposed data protection Regulation replacing Directive 95/46/EC: A sound system for the protection of individuals," COMPUTER LAW & SECURITY REVIEW, VOL. 28-2, APRIL, 2012, PP. 130-142; LUIZ COSTA & YVES POULLET: "Privacy and the Regulation of 2012," pp. 254-262; PATRICK VAN EECKE, CAMERON CRAIG & JIM HALPERT: "The first insight into the European Commission's proposal for a new European Union Data Protection Law," *Journal of Internet Law*, February, 2012, p. 19.

[66] The importance of this regulatory shift was soon stressed in ARTEMI RALLO, A.: "Que aguante el paso del tiempo," *El País*, 24 January 2012.

the doubts with an exhaustive (and allegedly feasible) regulation of the "right to be forgotten" in Article 17 of the GDPR Proposal.

However, regulation of the "right to be forgotten" under Article 17 of the GDPR Proposal still gave rise to confusion and new questions.

a) The inclusion of the right to be forgotten within the right to erasure

The heading of draft Article 17 (*"right to be forgotten and to erasure"*) already hinted at the inevitable and indivisible connection between both notions, which risked being confused. The former was included within the latter,[67] but their content and scope remained to be defined.

The fact that such a long provision did not make specific reference to the right to be forgotten aggravated that risk. Furthermore, the scope of both rights drew on the content of the "right to erasure," which had developed a profile its own under the long-standing Directive 95/46/EC.

The confusion between both concepts is well exemplified by both the Opinion of the LIBE Committee of the European Parliament of 22 October 2013[68] and the Final Report issued by the European Parliament on 12 March 2014. They eliminated the term "right to be forgotten," yielding to the enormous pressures of multinational corporations, but instead maintained the reference to the "right to erasure" and all the contents of Article 17 of the GDPR Proposal which were previously protected under the "right to be forgotten."

As a result, much of the content of Article 17 of the GDPR Proposal unequivocally referred to the rights of "rectification, erasure and objection" already enshrined in the EU legislation in force:

1′) The data right to erase personal data relating to them and the abstention from further dissemination of such data where: (a) the data are

---

[67] As stated in Recital 53 of the GDPR Proposal: "Any person should have the right to have personal data concerning them rectified and a 'right to be forgotten' where the retention of such data is not in compliance with this Regulation. In particular, data subjects should have the right that their personal data are erased and no longer processed, where the data are no longer necessary in relation to the purposes for which the data are collected or otherwise processed, where data subjects have withdrawn their consent for processing or where they object to the processing of personal data concerning them or where the processing of their personal data otherwise does not comply with this Regulation."

[68] http://www.europarl.europa.eu/meetdocs/2009_2014/documents/libe/dv/comp_a m_art_01-29/comp_am_art_01-29en.pdf

no longer necessary in relation to the purposes for which they were collected or otherwise processed; (b) the data subject withdraws consent or when the storage period consented to has expired, and where there is no other legal ground for the processing of the data; (c) the data subject objects to the processing of personal data; (d) the processing of the data does not comply with this Regulation for other reasons. Where the erasure is carried out, the controller shall not otherwise process such personal data (sections 1 and 8 of Article 17 of the GDPR Proposal).

2´) The controller shall carry out the erasure without delay, except to the extent that the retention of the personal data is necessary: (a) for exercising the right of freedom of expression,[69] (b) for reasons of public interest in the area of public health, (c) for historical, statistical and scientific research purposes[70], (d) for compliance with a legal obligation to retain the personal data by Union or Member State law to which the controller is subject (section 3 of Article 17 of the GDPR Proposal).

3´) Instead of proceeding to the erasure, the controller shall restrict (*blockage*) processing of personal data where: (a) their accuracy is contested by the data subject, for a period enabling the controller to verify the accuracy of the data (*rectification*); (b) the controller no longer needs the personal data for the accomplishment of its task but they have to be

---

[69] At the time of presenting this proposal, it was already obvious that one of the issues the European legislature would have to tackle to ensure the right to be forgotten was the potential accusations of censorship or restriction of freedom of expression. Viviane Reding's first words already accounted for the need to show that the right to be forgotten would not entail any threat to the freedom of information: "*The right to be forgotten is of course not an absolute right.* There are cases where there is a legitimate and legally justified interest to keep data in a data base. The archives of a newspaper are a good example. It is clear that the right to be forgotten cannot amount to a right of the total erasure of history. Neither must the right to be forgotten take precedence over freedom of expression or freedom of the media. The new EU rules *will include explicit provisions that ensure the respect of freedom of expression* and information. After all, I have been the EU's Media Commissioner for many years, and I will never compromise in the fight for the fundamental rights of freedom of expression and freedom of the media. This also holds true in the field of data protection, which is another important fundamental right, but not an absolute one" (Viviane Reding: "The EU Data Protection Reform 2012: Making Europe the Standard Setter for Modern Data Protection Rules in the Digital Age," Innovation Conference Digital, Life, Design, Munich, 22 January 2012 (http://europa.eu/rapid/press-release_SPEECH-12-26_en.htm).
[70] On the effects of this exception in the United Kingdom during the validity of Directive 95/46, see DAVID ERDOS: "Stuck in the Thicket? Social Research under the First Data Protection Principle," *International Journal of Law and Information Technology,* vol. 19- 2, 2011, pp. 133-152.

maintained for purposes of proof; (c) the processing is unlawful and the data subject opposes their erasure and requests the restriction of their use instead; (d) the data subject requests to transmit the personal data into another automated processing system (*portability*). These personal data, with the exception of storage, may only be processed for purposes of proof, or with the data subject's consent, or for the protection of the rights of another natural or legal person or for an objective of public interest. Where processing of personal data is restricted, the controller shall inform the data subject before lifting the restriction on processing (sections 4, 5 and 6 of Article 17 of the GDPR Proposal).

b) **The *novelty* of the right to be forgotten: the obligation to *inform* third parties on the request to erase "any links to, or copy or replication" of personal data**

The European Commission's willingness to enshrine a new "right to be forgotten" required providing a precise meaning to that which Article 17 of the GDPR Proposal contributed to the recognition of data protection *rights* (in particular, the right to erasure). What can be identified as *new* in such provision is the following:

1′) Article 17(1) of the GDPR Proposal made particular reference to the right of data subjects to obtain from the controller the erasure of their personal data and the refrainment from further dissemination, "especially in relation to personal data which are made available by the data subject while he or she was a child." Article 8 of the GDPR Proposal established a more specific regime in respect to the processing of personal data of children (under 13). From a strictly legal perspective, this provision called for different legal regimes governing the erasure of data depending on whether they had been made available when the data subject was a child or an adult. However, this would mean either lowering the protection of adults or duplicating the existing guarantees for children.[71]

Even if we admitted the establishment of different erasure regimes depending on the age at which the data were made available, this provision failed to cast light on their specific legal scope, since it did not provide any further obligations for the data controller.

In spite of the difficulties to define the legal scope of the said reference to

---

[71] These arguments were used to justify the proposed amendment to delete such reference to children in Article 17(1) of the GDPR Proposal; see Draft Report of 16 January 2013 on the GDPR Proposal, by the Committee on Civil Liberties, Justice and Home Affairs of the European Parliament (Rapporteur: Jan Philipp Albrecht).

children, the European Commission's intention was irreproachable and commendable:[72] to draw attention to the need for a "right to be forgotten" which was particularly appropriate considering the habits of children in their use of online services (especially, social networks[73]). Indeed, children's behavior invites to think of a future need to erase their data when they reach adulthood.[74] The right to be forgotten on the Internet will be all the more relevant when *privacy inconveniences* manifest themselves decades after, and people may want a "clean slate (…) against the negative use of past information."[75]

2) Article 17(7) of the GDPR Proposal included a reference –unique at this time– to the *establishment of time limits for the erasure* of data: "the controller shall implement mechanisms to ensure that the time limits established for the erasure of personal data and/or for a periodic review of the need for the storage of the data are observed." Erasure of data had been traditionally conditioned to withdrawal of consent or them no longer being necessary for the original purpose. That is why this new provision on fixed deadlines for erasure or for a periodic review of the data's need is noteworthy.

The scope of this provision was not limited to any specific sector (online-

---

[72] As shown by Recital 53 of the GDPR Proposal, recalling that the right to be forgotten "is particularly relevant, when the data subject has given their consent as a child, when not being fully aware of the risks involved by the processing, and later wants to remove such personal data especially on the Internet."

[73] On the effects on children's privacy in some Canadian social networks, see ARTEMI RALLO: "La protección de la privacidad en las redes sociales de Internet: la experiencia canadiense con facebook, google y otros," *Derecho y Redes Sociales*, A. Rallo and R. Martínez (eds.), 2nd edition, Civitas-Thomson Reuters, Pamplona, 2013, pp. 257-284.

[74] For a specific study on this issue, also focused on Canada, see KARIM BENYEKHLEF: "Minors, social network sites and le droit à l'oubli," *Rapport rédigé pour la Fundacion Solventia*, Madrid, Spain, March 2010, 40 pages (with Philippe-Antoine Couture-Ménard and Emmanuelle Paquette-Bélanger). On the problems of verifying the age of minors on the Internet, see RICARD MARTINEZ: "Menores y redes sociales. Condiciones para el cumplimiento del artículo 13 del Reglamento de desarrollo de la LOPD," *Derecho y Redes Sociales*, A. Rallo & R. Martínez (eds.), 2nd edition, Civitas-Thomson Reuters, Pamplona, 2013, pp. 203-230 and NATALIA MARTOS DÍAZ & OSCAR CASADO OLIVA: "Políticas de privacidad, redes sociales y protección de datos. El problema de la verificación de edad. Sistemas de autorregulación," *Derecho y Redes Sociales*, A. Rallo & R. Martínez (eds.), 2nd edition, Civitas-Thomson Reuters, Pamplona, 2013, pp. 231-256.

[75] LUIZ COSTA & YVES POULLET, Y.: "Privacy and the Regulation of 2012," p. 257.

offline), but the *establishment of expiration deadlines* for data[76] was one of the main preconditions to implement the right to be forgotten on the Internet. The imposition of a specific obligation requiring data controllers to set time limits for the periodic review of the need for processing was especially relevant in the online environment.

3´) Article 17(2) of the GDPR Proposal clearly evidenced the European Commission's understanding of the right to be forgotten and its scope:

a) A right to be forgotten confined to the virtual field of the Internet[77] (as shown by the unequivocal references to "links, copies or replications" and by Recital 54 of the GDPR Proposal[78]).

b) Imposition on controllers having erased the data of the obligation to *inform third parties* which are processing such data of the erasure: "Where the controller referred to in paragraph 1 has made the personal data public, it shall take all reasonable steps, including technical measures, in relation to data for the publication of which the controller is responsible, to inform third parties which are processing such data, that a data subject requests them to erase any links to, or copy or replication of

---

[76] Certainly, based on the approach taken by VICTOR MAYER-SCHÖNBERGER: *Delete: The Virtue of Forgetting in the Digital Age...*, p. 171.

[77] Viviane Reding confirmed this few days before the presentation of the GDPR Proposal: "So even tiny scraps of personal information can have a huge impact, even years after they were shared or made public. The right to be forgotten will build on already existing rules to better cope with privacy risks online. It is the individual who should be in the best position to protect the privacy of their data by choosing whether or not to provide it. It is therefore important to empower EU citizens, particularly teenagers, to be in control of their own identity online. By the way, 81% of German citizens are worried they are no more in control of their personal data! If an individual no longer wants his personal data to be processed or stored by a data controller, and if there is no legitimate reason for keeping it, the data should be removed from their system" ("The EU Data Protection Reform 2012: Making Europe the Standard Setter for Modern Data Protection Rules in the Digital Age," Innovation Conference Digital, Life, Design, Munich, 22 January 2012 (http://europa.eu/rapid/press-release_SPEECH-12-26_en.htm).

[78] Recital 54 of the GDPR Proposal established that: "To strengthen the 'right to be forgotten' in the online environment, the right to erasure should also be extended in such a way that a controller who has made the personal data public should be obliged to inform third parties which are processing such data that a data subject requests them to erase any links to, or copies or replications of that personal data. To ensure this information, the controller should take all reasonable steps, including technical measures, in relation to data for the publication of which the controller is responsible. In relation to a third party publication of personal data, the controller should be considered responsible for the publication, where the controller has authorised the publication by the third party."

that personal data. Where the controller has authorised a third party publication of personal data, the controller shall be considered responsible for that publication."[79]

Hence, this regulation of the right to be forgotten on the Internet was limited in its scope:

a) Like in the case of the right to erasure, providers of online services collecting data were obliged to erase them at the request of the data subject, as long as such data were under their control.

b) However, if such data were collected by third party services, the provider that originally obtained them was only required to "inform" these third parties on the data subject's request to erase "any links to, or copy or replication" of that personal data.[80]

c) The "conditions" established in the Commission's delegated acts for deleting links, copies or replications of personal data from publicly available communication services had to be complied with (Article 17(9) of the GDPR Proposal).[81]

2.4.- THE LONG EUROPEAN DEBATE AND THE PRESSURES OF MULTINATIONAL TECHNOLOGY CORPORATIONS AGAINST THE RIGHT TO BE FORGOTTEN (2012-2016)

---

[79] JEF AUSLOOS already stressed that the right to be forgotten should cover situations where data are shared with third parties: "To prevent data controllers from avoiding the right's application by transferring the data to a third entity (with whom the data subject has no direct consent-based relationship), the 'right to be forgotten' should follow the data when voluntarily (and legitimately) shared by the original data controller" ("The 'Right to be Forgotten' - Worth remembering?," *Computer Law & Security Review…*, p. 151).

[80] The EDPS, while welcoming this new provision, stressed the need to ensure actual effectiveness of the right to be forgotten, despite some obvious difficulties: "It may in some cases be a huge effort to inform all third parties who may be processing such data, as there will not always be clear understanding of where the data may have been disseminated. To have an effective right to be forgotten implies that the scope of the right should be clear from the moment the Regulation applies. Article 17 might need to be further developed in that respect" (*Opinion of the European Data Protection Supervisor on the data protection reform package*, 7 March 2012, http://www.edps.europa.eu/EDPSWEB/edps/Consultation/Reform_package).

[81] As pointed out by LUIZ COSTA & YVES POULLET, this does not preclude acknowledging that the exercise of these powers by the European Commission will be essential to ensure the effectiveness of a right to be forgotten which, under the GDPR Proposal, is inevitably based on a "techno-legal approach" ("Privacy and the Regulation of 2012," p. 257).

Despite the limited scope of the right to be forgotten under the GDPR Proposal, one year after its presentation the European Commission still felt the need to justify this new approach and to dispel the ghosts[82] that continually haunted the parliamentary debate. Such doubts were triggered by large technology corporations which would be subject to the new GDPR.[83]

At the Informal Justice and Home Affairs Council held in Dublin on 18 January 2013, Viviane Reding took the opportunity to stress the importance of the right to be forgotten as an effective guarantee for the control of one's one data, and as a response to a technology that provides unlimited possibilities of storage, exchange and dissemination of data.

Ambition and *pragmatism* were the drivers chosen by the European Commissioner to illustrate, on the one hand, the need to impose a clear obligation upon data controllers to erase the data and stop dissemination; and, on the other, the advisability of not establishing unreasonable obligations for companies: "That is why the right to be forgotten does not mean obliging companies to eradicate every digital trace that has spread on the web – we have simply suggested that a company informs third parties about a request for erasure ... In a nutshell: the Right to be Forgotten as proposed by the Commission is necessary, reasonable and workable. I am happy Ministers agree that this right should be one of the key pillars of the Regulation."[84]

---

[82] As exemplified by JOHN HENDEL's consideration that "two of the Western world's biggest transnational institutions may soon fall into a complex, ideological struggle: a right to free and open Internet v. a right to be forgotten." That is, an unsupported inference of a potential conflict between the European initiative to regulate the right to be forgotten and the submission of the *Report of the Special Rapporteur on the promotion and protection of the right to freedom of opinion and expression, Frank La Rue* on 16 May 2011 to the UN Human Rights Council ("The West's Coming Internet War," 7 June 2011, http://www.theatlantic.com/technology/archive/2011/06/the-wests-coming-internet-war/240044/).

[83] PETER HUSTINX: "European leadership in privacy and data protection," *Hacia un nuevo derecho europeo de protección de datos. Towards a new European Data Protection Regime* (eds.) A. Rallo Lombarte & R. García, Tirant lo Blanch, Valencia, 2015, p. 24.

[84] "Right to be forgotten: This is an important way of making sure that individuals are in control of their data. A response to the technologies that provide unlimited possibilities for the storage, exchange and dissemination of information. The principle is simple: if you have given your data to a company you should be able to get it back or delete it. Unless there are good reasons not to do so. To make this work in reality we have to be ambitious and pragmatic at the same time. *Ambitious* because we should impose a clear obligation on a

Reding's limited success is well exemplified by the *Report of the Irish Presidency of the Council of the European Union of 31 May 2013*. It significantly lowered the expectations of the European Commission by narrowing the scope of the right to be forgotten, which was made conditional on *available technology and the cost of implementation*: "*Article 17. Right to be forgotten and to erasure:* ... 2a. Where the controller (...) has made the personal data public and is obliged pursuant to paragraph 1 to erase the data, the controller, taking account of available technology and the cost of implementation, shall take (...) reasonable steps, including technical measures, (...) to inform controllers which are processing the data, that a data subject requests them to erase any links to, or copy or replication of that personal data... *Article 17b: Notification obligation regarding rectification, erasure or restriction:* The controller shall communicate any rectification, erasure or restriction of processing carried out in accordance with Articles 16, 17(1) and 17a to each recipient to whom the data have been disclosed, unless this proves impossible or involves a disproportionate effort."[85]

Feasibility[86] of the right to be forgotten was undoubtedly the main issue[87]

---

controller to erase data and to stop further dissemination of personal data where keeping the data is no longer necessary. *Pragmatic because we do not want to impose any unreasonable obligations on businesses*" (Viviane Reding, "Speech: Justice for Growth makes headway at today's Justice Council," Informal Justice Council, Dublin, 18 January 2013 (http://europa.eu/rapid/press-release_SPEECH-13-29_en.htm).

[85] http://register.consilium.europa.eu/pdf/en/13/st10/st10227.en13.pdf

[86] There is a very interesting study by ENISA (Network and Information Security Agency: *The right to be forgotten – between expectations and practice...*). From a technological approach, it points out the practical problems of the right to be forgotten as erasure of personal data. It puts forward a pragmatic proposal, stating the feasibility of requiring online search engines to erase search index results. This would contribute to achieving the intended purpose of the right to be forgotten: "While it is impossible in general to remove data from the Internet once it was published, it might be possible to limit its accessibility. One such approach relies on the observation that users typically find information on the Internet by issuing queries to a search engine, or by using a social networking, sharing, or tagging site. Data not identified by a search engine or shared via a service like Twitter is difficult to find. A natural way to "mostly forget" data is thus to prevent its appearance in the results of search engines, and to filter it from sharing services like Twitter. EU member states could require search engine operators and sharing services to filter references to forgotten data. As a result, forgotten data would be very difficult to find, even though copies may survive, for instance, outside the EU jurisdiction. To summarize, *all existing technical approaches to ensure the right to be forgotten are vulnerable to unauthorized copying while the date is publicly accessible and a re-dissemination of such*

raised by the American technology industry against the EU's strong commitment to ensure a modern and updated version of the right to erasure of data in the technological environment.[88]

This version of the right to be forgotten enshrined in Article 17(2) of the GDPR Proposal also elicited different responses from national authorities. Among them, Spain's stance on the initiative of the European Commission is particularly interesting.

On 27 November 2012, the Spanish Ministry of Justice made public Spain's position in favor of a European regulation on the right to be forgotten, seeking a balance between technology's theoretical possibilities and actual constraints on the Internet: a realistic analysis of the constraints still affecting technology's capabilities was essential to avoid false expectations regarding the protection of the right to be forgotten –expectations that could easily end in frustration.
Spain's position called for a realistic assessment, aware that the best human and technological efforts might not be enough to prevent data from being replicated and kept on servers and webs. The possibilities of disseminating information on the Internet are almost endless. Therefore, the obligation to fully erase not only the originally stored data but also their copies and any other trace can sometimes be excessive and unreasonable.

---

unauthorized copies once the data has expired. Therefore, the right to be forgotten cannot be ensured using technical means alone. A possible partial solution may be a legal mandate aimed at making it difficult to find expired personal data, for instance, by requiring search engines to exclude expired personal data from their search results" (p. 13). Indeed, one of its main recommendations is: "A possible pragmatic approach to assist with the enforcement of the right to be forgotten is to require search engine operators and sharing services within the EU to filter references to forgotten information stored inside and outside the EU region" (p. 14).

[87] Although in more general terms, it is worth recalling the wise words of MARTIN ABRAMS: "For the proposed regulation to be effective, those that implement and interpret must understand the challenges related to created data" ("Data origin and the proposed regulation," *Hacia un nuevo derecho europeo de protección de datos. Towards a new European Data Protection Regime* (eds) A. Rallo & R. García, Tirant lo Blanch, Valencia, 2015, p. 101).

[88] JEFFREY ROSEN stated that: "It's possible, of course, that although the European regulation defines the right to be forgotten very broadly, it will be applied more narrowly. Europeans have a long tradition of declaring abstract privacy rights in theory that they fail to enforce in practice" ("The right to be forgotten," *Stanford Law Review Online*, vol. 64, 2012, p. 92). On the problematic aspects regarding feasibility of the right to be forgotten, see EDUARDO USTARAN: *The future of privacy*, manuscript, 2013, p. 44.

In sum, Spain's stance aimed at a "viable understanding" of the right to be forgotten which should govern the obligation to inform third parties (provided they had been granted access to the data either expressly or tacitly). Such approach was based on the proportionality between the measures to protect the right to be forgotten and the effects thereof (without excessive or impossible costs). Spain suggested assessing the potential liability of Internet operators on a case-by-case basis, without holding the original data controller *strictly liable* for the actions of third parties.[89]

Another criticism of the right to be forgotten arises from its lack of *enforceability*. Despite its attempt to provide a more effective guarantee of the right to erasure in the digital environment, it manifested itself as an unclear right regarding its implementation and enforcement.

There were significant doubts concerning prosecution of violations: controllers were held accountable when personal data were made public or when third-party advertisement was authorized, but the obligations stemming from such liability were limited to taking "all reasonable steps" to inform third parties which are processing such data of the subject's request to erase any links, copies or replications.

The right to be forgotten thus became basically –or only– some sort of obligation to adopt technical measures that could be deemed objectively reasonable in order to achieve the intended purpose. This was not so much to effectively delete personal contents on the Internet as to eliminate the supply of information between online providers. In other words, as pointed out by the EDPS, Article 17 of the GDPR Proposal established an obligation of *endeavor*, which was more realistic from a practical point of view than an obligation of *result*.[90]

From the very beginning of the initiative, the right to be forgotten was somehow seen as a *threat to the freedom of expression and of the press*,[91]

---

[89] *Propuesta de Reglamento sobre Protección de Datos Personales* (Proposal for a Regulation on Personal Data Protection), Spanish Ministry of Justice, Posición Española/Versión 3.3, 27 November 2012, p. 18.

[90] *Opinion of the European Data Protection Supervisor on the data protection reform package*, 7 March 2012
(http://www.edps.europa.eu/EDPSWEB/edps/Consultation/Reform_package).

[91] JOHN HENDEL: "Why Journalists Shouldn't Fear Europe's 'Right to be Forgotten'," 25 January 2012
(http://www.theatlantic.com/technology/archive/2012/01/why-journalists-shouldnt-fear-europes-right-to-be-forgotten/251955/).

which loomed large in the parliamentary debate on the GDPR Proposal.[92] Freedom on the Internet[93] and the risk that the right to be forgotten could become some sort of censorship was voiced by the *prophets* of freedom on the Net, usually intermingled with the economic interests of powerful Internet corporations, producing effective results in the discussion process.[94]

Although it was obviously unnecessary, the European Commission had to deny the absolute nature of the right to be forgotten vis-à-vis the rest of rights and, in particular, the freedoms of expression and information. The Commission was also forced to assure that the right to be forgotten would not amount to a "right of the total deletion of history."[95]

Considering that the European Parliament Resolution of 6 June 2011 already warned of the need for "clarifying in detail and codifying the 'right to be forgotten'," while ensuring its full technical and

---

[92] For a critical analysis of how this regulation of the right to be forgotten affects freedom of expression and, in particular, its seeming incompatibility with the First Amendment of the US Constitution, see MUGE FAZLIOGLU: "Forget me not: the clash of the right to be forgotten and freedom of expression on the Internet," *International Data Privacy Law*, vol. 3-3, 2013, pp. 149-157.

[93] JEFFREY ROSEN concluded that: "Once the regulation is promulgated ... it's hard to imagine that the Internet that results will be as free and open as it is now" ("The right to be forgotten...," p. 92).

[94] As is evident from the amendments proposed to the Albrecht's Draft Report, or from the Commissioner Reding's speech at the Informal Justice Council held in Dublin on 18 January 2013: "Let me also just mention one thing, as I feel there has been some confusion on this aspect: the right to be forgotten cannot be absolute just as the right to privacy is not absolute. There are other fundamental rights with which the right to be forgotten needs to be balanced – such as freedom of expression and freedom of the press. We have taken account of these. In order to make this absolutely clear, we have specified that the Right to be Forgotten cannot lead to the deletion where individuals are exercising their right to freedom of expression or keeping data for historical purposes which would include newspaper archives (Article 17(3)(c)). We have also specified that freedom of expression includes processing for journalistic purposes (Art 80)," in "Speech: Justice for Growth makes headway at today's Justice Council...," (http://europa.eu/rapid/press-release_SPEECH-13-29_en.htm). The same concern regarding the need to settle the conflict between freedom of expression and the right to be forgotten can be found in the *Opinion of the European Union Agency for Fundamental Rights on the proposed data protection reform package*, Vienna, 1 October 2012, p. 16. These same doubts had already been raised in detail in *European Union data protection reform: new fundamental rights guarantees, 3rd Annual Fundamental Rights Agency Symposium*, Vienna, 10 May 2012, pp. 5 and 6.

[95] VIVIANE REDING: "The European data protection framework for the twenty-first century," *International Data Privacy Law*, 2012, vol. 2-3, p. 125.

---

organisational feasibility, it is hardly surprising that the "right to be forgotten" disappeared from the GDPR Proposal.

During the parliamentary debates on the GDPR Proposal,[96] there was some confusion between the notions of erasure and the right to be forgotten, to the extent that both the Opinion of the LIBE Committee of the European Parliament of 22 October 2013 and the Final Report adopted by the European Parliament Plenary on 12 March 2014 eliminated any reference to the "right to be forgotten." The heading "right to erasure," however, remained with almost the same content as Article 17 of the GDPR Proposal previously protected under the "right to be forgotten."

This position of the European Parliament was notably influenced by the doubts on the feasibility of the right to be forgotten raised by large Internet corporations[97] and by the 25 June 2013 Opinion[98] of the Advocate General of the CJEU in Case *Google versus Spain* (C-131/12), which rejected the existence of a right to be forgotten in the legal system of the European Union.

The AG warned about the potential dangers for Internet users resulting from an excessive application of the right to data protection in the reality of today's Internet. The AG put the interests of the information society and economic operators before the fundamental right to data protection. According to the AG, Internet users' interest to access information and an effective dissemination of online information (as a manifestation of the freedoms of information, expression, and enterprise) should prevail. The AG considered that the "right to be forgotten" could "prevent" or hinder the development of a crucial Internet service and, therefore, of information society itself.

In this context, it is not surprising that the European Parliament would lower the language of the right to be forgotten. This situation was

---

[96] ARTEMI RALLO: "El debate europeo sobre el derecho al olvido en Internet," *Hacia un nuevo derecho europeo de protección de datos. Towards a new European Data Protection Regime* (eds.) A. Rallo & R. García, Tirant lo Blanch, Valencia, 2015, pp. 703-737.

[97] The Chair of the LIBE Committee of the European Parliament, JUAN FERNANDO LÓPEZ AGUILAR, stated that there had never before been such an enormous lobbyist pressure: "Data protection package y Parlamento Europeo," *Hacia un nuevo derecho europeo de protección de datos. Towards a new European Data Protection Regime* (eds.) A. Rallo and R. García, Tirant lo Blanch, Valencia, 2015, pp. 29-81.

[98] http://curia.europa.eu/juris/document/document.jsf?text=&docid=138782&pageIndex=0&doclang=ES&mode=lst&dir=&occ=first&part=1&cid=1094085

radically reversed by the Judgment of the CJEU of 13 May 2014 (*C-113/12, Google v Spain*), which ruled exactly the opposite.

2.5.- RECOGNITION OF THE RIGHT TO BE FORGOTTEN IN THE GENERAL DATA PROTECTION REGULATION (2016)

The Judgment of the CJEU of 13 May 2014 (*C-131/12, Google v Spain*) is not the original cause, as we have seen, but it played a critical role in recovering the heading "right to be forgotten" in Article 17 of the GDPR finally adopted on 27 April 2016 –officially published on 4 May 2016 and scheduled to enter into force on 25 May 2018.[99]

The final content of Article 17 GDPR has not dispelled all criticism raised by the Proposal. The right to be forgotten is more clearly included within the right to erasure. In fact, while the Proposal seemed to hint at two different rights in its heading –"*right to be forgotten and to erasure,*" the final wording adopts a heading which undoubtedly includes the right to be forgotten within the right to erasure, without distinguishing between them –"*right to erasure ('right to be forgotten').*" In sum, Article 17 GDPR refers indistinctly as synonyms to the *right to erasure* and to the *right to be forgotten.*

Apparently, only the Recitals of the GDPR seek to give a different meaning to the right to be forgotten in two senses: online protection of minors, and erasure of data on the Internet. Recital 65 states that the right to be forgotten "is relevant in particular where the data subject has given his or her consent as a child and is not fully aware of the risks involved by the processing, and later wants to remove such personal data, especially on the internet. The data subject should be able to exercise that

---

[99] Regulation (EU) 2016/679 of the European Parliament and of the Council of 27 April 2016 on the protection of natural persons with regard to the processing of personal data and on the free movement of such data, and repealing Directive 95/46/EC (General Data Protection Regulation), *Official Journal of the European Union*, L 119, 4.5.15, pp. 1-88.

right notwithstanding the fact that he or she is no longer a child."[100] Recital 66 adds the following: "To strengthen the right to be forgotten in the online environment, the right to erasure should also be extended in such a way that a controller who has made the personal data public should be obliged to inform the controllers which are processing such personal data to erase any links to, or copies or replications of those personal data."

Article 17(1) GDPR enshrines the right to erasure (right to be forgotten) of personal data "without undue delay" in the following cases: (a) the personal data are no longer necessary in relation to the purposes for which they were collected; (b) the data subject withdraws consent or there is no other legal ground for the processing; (c) the data subject objects to the processing and there are no overriding legitimate grounds for the processing; (d) the personal data have been unlawfully processed; (e) the personal data have to be erased for compliance with a legal obligation in Union or Member State law; (f) the personal data have been collected in relation to the offer of information society services directly to a child.

The main manifestation of the right to be forgotten can be seen in Article 17(2) GDPR: "Where the controller has made the personal data public and is obliged pursuant to paragraph 1 to erase the personal data, the controller, taking account of available technology and the cost of implementation, shall take reasonable steps, including technical measures, to inform controllers which are processing the personal data that the data subject has requested the erasure by such controllers of any links to, or copy or replication of, those personal data."

The GDPR takes into account the significance of a wide dissemination of personal data in today's information society and, especially, through

---

[100] It is worth noting that Article 8 GDPR grants special protection to children: "Conditions applicable to child's consent in relation to information society services 1. Where point (a) of Article 6(1) applies, in relation to the offer of information society services directly to a child, the processing of the personal data of a child shall be lawful where the child is at least 16 years old. Where the child is below the age of 16 years, such processing shall be lawful only if and to the extent that consent is given or authorised by the holder of parental responsibility over the child. Member States may provide by law for a lower age for those purposes provided that such lower age is not below 13 years. 2. The controller shall make reasonable efforts to verify in such cases that consent is given or authorised by the holder of parental responsibility over the child, taking into consideration available technology. 3. Paragraph 1 shall not affect the general contract law of Member States such as the rules on the validity, formation or effect of a contract in relation to a child."

Internet services. Consequently, it establishes the obligation to inform those which are processing such personal data in order to limit the impact of this massive dissemination. Nevertheless, existing technical constraints call for a realistic and practical view limiting the right to be forgotten in the light of the *available technology* and the *cost of implementation*.

Furthermore, Article 19 GDPR significantly establishes an additional notification obligation –different from the obligation to inform: "The controller shall communicate any (...) erasure of personal data (...) to each recipient to whom the personal data have been disclosed, unless this proves impossible or involves disproportionate effort. The controller shall inform the data subject about those recipients if the data subject requests it."

The limits of the right to erasure (right to be forgotten) are clearly set forth in Article 17(3) GDPR: (a) the right of freedom of expression and information; (b) compliance with a legal obligation or the performance of a task carried out in the public interest or in the exercise of official authority; (c) public interest in the area of public health; (d) archiving purposes in the public interest, scientific or historical research purposes or statistical purposes;[101] (e) the establishment, exercise or defence of legal claims.

Although the GDPR Proposal included it within the right to be forgotten, Article 18 GDPR has replaced the former *right of blocking*, provided in Directive 95/46/EC, with a new *right to restriction of processing*, pursuant to which the data subject shall have the right to obtain from the controller restriction of processing when one of the following occurs: (a) the accuracy of the personal data is contested (for a period enabling the controller to verify the accuracy); (b) the processing is unlawful and the data subject requests the restriction of their use; (c) the establishment, exercise or defence of legal claims; (d) the data subject has objected to processing pending the verification whether the legitimate grounds of the controller override those of the data subject. In these cases, personal information can only be processed with the data subject's consent or for the establishment, exercise or

---

[101] Recital 156: "(...) Member States should be authorised to provide, under specific conditions and subject to appropriate safeguards for data subjects, specifications and derogations with regard to the information requirements and rights to rectification, to erasure, to be forgotten, to restriction of processing, to data portability, and to object when processing personal data for archiving purposes in the public interest, scientific or historical research purposes or statistical purposes."

defence of legal claims or for the protection of the rights of another natural or legal person or for reasons of important public interest of the Union or of a Member State. The data subject be informed by the controller before the restriction of processing is lifted.

CHAPTER II
THE RIGHT TO BE FORGOTTEN IN SPAIN (I): THE OBJECTION/ERASURE OF DATA INDEXED BY SEARCH ENGINES ON THE INTERNET

1.- THE SINGULARITY OF A *GENUINELY* SPANISH PROBLEM: INDEXATION OF OFFICIAL GAZETTES

1.1.- The "first case" regarding the right to be forgotten: notice of an administrative penalty published in the Official Gazette

The following resolutions, issued by the Spanish Data Protection Agency (*Agencia Española de Protección de Datos*, AEPD) against Google Spain, Google Inc. and the Official Provincial Gazette (BOP) at the request of the same individual, evidence the initial confusion on how to fulfill the alleged right to be forgotten.

1) Case BOP Valladolid I: X v. Google Spain

The complaint leading to the first case involving the right to be forgotten in Spain was filed before the AEPD on 24 May 2007. An individual required Google Spain not to index his personal data published in the digital version of an official gazette.

The dispute arose because, when the claimant typed his name in Google's search engine (Google Search), there was information on a penalty notice imposed by local authorities for breaching local provisions ("for urinating in public roadways"). The applicable legislation on the publicity of administrative resolutions allowed for the inclusion of this penalty notice in the Official Provincial Gazette only if it had been impossible to serve notice on the party at his/her home.

The claimant exercised his right to object against Google Spain. He claimed that the engine's search results indexes entailed an unreasonable public dissemination of his personal data, provided that such data were connected with an event leading to social rejection; this was prejudicial and caused him public damage because he was the Associate to the Headmaster at a school. However, Google rejected the claim, arguing that the problem was to be solved by the website owner, i.e. the Official Provincial Gazette, by blocking the web as well as by preventing crawling and indexation by the search engine.

The AEPD gave leave to proceed, i.e. it decided to hear the claim involving the right to object (proceedings no. TD/463/2007), and on 20

November 2007 it issued Resolution no. 1046/2007 upholding this claim. As a result, it ordered Google Spain to "adopt any measures necessary to remove the data from its index and to prevent access to the data in the future."[102]

The AEPD grounded its resolution on the right to object, enshrined in Directive 95/46/EC and duly transposed into Article 6(4) of the Spanish Data Protection Organic Act (LOPD): "In the cases where the consent of the data subject is not required for processing personal data, and unless provided otherwise by law, the data subject may object to such processing when there are compelling legitimate grounds relating to a particular personal situation. In such an event, the controller shall exclude the data relating to the data subject from the processing."

The personal information made public by a City Council in the Official Provincial Gazette is covered by Act 5/2002, of 4 April, governing Official Provincial Gazettes. This Act required Provincial Councils to publish in the Official Provincial Gazette "any provision, local regulation, resolution, edict or public notice, announcement, act or agreement from public authorities and courts of justice that must be included therein under a legal or regulatory provision" (Article 6(1)). Similarly, Articles 58 and 59 of Act 30/1992, of 26 November, on the Legal Regime of Public Authorities and Common Administrative Procedure, allow for notifying administrative resolutions by publishing them in the Official Gazette when it has been impossible to serve notice at the mailing address. In sum, Spanish legislation allows for including such notice in the digital version of the Official Gazette.

However, in contrast to the digital version of the Official Gazette, no law provides either that personal data must be included in Google search indexes to facilitate user access to certain websites, or that such data must be temporarily stored in cache memories.

The admissibility of the right to object requires assessing whether there are "compelling legitimate grounds relating to a particular personal situation." The AEPD considered there were indeed compelling and legitimate interests for a threefold reason. First, the personal information at stake concerned an infringement in a matter of citizen coexistence. Second, the claimant worked at an educational institution. Third, although

---

[102] Recital 45 of Directive 95/46/EC clarifies the scope of this right: "In cases where data might lawfully be processed on grounds of public interest, official authority or the legitimate interests of a natural or legal person, any data subject should nevertheless be entitled, on legitimate and compelling grounds relating to his particular situation, to object to the processing of any data relating to himself."

the territorial scope of the official publication was limited to the province, Google's data processing allowed for general and universal access to such information. The AEPD acknowledged that search engines enable Internet users to access websites through a list of indexed links. According to Spanish legislation, this falls within the definition of "information society services." These services must "respect human dignity," or otherwise "the bodies responsible for its protection, duly exercising the powers legally vested in them, shall adopt any measures necessary to suspend the provision of these services or to withdraw any data [breaching the principles set out below]" -Article 8 of Act 34/2002, of 11 July, on Information Society Services and Electronic Commerce (LSSI).[103]

The LSSI made it possible to bring a claim against the search engine when the competent authority (AEPD) found a violation of the fundamental right to data protection as well as of human dignity.[104]

In sum, the AEPD held that the data indexed by Google affected the claimant's dignity and violated his fundamental right to data protection. In its condition as the competent body, it required Google Spain (i.e., the data controller) to adopt any measures necessary to comply with Spanish legislation (LOPD and LSSI).

2) Case BOP Valladolid II: X v. Official Gazette

---

[103] It is worth recalling that Spanish Constitutional Court Judgment (STC) no. 292/2000 stated the following: "Article 18(4) of the Spanish Constitution guarantees the rights to privacy and honor, along with a full enjoyment of the remaining individual rights. Additionally, this guarantee is in itself a fundamental right or freedom, i.e. the right to be free from potential attacks on personal <u>dignity</u> and freedom stemming from an unlawful processing of personal data by automatic means, designated by the Constitution as "information technology." Accordingly, "the fundamental right to data protection is aimed at ensuring that the data subject is under control of his/her personal data, i.e. of the use and destination thereof, in order to prevent unlawful data traffic that could damage the data subject's <u>dignity</u> and individual rights."

[104] A different issue altogether is how search engine providers can be held liable, since Article 17 LSSI ("Liability of service providers that provide links to contents or search tools") made liability conditional on: (a) being aware that the information to which they refer or which they suggest is unlawful or in breach of third party interests or rights subject to compensation; (b) and, if they are aware, failing to act diligently to remove or disable the relevant link. Furthermore, awareness is deemed to exist when a competent body (such as the AEPD) has taken action (declaring that the data are unlawful, ordering their withdrawal or preventing access to them, or declaring that there has been an injury) and the search engine is aware of such decision.

Following the previous resolution, the claimant brought another claim (proceedings no. TD/980/2008). On 28 January 2008, he exercised his right to object to the publication of the municipal edict notifying the penalty for breaching the local regulation on citizen coexistence against the City Council and the Official Provincial Gazette.

Although this individual required the deletion of his data both from the municipal edict and the Official Gazette's website, Resolution no. 1531/2008, issued by the AEPD on 13 January 2009, dismissed the first claim. The Spanish Data Protection Agency considered that the City Council's edict publication complied with Articles 59(5) of Act 30/1992 and 6(1) of Act 5/2002, of 4 April, whereas it upheld the complaint against the Official Provincial Gazette.

During the proceedings, the Valladolid Provincial Council, responsible for the Official Provincial Gazette, had reported to the AEPD that it had erased and replaced the data subject's personal information. However, it had failed to limit the page view where the notice was, as well as the rest of the Official Gazette.

The Official Gazette anonymized the claimant's identity by replacing his name and last name with other characters. According to the AEPD Resolution, this prevented "the multiplier effect of dissemination through the Internet and, to a greater extent, through search engines, along with its impact on data protection of persons, particularly those who do not play a role in public life." This anonymization also avoided any potential "permanent unwanted effects of search engine data processing against the data subject's will."

This *forward-looking doctrine* is tied to the pioneering approach of the 1978 Spanish Constitution (CE), which was able to foresee the potential risks of information technology for the enjoyment of certain fundamental rights. In 1978, the drafters of the Constitution could only address an emerging and primary use of computers. Nevertheless, the omnipresence of the Internet nowadays and the extremely significant impact of some of its services (particularly search engines) call for a reformulation of the constitutional protection in line with the current "use of information technology."[105]

3) Case BOP Valladolid III: X v. Google Inc.

Finally, on 22 May 2008, this individual filed a complaint against Google Inc. to claim for protection of his right to object. The proceedings (TD/833/2008) concluded on 21 November 2008. The AEPD issued Resolution no. 1616/2008 dismissing the claim against Google Inc., on the grounds that the claims had already been fulfilled, since the claimant's data were not included in the Official Provincial Gazette and his name and last name had not been indexed by Internet search engines.

In the context of this AEPD Resolution, Google Inc. put forward, <u>for the first time</u>, the legal grounds that founded (from the first instances up to the Court of Justice of the European Union) its rejection to enforce AEPD resolutions, thereby undermining the right to be forgotten:

1′) the search engine's automatic nature based on a keyword search;
2′) the neutral nature of the search engine vis-à-vis the webmaster's liability for being the only one capable of withdrawing the information;
3′) the inapplicability of Spanish legislation -since Google Spain acts solely as an exclusive commercial representative of Google Inc. to sell advertising space, but with no responsibility over the search engine- and European legislation -since the search engine services are provided by Google Inc. in the United States, and therefore the EU Data Protection Directive does not apply.

Nevertheless, the AEPD took advantage of these proceedings to lay the

---

[105] This AEPD Resolution quoted Constitutional Court Judgment (STC) no. 292/2000: "By including Article 18(4) of the Spanish Constitution, currently in force, the drafters emphasized their awareness of the risks attached to the use of information technology. This constitutional provision empowered the legislature to guarantee certain fundamental rights as well as the full exercise of individual rights (...). On the one hand, the aim and concerns of the drafters are evidenced by the Draft Constitution, which already included a paragraph similar to current Article 18(4), and by the subsequent broadening of this provision through the inclusion of a final indent. On the other hand, these concerns are more clearly evidenced by the debate in the Senate. Although the need for this paragraph was questioned given the enshrinement of the rights to privacy and honor in the first paragraph, all doubts were dispelled as soon as it was stated that those rights (having regard to their content) did not provide sufficient guarantees vis-à-vis the potential threats of computers for private life. Accordingly, by means of Article 18(4), the drafters did not only want to ensure a specific scope of protection, but a more suitable one."

main legal foundations of the "Spanish model" of the right to be forgotten against Google:

1′) the recognition of the right to object to data processing on compelling legitimate grounds relating to a particular personal situation (Articles 18 LOPD and 34-35 of the Implementing Regulation of the LOPD, RLOPD);

2′) the applicability of Spanish legislation when the data controller is not established in the EU but the equipment used for the processing is located in Spain;[106]

3′) the applicability of Spanish legislation when the processing is carried out "in the context of the activities of an establishment" of that controller on the territory of a Member State implying the effective and real exercise of activity, regardless of the legal form of the establishment (a local office, a subsidiary with legal personality or a third party agency), i.e., when the controller establishes an office in a Member State that is involved in the selling of targeted advertisements to the inhabitants of that state or complies with court orders and/or law enforcement requests by the competent authorities of a Member State with regard to user data;[107]

4′) search engines resort to "equipment" located on the territory of the Member State: data storage centers, use of personal computers, terminals and servers or cookies and similar software devices;[108]

5′) in order to protect human dignity, the competent domestic bodies may adopt any necessary measures to suspend the provision of services or to withdraw any data in breach of human dignity (Articles 4 and 8(1) LSSI).

1.2.- The indexation of Constitutional Court (*Tribunal Constitucional*, TC) judgments and orders. The anonymization of European Court of Human Rights (ECtHR) judgments

---

[106] In order to prevent individuals from being deprived of the protection guaranteed under the Directive, any processing of personal data must be carried out in accordance with the law of Member States and, if the controller is established in a third country, that must not stand in the way of the protection of individuals provided for in the Directive. In these cases, the processing should be governed by the law of the Member State in which the equipment used is located, and there should be guarantees to ensure that the rights and obligations provided in the Directive are respected in practice (Articles 3 RLOPD and Recital 18 of Directive 95/46/EC).

[107] Article 29 Working Party, 148, 4 April 2008, Opinion on search engines.

[108] Article 29 Working Party, 148, 4 April 2008, Opinion on search engines.

One of the most prominent dimensions of the publicity of public acts in the Spanish constitutional system is the dissemination of judgments and court orders issued by the Constitutional Court. This publicity collides with data protection very intensely, given its tremendous reach in the Internet era.

1) The anonymized publication, as an exception, of Constitutional Court decisions in the Official State Gazette (BOE) as well as on its website

The Constitutional Court (TC) has laid down a general criterion regarding the reach of the publicity and publication of its judicial decisions, i.e., a criterion on anonymizing or concealing data subjects' personal identities. Furthermore, the TC has provided an exception to the full identification of the parties by referring to them by their initials (Constitutional Court Judgment, STC, no. 114/2006, of 5 April, following its previous Court Order no. 516/2004, of 20 December).

Constitutional Court Order no. 516/2004 rejected the appellant's claim, who requested that published judgments only include his, his wife's and other persons' initials mentioned in the court decision. The appellant's claim was based on grounds of personal safety, professional activity, and personal standing and reputation. However, the TC rejected the claim, although admitting to the possibility of exceptionally overcoming the principle of publicity on grounds of public order and protection of fundamental rights and freedoms (Articles 120(1) of the Spanish Constitution, CE, and 232(2) of the Organic Act on the Judiciary, LOPJ).

The TC had been taking "special care" in order not to include any piece of personal information that was not strictly necessary for the Court's legal reasoning and ruling. Exceptionally, it had not identified persons mentioned in its decisions to protect children's privacy (Constitutional Court Judgments, no. 114/1997, of 16 June; no. 288/2000, of 27 November; no. 94/2003, of 19 May, and no. 127/2003, of 30 June), or to preserve the privacy of victims of sex crimes (STC no. 185/2002, of 14 October).

Nevertheless, in this specific case, the TC held that the claim was not sufficiently grounded as to override the general principle of publicity, since no personal data were mentioned making it possible to trace the appellant. There was therefore no threat to his personal safety.

Finally, STC no. 114/2006, of 5 April, following another request for anonymization of the Constitutional Court Judgment's publication "on the Internet and in the online version of the BOE," rejected the claims and established the applicable Constitutional Court's doctrine regarding the clash between data protection and publicity of TC decisions:

1') Utmost formal and substantive dissemination of TC decisions

The publicity and publication of Constitutional Court decisions must abide by the following rules: 1') "Judicial proceedings shall be public, with the exceptions specified in procedural laws" (Article 120(1) CE); 2') "Constitutional Court judgments shall be published in the Official State Gazette, including the dissenting opinions, if any" (Article 164(1) CE; 3') "Judgments (...) shall be published in the Official State Gazette (...). The Court may also choose to publish its Orders in the same manner as it deems appropriate" (Article 86(2) of the Organic Act on the Constitutional Court, LOTC).

When providing for the publication of TC decisions in the Official State Gazette (BOE), the purpose of the Spanish Constitution at the time of its drafting was to fully disseminate TC rulings over any other decision (judicial decisions, etc.). Pursuant to Article 9(1) CE and Article 5(1) LOPJ, all citizens and public authorities and particularly judicial bodies-are bound by the Constitution. Effectively guaranteeing these provisions requires a clear knowledge of the Constitutional Court's case law, which must be advanced by the TC itself using any available means. As stated by the TC, there is "a substantive obligation to provide the greatest possible accessibility and public dissemination to those Court's decisions setting forth constitutional doctrine, regardless of the nature of the decisions and the proceedings within which they are issued" (STC no. 114/2006). This TC argument is irreproachable, since it fulfills the requirements of the principle of publicity within a State governed by the rule of law where the constitutional jurisdiction fully and consistently structures the legal system.

2') The obligation to publish TC decisions in full as a general principle

STC no. 114/2006 concluded that the abovementioned provisions also impose on the TC "an implied substantive obligation to publish full decisions." The Constitutional Court understood that the constitutional obligation of giving the utmost dissemination to its doctrine required the publication of its decisions "in full," which necessarily imposed a twofold behavior: first, to disregard summarized publications or brief excerpts of its case law; second, to publish the entire decisions, thereby enabling the best possible understanding and knowledge thereof. This interpretation of the obligation to publish TC decisions "in full" is totally in line with the purpose of the Constitution at the time of its drafting, i.e., to ensure the greatest possible knowledge of the constitutional doctrine.

Nevertheless, the TC understood that, in order to comply with the obligation of maximum dissemination of its case law, the publication of its decisions "in full" should not be limited to ensure a "complete" dissemination "of its doctrine." In the Court's view, the publication had to be "unamended," i.e., unredacted and unmodified (as was the case for the anonymization of decisions, since the parties' identification information was erased and/or replaced with alternative marks). This rule could only be breached under exceptional circumstances, and in order to preserve certain legal interests.

The TC argued in favor of "full" publicity ("including the full identification of parties to the constitutional proceedings"), based on the need to "ensure highly relevant constitutional interests:" 1′) the impartiality of constitutional jurisdiction; 2′) everyone's right to be informed of the circumstances, including personal circumstances, of those cases heard by the Constitutional Court because of their significance. It drew a clear conclusion: "Any matter regarding the potential non-identification of parties to constitutional proceedings (...) has a strictly jurisdictional nature and must be solved *solely and exclusively* by this Court," which shall only be subject to the Spanish Constitution (CE) and the Organic Act on the Constitutional Court (STC no. 114/2006, legal basis 6).

There is no denying that the Constitutional Court is responsible for anonymizing its own decisions. However, the remaining arguments do not seem entirely conclusive as to forbid the deletion of certain identification information of parties (name and last name) in TC rulings. It is hard to imagine that those reasons could lead to impartiality issues or hinder the actual knowledge of constitutional doctrine. This is not the case when judicial decisions (the Spanish Supreme Court's, for instance) are anonymized.[109]

3´) The exceptions to the utmost dissemination of full decisions provided by the TC and the ECtHR

Notwithstanding the foregoing, the Spanish Constitutional Court has concluded that the constitutional requirement of utmost dissemination and publicity of its full decisions does not have an absolute nature. In other words, there are exceptions thereto when so provided by procedural law or when in conflict with other prevailing fundamental rights or constitutional guarantees.

The TC recalls that Organic Act 19/2003, of 23 December, modified Article 266(1) LOPJ, so that the publication of a full judicial decision may be exempted. The amended provision was reworded as follows: "Access to the text of judgments, or certain aspects thereof, may be restricted when such access can affect the right to privacy, the rights of persons in need of special protection, or the guarantee of anonymity regarding victims and injured parties, where appropriate. Access will also be restricted, on a general basis, to prevent judgments from being used for purposes contrary to the law."[110]

According to the TC, the possibility of not identifying the parties will be more restricted in constitutional than in judicial proceedings , given the substantive obligation of maximum dissemination of Constitutional Court's decisions. Nevertheless, the TC acknowledges that Article 266(1)

---

[109] The AEPD has heard disputes regarding the mandatory anonymization of rulings when they are subject to universal dissemination: the "Case Aranzadi-Westlaw" on the anonymization of judgments triggered Resolution no. 486/2004. The proceedings revolved around the claim that a judgment had been published on the Internet by Editorial Aranzadi through www.westlaw.es, showing the claimant's name and last name in full. According to the publishers Editorial Aranzadi, the mistake was attributable to the entity providing the rulings: CENDOJ, the judicial documentation center which collects and disseminates Supreme Court's, Regional High Courts' and Provincial Courts' case law. However, CENDOJ claimed that Aranzadi had committed to anonymize the rulings under the agreement concluded between them. The AEPD found a breach of Article 6 of the Spanish Data Protection Organic Act (LOPD), which qualified as a "serious" violation, and thus the AEPD imposed a penalty on the publishing house.

[110] A broader analysis on the effectiveness of the right to data protection in the judicial sphere can be found in ARTEMI RALLO: "La garantía del derecho constitucional a la protección de datos personales en los órganos judiciales," *Nuevas Políticas Públicas: Anuario multidisciplinar para la modernización de las Administraciones Públicas*, vol. 5, 2009, pp. 97-116.

LOPJ, jointly with Article 6(4) LOPD, "can be a reference" to limit the publicity of parties' information through "individual weighing" of the constitutional interests at stake. Such provisions may also serve to determine the prevailing interests (privacy, protection duties, victims and injured parties, etc.).

The Spanish Constitutional Court disregards the LOPD as a binding legal framework. However, it concedes its "utility" as a "procedural-subjective parameter" to establish exceptions to the full publicity of its decisions, focusing on the "right to object" enshrined in Article 6(4) LOPD. The TC safeguards, indirectly and in an implied manner, the rights of the parties to object to data processing (i.e., to request the anonymization of their data) when there are compelling legitimate grounds relating to a particular personal situation. Obviously, such grounds must be determined by the TC.

Moreover, the TC warns that Article 266(1) LOPJ cannot entail a limitation of fundamental rights and constitutional guarantees that may collide with the constitutional principle of maximum dissemination of TC's decisions -as would be the case for the fundamental right to data protection enshrined in Article 18(4) CE. The scope and autonomy of this right are defined by STC no. 292/2000. In that regard, the grounds listed in Article 266(1) LOPJ could not exclude any others that should be weighed against the publicity of jurisdictional decisions issued by judicial bodies and the Constitutional Court.

As a general criterion, the TC has stated that "individuals engaging in a public procedure by choice (...) may not invoke their fundamental right to privacy or the guarantee regarding the use of information technology (Articles 18(1) and (4) CE) merely because the Constitution provides or allows for the official publication, publicity and accessibility of those proceedings including the individual's name (as required by the significance of the case)" (STC no. 68/2005, of 31 March, legal basis 15).

However, STC no. 68/2005 points out that, if "the content of such proceedings eventually includes information that can be deemed inherent to the individual's privacy," such constitutional guarantees will apply. The TC has often anonymized its decisions omitting identification information of the parties to the constitutional proceedings in order to ensure victims' anonymity (STC no. 185/2002, of 14 October, or STC no. 127/2003, of 30 June), to protect children in parenthood or custody cases (STC no. 7/1994, of 17 January, or STC no. 144/2003, of 14 July), or adoption or abandonment cases (STC no. 114/1997, of 16 June; STC no. 124/2002, of 20 May; STC no. 221/2002, of 25 November; or STC no. 94/2003, of 19 May), or where they have been accused of criminal offences (STC no. 288/2000, of 27 November, or STC no. 30/2005, of 14 February).

This is common practice in supranational courts,[111] such as the European Court of Human Rights. Article 47(4) of its Rules of Court provides that applicants who do not wish their identity to be disclosed to the public shall so indicate and shall submit a statement of the reasons justifying such a departure from the normal rule of public access to information in proceedings before the Court. The President of the Chamber may authorize anonymity in exceptional and duly justified cases. Although on 25 February 1997 (Case *Z. v. Finland*) the ECtHR declared that there is a public interest in ensuring the transparency of court proceedings and thereby the maintenance of the public's confidence in the courts, the ECtHR has anonymized its judgments in many cases. A paradigmatic case is *C.C. v. Spain* (Application no. 1425/06), which was decided by the ECtHR on 6 October 2009. The Court ruled against Spain for breaching Article 8 of the European Convention on Human Rights (ECHR), since Spain failed to dissociate the applicant's health

---

[111] Conversely, the United Nations Human Rights Committee acts differently. The AEPD -in proceedings no. TD/1486/2009, decided on 12 March 2010 (R/572/2010)- upheld the complaint and urged Google to adopt any necessary measures to remove from its index, subsequently preventing any future access, the personal data included in a 2003 Decision issued by the United Nations Human Rights Committee. However, the AEPD refused to rule on the webmaster's obligations, since the claimant had not exercised his right to object against the webmaster. Notwithstanding its decision against Google, the AEPD suggested the claimant to claim against the webmaster. Accordingly, the claimant exercised his right to object against Google, arguing that when he entered his name and last name in the search engine, the list of results displayed links regarding a Decision issued by the United Nations Human Rights Committee. This Decision rejected the appeal for protection for an alleged breach, by the contentious administrative court that heard his claim, of the right to an effective remedy enshrined in the International Covenant on Civil and Political Rights. The claimant asserted that the publication of the Decision on Google was causing severe damage to him both personally and professionally, since the publicity of certain personal and family-related circumstances had a serious impact on his standing and reputation. This was due to the fact that the claim involved a local event, and Google links appeared right by his professional data; given his position as digital media manager, these links were undermining his reputation and professional standing. In the claimant's view, it amounted to an unreasonable public dissemination of personal information which was not newsworthy and affected solely and exclusively his private and family life, and damaged his right to honor.

information from his identity.[112]

The ECtHR's legal reasoning to rule against Spain in *C.C. v. Spain* (Application no. 1425/06) is extremely interesting, since it focuses on whether or not judgments must be anonymized in certain cases.

The ECtHR deemed necessary that the judge have access to the medical records, in order for him to have sufficient knowledge of the case at stake, thereby "protecting" the counterparty's "rights and freedoms."

The ECtHR appraised the fundamental importance of the "protection of personal data" -particularly medical data- regarding the respect for private life. The Court highlighted the importance of confidentiality of

---

[112] This application against Spain was filed by a Spanish national. He considered that his right to private life enshrined in Article 8 ECHR had been violated due to the dissemination of his identity, connected to his health status, in a first instance ruling. The applicant, who was HIV-positive and had another serious medical condition, had taken out life insurance with a company that refused to compensate him when his permanent occupational disability was declared. The applicant brought a claim before the Court of First Instance, and the insurance company requested the judge to ask for his full medical records to the hospital and Social Security authorities. Upon the acceptance of this request by the judge, the applicant challenged the judicial decision and requested the judge: 1´) to remove any reference to his identity and HIV in the trial documents as well as in the future ruling; 2´) to hold the hearing *in camera*; 3´) not to mention his full name in any judicial decisions. The judge rejected all three claims, arguing that there would be no publicity whatsoever to this medical information outside of the proceedings. The Judgment delivered by the First Instance Court dismissed the applicant's claim -on the grounds that by the time he entered into his insurance policy he had not declared the abovementioned conditions and, in the actual Judgment, the seriousness of his diseases was referred to -expressly mentioning lymphoma and AIDS. This first instance ruling was appealed, and the Provincial Court subsequently upheld the judgment on the merits and, although it did not tie his identity to AIDS, ratified the impossibility of overturning the first instance ruling for the violation of the appellant's right to privacy. Finally, the appellant's filed an appeal for constitutional protection before the Constitutional Court, arguing that Article 18 of the Spanish Constitution had been breached for a threefold reason: the production of his medical records, the connection between his identity and his medical conditions in the first instance ruling, as well as the public nature of the proceedings. However, the Constitutional Court dismissed the appeal on 20 June 2005, and it founded its decision on the principle of proportionality. The Court considered that the subject-matter of the proceedings was the appellant's health, and therefore the insurance company could not be prevented from accessing his medical records, particularly when the judge had stated that the data would not be used outside of the proceedings. Accordingly, the Constitutional Court ruled that all previous judicial decisions had been well-founded and not arbitrary.

---

sensitive health information as a "vital principle in the legal system," since it is essential not only to protect patients' privacy, but also their confidence in the medical profession and in the health services in general. Otherwise, patients could be deterred from revealing such information of a personal and intimate nature, thereby endangering their own health and, in case of transmissible diseases, that of the community.[113] In particular, disseminating information on AIDS could have "devastating consequences" on the concerned party's private life, as well as on his/her social and professional status, since he/she could be "exposed to opprobrium and the risk of ostracism." This flawless overview of the importance attached to the protection of certain sensitive data leads to the following warning by the ECtHR: when determining whether the interference is necessary and proportionate to the legitimate aim pursued, the weighing must take into account the preservation of an essential aspect of public interest. Given the extremely intimate and sensitive nature of information about a person's HIV infection, any measure adopted by States to disseminate it will call for "the most careful scrutiny" by the Court.

The ECtHR could not disregard that the publicity of judicial decisions is meant to preserve confidence in courts. The ECtHR confirmed that Spanish legislation entitles judges to limit the publicity of the abovementioned data and access to judgments if privacy or the guarantee of anonymity are at risk.

Finally, having regard to all circumstances, and particularly to the special protection to be granted to information concerning AIDS, the ECtHR found that fully identifying the appellant in connection with his health status in the first instance ruling "was not justified by compelling reasons," thus violating the right to private life enshrined in Article 8 ECHR.

<u>4´) The maximum dissemination of TC decisions on the Internet</u>

STC no. 114/2006 puts forward the substantive obligation leading to the use of any other suitable means of dissemination that enable the best knowledge of constitutional doctrine. The TC acknowledges that the requirement of utmost accessibility could be "formally" ensured by the publication of its judgments in the Official State Gazette (BOE). However, from a "substantive" perspective, the Court must definitely seek to publish judgments through any additional means that are appropriate and suitable to fulfill the obligation of effective dissemination. Substantive publicity is also required by law, and makes

---

[113] As the ECtHR had already stated in Z. v. Finland, 25 February 1997.

case law compilations necessary, which must be awarded full dissemination through any means: paper, digital means or on the Internet.[114]

2) TC judgments indexed by Internet search engines

The utmost dissemination of TC rulings finds its maximum expression in the possibility that Internet search engines (Google) index and disseminate them on a universal and permanent basis. This potentiality fulfills the constitutional case law doctrine established in STC no. 114/2006. However, it leads to growing concerns about the need to reconcile the utmost dissemination of constitutional doctrine with the right to data protection.

Search engines achieve their full potential in two situations identical in substance yet formally different: a) the publication of TC judgments in the BOE pursuant to constitutional provisions; b) the publication of such rulings on the Constitutional Court's official website pursuant to constitutional provisions. In both cases, search engine providers will index the judgments and will disseminate them on the Internet, thereby multiplying knowledge about constitutional doctrine but also the intrusive effects on personal data protection.

The case of the Constitutional Court Order (TD/00569/2008) provides a good picture of this situation.

On 4 October 2008, the right to object was exercised against Google Spain before the AEPD. The claim was that there was a reference to Constitutional Court Order no. 386/2005, of 7 November 2005, in Google search index. The claimant (RRR) alleged that, when she typed in her name (RRR) in the search engine, the following excerpt appeared as a search result: "Constitutional Court, RRR, a penalty amounting to 500,001 pesetas imposed for a very serious infringement (...). In the first case, it involves Ms. RRR, (...)." In other words, there was a short reference implying that the data subject could be involved in constitutional proceedings, and that previously she could have been subject to a penalty for a very serious offence. The data subject claimed that she had not been found liable for a very serious infringement, since back in the day she had been discharged. She added that the

---

[114] On the issues regarding the publication on the Internet of judicial decisions, ROSARIO DUASO CALES: *La protection des données personnelles contenues dans les documents publics accessibles sur Internet: le cas des données judiciaires*, Mémoire présenté à la Faculté des études supérieures de l'Université de Montréal, December 2002.

abovementioned reference had been included in the Constitutional Court Order (ATC) as an example for other proceedings, but not as part of the actual constitutional case. Indeed, the wording of ATC no. 386/2005 supported that claim in the factual background.

Google Spain contended that personal data included on websites indexed by Google were not used by Google, adding that Google lacked the ability to make decisions about their uses. Apparently, Google merely indexed data for users without handling them, and any decisions regarding the use of these data could have only been previously made by the webmaster when the data were made public. Ultimately, the decision regarding the purpose and content of the processing had been previously made by the webmaster, and only the latter could be held liable.

Nevertheless, the AEPD understood that Article 6(4) of the Spanish Data Protection Organic Act (LOPD) excluded liability of the TC, insofar as such provision sets out that where the consent of the data subject is not required for processing personal data, and except where otherwise provided by law, the data subject may object to such processing on compelling legitimate grounds relating to a particular personal situation. The applicable legislation empowered the Constitutional Court to order the publication of personal data in its judicial decisions. However, this does not apply to Google, since no piece of legislation required the claimant's data to be included in Google Search indexes to facilitate access to certain pages, nor required personal data to be included in those pages temporarily stored by Google in the cache.

Finally, on 24 September 2008, the AEPD decided (R/01304/2008) to uphold the right to object against Google Spain. It urged Google to adopt any measures necessary to remove the data from its index and to prevent future access thereto.

It is worth noting that the President of the AEPD submitted this Resolution to the Presiding Judge of the Constitutional Court for information purposes, and he concluded that it was unnecessary to include identifying data of non-parties to the constitutional case. Accordingly, the Presiding Judge of the TC decided to anonymize the claimant's personal data in Constitutional Court Order (ATC) no. 386/2005, replacing her name and last name with the initials "María Isabel R.R."

However, the previous criterion[115] was partially reviewed in AEPD Resolution no. 67/2012 dated 31 January 2012. Google Spain was only required to prevent the indexation of personal data contained in a Constitutional Court judgment mentioned in elpais.com and in another private website. Nevertheless, no such obligation was imposed on Google with regards to the Official State Gazette's website where the said TC judgment was published.

This resolution stripped the AEPD of its prerogatives regarding data dissemination in TC rulings: "The Constitutional Court claims for itself, solely and exclusively, the power to determine whether the publicity of a TC ruling can be restricted. Consequently, the AEPD is not entitled to examine this matter. Only the Constitutional Court is empowered to provide for any exceptions, following a jurisdictional decision, to the constitutional requirement of maximum dissemination and publicity of its full decisions including constitutional doctrine in the identification of the parties to the case (...). [T]he AEPD cannot assess if the ruling published in the Official State Gazette (BOE), against which the right to object is exercised, is obsolete or inaccurate, since such assessment falls outside the scope of its powers -according to the Constitutional Court. The TC is exclusively responsible for determining this matter, based on its considerations and powers (...), and Google must not be required to prevent the indexation of the disputed publication."

1.3.- The publication of pardons in the BOE

The publication of pardons has traditionally collided with the right to data protection. Spanish legislation requires their publication and utmost dissemination in each relevant official gazette. The currently applicable regulation is established in Act 1/1988, of 14 January. Article 30 of this piece of legislation provides that "[a]ny form of pardon shall be granted through a Royal Decree, which shall be published in the Official State Gazette." Moreover, the publication of pardons was also provided by the Act on Pardons of 18 June 1879 ("(...) in the Gazette").

The original rationale for publishing pardons was, on the one hand, to render such pardons legally effective through formal means, and, on the

---

[115] This approach was reiterated in AEPD Resolution no. 643/2012, of 30 March 2012 (TD/1692/2011), concerning the personal data published in a court order issued by the Constitutional Court and contained in tribunalconstitucional.es. Additionally, Resolution no. 645/2012, of 30 March 2012, (TD/1826/2011) also reiterated this doctrine. This decision related to personal data published in a TC court order suspending enforcement of a judgment delivered by the Barcelona Provincial Court, which appeared in boe.es or tribunalconstitucional.es among other links.

other, to promote the maximum dissemination of an "act of grace" o "executive clemency" with unquestionable personal benefits for the pardoned person. Originally, the publication of pardons in each relevant official gazette sent an unequivocally positive message for the pardoned person that society received. Indeed, the pardoned person had been graced with a substantially better personal-criminal situation.

Nonetheless, in the context of the information society, the publication of pardons in the BOE is perceived as having a prejudicial dimension by many "pardoned persons." Accordingly, far from seeking maximum dissemination, they try to avoid it, or at least to minimize it. Although some time ago the granting of pardons and their maximum dissemination had net and desired benefits, many pardoned persons nowadays perceive it as prejudicial. Rather than the inclusion in the traditional hard copy edition of the Official State Gazette -required to render legally effective the granted pardons yet not very helpful in terms of dissemination, the prejudicial effects perceived by pardoned persons are attached to the publication on the digital version of the BOE. The core issue is not the possibility of searching the pardon on the BOE's official website through internal search engines (which third parties will rarely do), but rather the universal and permanent dissemination provided by Internet search engines (Google) when the pardon is crawled in the said official website. This is evidenced by the complaints brought before the AEPD by several pardoned persons when they "agree with the inclusion of their personal data in the BOE's hard copy version, but they reiterate their request that such data not be accessible through the Internet" (TD/220/2004).

The following cases heard by the AEPD show how difficult it is to balance the right to data protection regarding data included in pardons with the legally required publication in the relevant official gazette. In this regard, these cases exemplify the complexity of allocating responsibilities amongst the various actors involved, i.e., the BOE, the Ministry of Justice and Internet search engines (Google).

1) Cases involving pardoned persons against the BOE. The protocol "robots.txt" as a guarantee of the right to be forgotten vis-à-vis official gazette indexation

The shift in society and the technological revolution have led the AEPD to change its criterion regarding the BOE's liability when publishing pardons.

On 27 May 2004, the AEPD received a request for deletion of data in a pardon published on the BOE's website. The Official State Gazette rejected the request, arguing that including the pardon in the BOE, through the relevant Royal Decree, was required by the applicable legislation on pardons. It added that the Official State Gazette's website faithfully reflects the BOE's hard copy version, and thus any modification online would amount to manipulating the official gazette.

On 4 November 2004, the AEPD dismissed the claim against the Official State Gazette (R/602/2004) based on the following: the BOE is a publicly accessible source under Article 3(j) LOPD, "available for consultation by any person not excluded to do so under a legal provision," where including the pardon granted to the claimant is required by law (Article 30 of Act 1/1988, of 14 January). In the AEPD's view, the nature of the BOE as a publicly accessible source applies both to the hard copy and the digital version. In other words, the AEPD excluded liability of the Official State Gazette regarding the deletion of data included in pardons published either in hard copy format or on the Internet. However, the BOE replaced the claimant's name and last name with his initials in the search engine of the gazette's digital version, without erasing his data from the specific page where the pardon was made public. Therefore, the desired result was achieved through the anonymization of the pardoned person's identity.

Notwithstanding the foregoing, this AEPD approach evolved, as shown by Resolutions dated 20 December 2010 (no. 2553/2010) and 13 July 2012 (no. 1777/2012), amongst many others.[116]

On 5 June 2010, a pardoned person exercised the right to delete (or right to erasure) against the BOE. The pardoned person requested the deletion from BOE web addresses of the identifying data contained in the Royal

---

[116] The controversy regarding the processing of pardoned persons' data is well exemplified by AEPD Resolution no. 229/2013. This Resolution was issued in the Case Pardoned Person against the Ministry of Justice (TD/123/2013) to decide on the request for deletion of a pardoned person's data addressed to the Ministry of Justice, which handled the pardon proceedings. The AEPD rejected the complaint on the basis that there were legal grounds to retain the data, and that the Ministry of Justice had responded to the claimant arguing that the said Ministry's actions were reasonable and in compliance with the applicable legislation. In order to avoid liability for the publication of personal data, the BOE often contends, inter alia, that it is neutral vis-à-vis those bodies and institutions adopting the relevant resolutions and ordering their publication -without any discretion, at least *a priori*, to alter or modify such decisions. Particularly, Royal Decrees on pardons are enacted by the Council of Ministers on the motion of the Ministry of Justice, which handles pardon proceedings and ultimately decides on the personal data to be included in the Royal Decree, in order to fulfill the publication obligation under the Act on Pardons. Consequently, indexation of pardons by Internet search engines stems from the decisions made by the Ministry of Justice.

Decree granting his pardon in 2003. This Royal Decree mentioned previous convictions and prison sentences for embezzlement and falsification of commercial documents.[117]

Nevertheless, in response to the BOE's arguments against the deletion of the pardoned person's data, the AEPD (no. 2553/2010) held that personal data protection regulations could not simply consider official journals and gazettes as "publicly accessible sources" (Article 3(j) LOPD). Rather, it pointed out that consideration must be given to the recent case law established in the High Court (*Audiencia Nacional*, AN) Judgment dated 20 April 2009: "Any reference on a website to persons, identifying them by their names or otherwise (...) amounts to the processing of personal data wholly or partly by automatic means as provided by Article 3(1) of Directive 95/46/EC."

Consequently, when the BOE published personal data on its website, it was processing data wholly or partly by automatic means. Additionally, even if there was a legal obligation to publish certain administrative acts, the BOE was subject both to the rules and regulations on the publishing of acts and provisions, and to data protection legislation. Therefore, the BOE was under the obligation to prevent indiscriminate dissemination of data contained in its digital version, which took place through unlimited access by Internet search engines.

Finally, the AEPD upheld the claim against the Official State Gazette. However, instead of acknowledging the pardon person's right to deletion (which could have been fulfilled by replacing the name and last name with the initials), urged the BOE to adopt any measures necessary to "prevent indexation of the claimant's personal data in its pages, so that Internet search engines are unable to associate them to the claimant."

The AEPD did not only tackle the issue of the indexation of official gazettes by Internet search engines (Google). It also imposed on the BOE the obligation to establish any "measures necessary" to prevent such indexation with no need to delete or modify the gazette's contents.

---

[117] The BOE further stated that official journals and gazettes must be deemed as publicly accessible sources. Also, the BOE asserted that those provisions, acts and notices published in the Official State Gazette with personal data are the ones that must be officially disseminated on grounds of public interest or other legal grounds according to the relevant procedural rules and regulations. Finally, the BOE added that the principles of publicity, access to public decisions and administrative transparency had to be taken into account, since they are essential in a democratic State under the rule of law.

In subsequent decisions,[118] the AEPD has added arguments such as those exposed in Resolution no. 1777/2012. The Spanish Data Protection Agency acknowledges the citizen's right to object -on compelling legitimate grounds relating to a particular personal situation (Article 6(4) LOPD)- to the processing of personal data to prevent them from being captured by Internet search engines. The right to object allows for a subjective and individualized assessment of the citizen's right. Such right may be fulfilled -with no need for deletion- if access to personal information is prevented through the existing techniques as well as through proportionate means in relation to the aim pursued. The applicants often state that their objection does not focus on the publication of the pardon on the BOE's official website, but rather on the crawling and indexation carried out by search engines (Google), which enables a tremendously intrusive dissemination.[119]

Acknowledging this "form" of the right to object in a distinct technological environment led the AEPD to adopt two significant criteria: 1′) the BOE's obligation to adopt necessary and appropriate measures to prevent website indexation by search engines must consider the "current state of technology"; 2′) the AEPD deems the robots exclusion standard "robots.txt" as a necessary and appropriate measure to prevent indexation by Internet search engines. This protocol allows the webmaster to create a "negative file" with content that search engines (Google) can neither crawl nor index. In spite of the considerable reluctance expressed to the AEPD, the BOE was already using these "robots.txt" files to prevent the indexation of certain content by Internet search engines.

2) Case *Pardoned Person against Google Spain*: explicit rejection of

---

[118] AEPD Resolution no. 2037/2012, of 29 August 2012, issued in proceedings no. TD/1018/2012, which rejected the right to object against the BOE. The Spanish Data Protection Agency considered that there was not "sufficient evidence that the Royal Decree [from 2012] through which the pardon was granted was obsolete or that the formal and time requirements laid down in such Royal Decree had been met." Likewise, see Resolution no. 02478/2012, of 17 October 2012, issued in proceedings no. TD/015181/2012.

[119] In Resolution no. 1777/2012, the AEPD found that there were compelling legitimate grounds for the pardoned person to seek the preservation of his privacy as well as a limited access to his personal information, having regard to the time elapsed since the publication of Royal Decrees of 2000 and 2002 through which the pardon was granted.

the applicability of Spanish legislation[120]

On 26 May 2008, the AEPD received a deletion request that had been previously rejected by Google. A Royal Decree issuing a pardon published in the BOE mentioned the conviction of the pardoned person for a crime against public health, as well as the corresponding prison sentence. Such sentence was "pending enforcement, on the condition that she does not leave the ongoing treatment until achieving full rehabilitation." The published pardon did not only disclose the criminal conviction, but also the drug rehabilitation treatment to be followed by the pardoned person.

Google Spain claimed to be a mere a commercial representative of Google Inc. for the sale of advertising space available on its website. It also alleged that it did not carry out search engine activity, and that it simply submitted to Google any requests for deletion. Google Inc. would be the only company that could be required to ensure the right to delete (or right to erasure), yet subject to United States legislation: search services are provided from the United States, and neither the EU Directive nor Spanish data protection legislation would be applicable. Google Spain understood that according to Opinion 1/2008 on data protection issues related to search engines of Article 29 Working Party, adopted on 4 April 2008, the main responsibility for the data lies with webmasters and not with search engines.

The AEPD yet again declared its jurisdiction and the applicability of Spanish legislation to guarantee the rights to delete/object by search engine providers. It ultimately urged Google (R/02676/2009) to "adopt any measures necessary to remove the data from its index and to prevent access to the data in the future." Although the Act on Pardons allowed for the inclusion of data in the Official State Gazette, no legal provision

---

[120] Google's stance has been identical in other cases heard by the AEPD. For instance, in proceedings no. TD/420/2008, the AEPD upheld the complaint against Google Spain on 29 December 2008 regarding the data contained in a Royal Decree issuing a pardon and published in the BOE. Such Royal Decree contained information on the data subject related to his prior conviction for child abduction and threats. In proceedings no. TD/336/2010, on 30 July 2010, the AEPD (R/1694/2010) upheld the complaint against Google Spain about the data included in a Royal Decree issuing a pardon of 1995. This Royal Decree mentioned the prior conviction of the pardoned person for forgery of official documents back in 1979 and 1981. In proceedings no. TD/627/2009, on 5 October 2009, the AEPD (R/1795/2009) upheld the complaint against Google Spain for the data contained in a Royal Decree issuing a pardon of 2007, which referred to the previous conviction.

requires such data to be included in Google indexes nor in its cache memories.

In spite of the fact that the claim was exclusively brought against Google, and that the AEPD's decision only affected the search engine, the Agency's Resolution addressed the BOE through *obiter dictum*: "In order to effectively fulfill the right invoked in the proceedings, we hereby require the Official State Gazette to implement any measures necessary to prevent indexation of the data subject's personal data included in the document published by the said Gazette, as well as to prevent such data from being captured by Internet search engines."

3) Case *Pardoned Person against Yahoo*: tacit acceptance of Spanish jurisdiction

It is worth noting the contrasting legal response that other Internet search engines received in an identical situation.

On 20 January 2011, the AEPD received an objection request -and, alternatively, a request for deletion- against Google Inc., Google Spain, the BOE and Yahoo Iberia for the data contained in a Royal Decree issuing a pardon published in 1991. AEPD Resolution no. 2795/2011, of 9 December 2011, on the one hand, upheld the complaint against Google Spain (which had again refused to apply European and Spanish legislation to the search engine provider, thereby attributing responsibility to Google Inc.); on the other, it dismissed the claim against the BOE (which had met the data subject's request, i.e., erasing the name mentioned in the Royal Decree from its digital version's search engines) and Yahoo Iberia.

The AEPD dismissed the complaint against Yahoo Iberia, who had timely replied to the claimant's request by stating that Yahoo Search was a search engine unrelated to the linked websites and not responsible for the data available therein. Yahoo Iberia suggested the data subject to request deletion from the webmasters. However, Yahoo Iberia erased the search results. Additionally, Yahoo Iberia never challenged the applicability of EU and Spanish legislation to the activities carried out by the search engine, and fulfilled the right to delete.

1.4.- The publication of electoral nominations in the BOE

On 18 January 2011, a complaint was filed before the AEPD against Google Spain and the BOE. Apparently, there had been a breach of the right to object regarding personal data included in the nominations for the 2004 European election. These nominations had been published in the

BOE as required by the Spanish Electoral Board and under Articles 47(1) and 220(5) of Electoral Organic Act 5/1985, of 19 June (LOREG).[121]

Through Resolution no. 1522/2011, of 18 July 2011, the AEPD rejected the objection request regarding both Google Spain and the BOE. Publishing electoral nominations in the Official State Gazette is permitted by law. The AEPD assessed whether there were compelling legitimate grounds relating to a particular personal situation that enabled the protection of the right to object and the prohibition of the relevant data processing both by the BOE (for instance, through technologies preventing indexation by Internet search engines) and by Google (which is not specifically entitled by law to enable such indexation). The AEPD dismissed both claims arguing that, based on current constitutional case law, there were no compelling and legitimate interests at stake.

The Constitutional Court entered judgment on the applicability of the right to object to data processing in connection with the publication of nominations during the 2003 municipal elections.

Constitutional Court Judgment STC no. 85/2003, of 8 May, entered judgment on an election-related appeal brought against Supreme Court Judgments (delivered by the Special Chamber under Article 61 of the Organic Act on the Judiciary) revoking certain nominations for the 2003 municipal elections. The appellants invoked a violation of the right to privacy (Article 18 of the Spanish Constitution, CE) and the right to freedom of thought (Articles 16 CE, 9 ECHR and 17 of the International Covenant on Civil and Political Rights), arguing that the judgment under appeal used personal data contained in police reports related to the involvement of several candidates in previous elections: in the absence of unambiguous consent by the data subject, the data could have been unlawfully obtained and produced in the proceedings, thereby violating the candidates' right to privacy.

STC no. 85/2003 (legal basis 21) draws a distinction between the scope of the right to privacy (Article 18(1) CE) and the right to data protection (Article 18(4) CE): a) The Spanish Constitutional Court narrows the scope of protection when asserting that the purpose of the fundamental

---

[121] As usual, Google Spain denied its responsibility for the searches, rejected that Google Inc. be subject to EU or Spanish legislation, and excluded responsibility of the search engine provider for the indexed results, thereby holding the webmaster liable, i.e., the BOE. Nevertheless, the AEPD remained consistent with its doctrine on Google Spain's responsibility, as well as regarding the applicability of Spanish data protection legislation and the possibility of guaranteeing the right to object on individual compelling legitimate interests.

right to privacy (Article 18(1) CE) is to guarantee a private sphere for the individual vis-à-vis the action and knowledge of public authorities and other individuals, concerning only "the most basic aspects of personal self-determination (...) that may be reasonably required in a social context having regard to the prevailing social criteria." b) The Constitutional Court clearly excludes data related to political participation from such "basic aspects." Such data, by their very nature, are necessarily public within a democratic society: "Exercising the right to political participation (Article 23(1) CE) generally entails assuming that such aspect of one's private life will not stay away from public knowledge." The Court also asserts that "if an individual freely decides to run for office, he/she cannot invoke an alleged right to privacy regarding that aspect of one's private life." c) Social publicity of candidates' activity, which is inherent to political involvement, is closely tied to the formal publicity given by electoral legislation to many actions within electoral processes -publication of nominations in official provincial gazettes or the BOE- to ensure a safe and transparent democratic process. d) Upon assessing the power over one's personal data (Article 18(4) CE), the Constitutional Court concludes the following: "Such power cannot be sought regarding the only relevant data at stake, i.e., the political links of candidates in an election. As has been stated, these are published data accessible by any citizen, and thus beyond the control of the data subject. A candidate's political affiliation is and must be public information within a democratic society, and therefore data subjects cannot claim any power over such data."[122]

The AEPD issued Resolution no. 1522/2011 dismissing the claimant's right to object. It argued that running for office and the formal publicity obligations provided by law entail waiving the power over one's own data attached to the right to data protection.

There is no doubt that anyone who runs for office does not only give up the secrecy regarding his/her political ideology, but also, self-evidently, the candidate will seek utmost social publicity and will assume any legal effects stemming from the provisions on official publicity in electoral processes. Although, as stated by the Constitutional Court, an "anonymous" individual's political ideology is sensitive information and it deserves special protection in terms of data protection, the fact remains that "a candidate's political affiliation is and must be public information within a democratic society." As soon as a "citizen" becomes a "candidate," he/she inevitably gives up this special protection in the interest of the utmost publicity for his/her nomination, as well as for the

---

[122] This doctrine was reiterated in similar cases heard by the Constitutional Court. See Judgments no. 99/2004 (legal basis 13) and 68/2005 (legal basis 15).

sake of a safe and transparent democratic process, the keystone of which is the election. Therefore, the AEPD considered there were no compelling legitimate grounds that overrode the publicizing of these data by the BOE and Google Search.

It is worth examining whether the candidate loses the power over his/her data forever, as well as if he/she definitely gives up the secrecy regarding his/her political affiliation disclosed when running for office.

The AEPD's general doctrine on the right to be forgotten regarding personal data published by official gazettes would entail imposing on Google the obligation to prevent data indexation, as well as requiring the BOE to adopt technical measures in order to prevent such indexation if there are individualized compelling legitimate interests at stake. This will be the case, preferably, when the dissemination of data in official gazettes stems from a legal obligation beyond the individual's knowledge and power (for instance, when administrative penalties are notified). Nevertheless, this data subject's power will be significantly diminished when an official publicity requirement is attached to the relevant data, as it often happens when someone runs for office.

The publicity as a candidate or as the winner of an election certainly constitutes the weakest dimension of the right to be forgotten. Indeed, a candidate who sought to represent society -or even managed to effectively represent it in public office- can hardly demand digital oblivion in order to regain some sort of social anonymity entirely alien to the historical reality of politics.

1.5.- The publication in the BOE of disciplinary sanctions imposed on public officials

1) Case *Sanction imposed on a Public Prosecutor of the Supreme Court*

On 8 January 2008, a data subject exercised his right to object against Google before the AEPD. The claim concerned the data published in the Official State Gazette upon notification of a ruling on a contentious administrative appeal filed by the data subject, a Public Prosecutor of the Supreme Court. The appeal had been brought against two sanctions. According to the claimant, this publication "causes moral and professional damage, and it is particularly unfair considering that the sanction had been complied with and was cancelled years ago, also taking into account that it contained sensitive information."

In accordance with Articles 58 and 59 of Act 30/1992, this notice was included in the BOE so that the addressee could become aware of it, since such notice could not be served in person. The information published by Google related to disciplinary action taken for an offence that was time-barred and overridden by the claimant's professional achievement discretionally acknowledged by the Government. According to the claimant, the published information "caused permanent, arbitrary and unnecessary prejudice to the claimant's dignity, thereby largely exceeding the scope of the penalty provided by law."[123]

On 17 July 2008, the AEPD found (R/924/2008) compelling legitimate grounds to consider that publishing in the BOE the ruling on a contentious administrative appeal against two sanctions imposed on a Supreme Court Prosecutor affected the claimant's personal situation. According to the AEPD, "considering particularly that the sanction published years ago had been complied with and cancelled, and considering also that the Official State Gazette had prevented access to the relevant data through BOE search engines with access to the document." The AEPD decided that Google had to comply with the data subject's right to object, and ordered Google to adopt any measures necessary to remove the data from its index and to prevent access to the data in the future.

In case the abovementioned measures did not suffice to effectively guarantee the right to object, on the same date, the AEPD sent the BOE a written requirement to implement any measures necessary to avoid data indexation as well as to prevent Internet search engines from capturing them.

2) Case *Sanction imposed on a prison officer and threats from ETA*

On 23 April 2008, a complaint against Google Spain was filed before the AEPD. In this case, Google Spain had allegedly breached the right to object due to certain data indexed in the search engine. These data

---

[123] The BOE had previously reported to the claimant that it was no longer possible to access those data through those Official Gazette's search engines with access to the relevant document, although the public prosecutor originally requested that his identification information be replaced with his initials. Google Spain replied that it was unable to fulfill his right to object because the BOE had blocked the page to prevent access. Furthermore, the claimant alleged before the AEPD that the content of his searches was in publicly accessible third party websites. Thus, in order to permanently erase content from the results, the help of the third party's webmaster was necessary -being the only one capable of preventing a page from appearing in Google by including a robot exclusion protocol. Otherwise, even if the page was removed from the search index, it would remain published on the Internet. Furthermore, given that Google robots are constantly searching the web for content, it would be selected and re-added to the indexes.

concerned two resolutions issued by the General Directorate for Correctional Facilities in 1996 and 1998, which were published in the Official State Gazette.

The alleged compelling legitimate grounds relating to the claimant's personal situation, a prison officer, were the following: first, the need to avoid an unreasonable public dissemination of a set of personal data which led to social rejection, since the personal data at stake related to a disciplinary sanction; second, his identity was revealed to the terrorist group ETA, which targeted prison officers.

Google Spain claimed that it was unable to fulfill the data subject's right to object, because the said search results were included in publicly accessible third party websites and it needed the webmaster's cooperation to prevent the indexation of these data. The BOE had lawfully included this information, in accordance with Act 30/1992. The resolutions issued by the General Directorate for Correctional Facilities made public that the claimant had complied with the contentious administrative judgments dismissing his appeals against disciplinary sanctions for serious misconduct under the Disciplinary Regulations for Public Officials.

In its Resolution no. 1783/2008, of 20 January 2009, the AEPD put forward that there was no piece of legislation entitling Google Spain to keep the claimant's data in its search indexes or in the pages temporarily stored in the cache. The AEPD also confirmed that, having regard to the data subject's position as a prison officer, there were compelling legitimate grounds to consider that the personal information published in the BOE had an impact on the data subject's personal situation.

Accordingly, the AEPD upheld the right to object exercised against Google Spain. The Spanish Agency "ordered" Google Spain "to adopt any measures necessary to prevent indexation of the data subject's personal data, as well as to prevent such data from being captured by Internet search engines in the future." Additionally, the AEPD urged the BOE to "implement any measures necessary to avoid indexation of the data subject's information" as well as to prevent future searches.

1.6.- The publication of announcements and judicial decisions in official gazettes

On 24 January 2008, a data subject exercised the right to object before the AEPD. The complaint was brought against the A Coruña Official Provincial Gazette for allowing Internet search engines to access personal information from the data subject and his minor children when publishing a court notice dated 15 November 2000. This notice contained personal information regarding the data subject's marital status, the contentious divorce, and the custody of his minor children.

The complaint was addressed to the Official Gazette. Therefore, AEPD Resolution no. 1303/2008, of 23 October 2008, only referred to the Gazette when it upheld the right to object exercised against the A Coruña Provincial Council, responsible for the Official Provincial Gazette (BOP). The AEPD ordered the BOP to adopt "any measures necessary to withdraw the indexation of the name and last name in the said document, so that Internet search engines are not able to associate it to the data subject in the future."

The AEPD deemed lawful the inclusion of the notice of judgment based on Articles 58 and 59 of Act 30/1992, which allow for an edict notice if the official notice cannot be served in person.[124]

Nevertheless, the AEPD considered that there were compelling legitimate grounds relating to a particular personal situation of the claimant to exercise the right to object against the BOP publication of that divorce

---

[124] The AEPD has also dealt with the publication of decisions in official gazettes in the following cases: Trial of minor offence (TD/17/2009) and Executory process (TD/444/2008). On 20 November 2008, another complaint was filed before the AEPD. The claimant alleged that Google Spain (the defendant) had not fulfilled the right to object regarding the publication of a court notice in an Official Provincial Gazette. The data subject requested that her personal data contained in a summons for a minor offence published in a BOP in 2007 should not be processed, since those data caused her personal and health-related problems. Google Spain denied responsibility for the search service on the Internet. On 26 June 2009, the AEPD upheld the complaint against Google Spain (R/1388/2009), ordering the latter to adopt any measures necessary to withdraw the data from its index and to prevent access to the data in the future. The AEPD considered that Spanish legislation was applicable to the search engine, and that the claimant had compelling legitimate grounds relating to a particular personal situation supporting her right to object. The AEPD decided that the Official Provincial Gazette had lawfully published the data. However, although there was no direct claim against the gazette, and in order to effectively comply with the right to object, the AEPD urged the Gazette to implement any measures necessary to prevent indexation of the personal data, as well as to prevent such data from being captured by Internet search engines. Through Resolution no. 1488/2008 dated 4 November 2008, the AEPD had upheld the right to object exercised against Google Spain by a local police officer whose personal data appeared in an Official Provincial Gazette. A court of justice had ordered to publish an Executory process notice about some debt from 2001, which caused serious prejudice both personally and professionally in light of two overlapping circumstances: 1´) he was a local police officer; 2´) the debt mentioned in the court notice was due.

judgment. Particularly, the AEPD focused on two aspects: 1') the need to take into account "that the ruling's publication years ago had fulfilled its purpose," i.e., the AEPD added to its line of reasoning an assessment of the expiration or obsolescence of the act of publishing in connection with the effects of court notices; 2') the "the multiplier effect of dissemination through the Internet and, to a greater extent, through search engines, along with its impact on data protection of persons, particularly those who do not play a role in public life." Therefore, it was necessary to avoid that search engine data processing could have "permanent unwanted effects against the data subject's will."

1.7.- The publication of social inclusion and unemployment benefits and of traffic penalties in official gazettes

Proceedings no. 175/2009 highlight the wide array of cases that can be triggered by the provisions protecting the publication of decisions in official gazettes, thus generating a legitimate feeling of loss of social reputation on which the right to be forgotten can be founded.

On 18 December 2008, the AEPD received a complaint against Google Spain, several official gazettes, and Jurisweb Interactiva S.L. for the processing of data published in the said official gazettes regarding notices of social inclusion and employment benefits (2003, 2004 and 2005) as well as traffic penalty notices (2004 and 2008). The dissemination of these notices through Internet search engines seriously undermined the claimant's dignity and right to honor, causing professional damage.

The involved official gazettes argued that the publication of the abovementioned decisions stemmed from the obligation imposed by Article 6(1) of Act 5/2002, of 4 April, governing Official Provincial Gazettes. Furthermore, Article 9 of this piece of legislation provides that under Article 45 of Act 30/1992, Provincial Councils must promote the use of telematics, and electronic and computer means regarding the services provided by Official Provincial Gazettes, guaranteeing at all times the authenticity of the documents published.

Through Resolution no. 1637/2009 of 24 July 2009, the AEPD dismissed the appeal for protection against official gazettes. Nevertheless, it stated the following: "since the data subject has already acknowledged receipt of the abovementioned administrative acts, which was the aim of publishing such acts in the relevant official gazettes, the Cordoba and Cadiz Provincial Councils should issue the relevant orders to limit the indexation of the data subject's name and last name (...) in the said documents by using a code (...), so that Internet search engines are not able to associate them to the data subject in the future." The AEPD assessed the purpose of the notification, assuming that once an individual acknowledged receipt of a given notice, the latter's purpose was fulfilled. Accordingly, it restricted general access to those data. Based on the legal framework safeguarding the intangibility of official gazette content, the AEPD considered that the right to object was sufficiently fulfilled by preventing data indexation by Internet search engines through the existing technology.

The complaint was also filed against a private entity's website (Jurisweb Interactiva S.L.), which apparently reproduced the content of official gazettes' digital versions and which ultimately deleted the data.

Finally, the AEPD upheld the complaint against Google Spain, thereby reassuring its condition as responsible for the search engine and confirming the applicability of Spanish data protection legislation. The AEPD urged Google to remove the data from its index and to prevent any future access thereto. The Spanish Agency acknowledged that, under Article 6(4) of the Spanish Data Protection Organic Act (LOPD), the right to object was duly invoked, since "the information, from long ago, refers to personal situations which, if learned through Internet search engines, according to the data subject, violate his/her dignity and right to honor. In this vein, it is worth noting that the official publication is limited to a restricted territorial scope (the official gazettes were the Cordoba and Cádiz BOPs) whereas data processing by Google leads to a general and universal access to information." The AEPD came up with two appealing elements of evaluation: *time* and *territory*. Vis-à-vis the universal and permanent nature inherent to information contained on Internet search engines, the AEPD puts forward the restricted, time-limited and confined scope of traditional official publications. In the Internet era, one can notice the shift of the original purposes and benefits sought, which have turned into sources of individual damage.

2.- THE INDEXATION OF MEDIA ON THE INTERNET

Online media represent the most controversial battleground in the context of the right to oblivion on the Internet, since they give rise to a clash between the right to data protection, on the one hand, and freedom of expression and the right to information, on the other.[125]

Equating "oblivion" and "censorship" is more than risky, and is usually suggested by "evangelists" advocating for unrestrained freedom on the Internet. It is common ground that there are no absolute or unlimited rights, and particularly that information freedoms must abide by all fundamental rights. However, the fundamental right to data protection does not enjoy (neither socially nor amongst legal scholars) the tremendously prominent status awarded to other individual rights (right to honor, privacy, etc.) vis-à-vis the right to information.

In conflicts such as honor vs. information or privacy vs. freedom of expression, there are well-established hermeneutic resolution techniques. Nevertheless, the clash between data protection and media is somewhat unexplored. That is why the principles and rights inherent to data protection (quality, consent, access, deletion, rectification, objection, etc.) are very difficult to apply to the media.

The exercise of the right to be forgotten -construed as the individual's entitlement to request the deletion or the limitation of the use of personal data in a given communication media- is hard, but not impossible.

In the event of conflict, the right to be forgotten is in principle considerably weak vis-à-vis information freedoms. Three drivers strengthen the prevalence of the right to information:[126] 1) the superior and institutional value of information within a democratic society (the free shaping of public opinion is a basic pillar) provides many examples of how information on the Internet considerably strengthens individual freedoms, even in authoritarian regimes. 2) The Internet is the backbone of information societies, and search engines are the perfect match to promote culture, progress and freedom. 3) If the right to information could always be expressed through the plurality of media, the Internet turns every user into a potential provider of information; on the one hand,

---

[125] On the impact of the Internet on freedom of expression and freedom of information: YAMAN AKDENIZ: "To block or not to block: European approaches to content regulation, and implications for freedom of expression," Computer Law & Security Review, vol. 26, 2010, pp. 260-272; ALTHAF MARSOOF: "Online Social Networking and the Right to Privacy: The Conflicting Rights of Privacy and Expression," International Journal of Law and Information Technology, vol. 19-2, 2011, pp. 110-132.

[126] For further information on this, see JEFFREY ROSEN: "Free speech, privacy and the web that never forgets," Telecommunications and High Technology Law, vol. 9, 2011, pp. 346-356; MUGE FAZLIOGLU: "Forget me not: the clash of the right to be forgotten and freedom of expression on the Internet," International Data Privacy Law, vol. 3-3, 2013, pp. 149 to 157.

it blurs the traditional notion of media and, on the other, it broadens such notion.

Thanks to the numerous complaints filed before the AEPD, we have been able to solve many cases illustrating that it is possible to make the right to be forgotten compatible with online media information. First, a distinction must be drawn between the general issues posed by current data included in online media and the conflict triggered by the digitalization of newspaper archives and libraries -the indexation by Internet search engines of personal information that was current decades ago.

2.1.- Digitalization of newspaper archives: travelling back in time to old information

1) Drug trafficking and withdrawal syndrome: *El País*[127]

In 1985, the print edition of *El País* published that the brother of an important Spanish city's mayor had been arrested for alleged drug trafficking. The story was rich in details, including the personal and professional identity of other detainees, as well as their health status. In particular, there was mention of "withdrawal syndrome" for which two sisters were being treated. They were both put in a correctional facility after they were arrested.

Almost twenty five years later, on 3 August 2009 (TD/1436/2009 and TD/1437/2009), those sisters exercised their right to object before the AEPD against *El País* and Google. According to them, when they entered their personal data in Internet search engines, the full digitalized story popped up, and it had become easier to access such story now that it was

---

[127] The AEPD heard a similar case (TD/487/2010). On 26 February 2010, a claim based on the right to erasure was brought before the AEPD. The claimant requested the newspaper *ABC* to erase data published in 1975 in a story under the heading "*Más de 20 jóvenes detenidos en Madrid como implicados en el consumo y tráfico de drogas*" ("More than 20 minors involved in drug use and trafficking were arrested in Madrid"). Based on his right to erasure, the claimant alleged that the information concerned an arrest performed in 1974, when he was still a minor student, and that the proceedings had been permanently stayed. He added that he was currently a liberal professional, and thus his reputation and professional standing were being prejudiced, since the facts appeared when his name was entered in Google Search. On 18 June 2010, the AEPD (R/1044/2010) dismissed the claim against *ABC*, arguing that the digitalized publication was covered by the constitutional right to freedom of information. Nonetheless, *ABC* told the AEPD that it would try to exclude name-based searches. The claimant's personal data continued to appear in Google search index.

online. The claimants contended that: 1′) the public relevance of the facts and the focus of media coverage were on the family ties of one of the arrested persons with the mayor; 2′) the amount of drugs seized was not of public interest. The claimants never denied the veracity of the information, but they held that the story was not accurate in light of the outcome of the judicial proceedings and their current health status.

El País contended that both elpais.com and the print newspaper *EL PAÍS* were social communication media covered by the fundamental right "to freely communicate or receive truthful information by any means of dissemination whatsoever" enshrined in Article 20(1)(d) of the Spanish Constitution. The facts remained online just like any other information stored in their paper records and electronic files.

The AEPD did not impose any specific obligations on Google or *El País*, but these Resolutions (R/85/2010 and R/94/2010), of 12 and 24 March 2010, did provide certain defining arguments for the Agency's position towards the clash between the right to oblivion and the media.

The AEPD concedes that when there are compelling legitimate grounds relating to a particular personal situation, the media might have to limit the indexation of certain news stories by Internet search engines:[128]

Obviously, the publication of a news story in online media is covered by Article 20 of the <u>Constitution</u>, which enshrines freedom of speech and

---

[128] In fact, well before that, on 26 January 2009 (R/1871/2009), the AEPD had already decided on Proceedings no. TD/1164/2008, where it dismissed the complaint against Prisacom, yet upholding the claim against Google Spain, subsequently ordering the latter to adopt any measures necessary to withdraw the data contained in a story published in 1987 by *El País* and to prevent future access thereto; according to the claimant, those data exposed him to personal danger due to the activity of terrorist groups that targeted military officers. On 4 February 2009, the AEPD issued an identical Resolution (R/155/2009) regarding the data contained in a 1991 news report from *El País*. In the claimant's view (also a military officer), such news report entailed an unreasonable dissemination which put him at risk with terrorist groups. On the same date, R/155/2009 (TD/1335/2008), the AEPD solved the "Plastic Surgeon Case." Apparently, a story from 1991 published in *El País* stated that a plastic surgeon had been accused of a crime. However, there was no subsequent information on his acquittal. Since this information had been indexed by search engines online, it "damaged his reputation and professional standing, whilst breaching the privacy and confidentiality of his data." The AEPD upheld the claim against Google Spain, but failed to uphold the complaint brought against *El País*. Nevertheless, it recommended the newspaper to use electronic means in order to prevent the indexation of the news story by Internet search engines if it considered that a legitimate personal interest was at stake or that the facts were not newsworthy.

freedom of information, whilst protecting the right to "receive truthful information by any means of dissemination whatsoever."

In line with settled constitutional case law,[129] the right to receive truthful information (since it plays an institutional role within a democratic society to shape a free public opinion) should prevail over other constitutional rights (including the right to data protection) when the facts are deemed of public relevance (i.e., related to public affairs of general interest based on the subject matter and the persons involved) and the information is truthful.[130]

The AEPD advanced the *ratio decidendi* of future cases: "Although the publication of a story in the press is protected by freedom of speech and freedom of information (...), the development of the Internet and the wide establishment of search engines entail an exponential and permanent dissemination of personal data included in press reports. Therefore, if there is a legitimate interest relating to a personal situation, and provided that the information remains unaltered in its original form -since it would not be erased from historical records or files, it could be desirable for the webmaster to prevent the indexation of the news story by Internet search engines. This would limit an indiscriminate and permanent dissemination, which can also be prejudicial. Accordingly, we suggest this newspaper to carry out any necessary action in order to limit the indexation of Ms. AAA's name and last name in the abovementioned document, so that Internet search engines are unable to associate them to the data subject in the future" (R/85/2010 and 94/2010).

The quest for striking a fair balance between freedom of information and data protection in online news will therefore revolve around the following

---

[129] See Constitutional Court Judgments no. 6/1981, 105/1983, 168/1986, 165/1987, 6/1988, 107/1988, 105/1990, 240/1992, 176/1995, 4/1996.
[130] Recital 37 of Directive 95/46/EC is more nuanced when addressing the need to *reconcile* (and not only to weigh) the right to data protection and the freedoms of speech and information: "the processing of personal data for journalistic purposes or for purposes of literary or artistic expression, in particular in the audiovisual field, should qualify for exemption from the requirements of certain provisions of this Directive in so far as this is necessary to reconcile the fundamental rights of individuals with freedom of information and notably the right to receive and impart information, as guaranteed in particular in Article 10 of the European Convention for the Protection of Human Rights and Fundamental Freedoms."
Also, the Spanish Constitutional Court has also pointed out the following: (a) any person or media outlet reporting truthful news, along with the audience of such news, are entitled to freedom of information; (b) media or journalists do not have a strengthened fundamental right (although they are granted specific protection) with respect to any other citizen (STC no. 225/2002).

core principles:

a) Reinforcing the lawfulness of the media to publish the information, as well as to preserve it unaltered in its original form, without deleting historical files (such as those stored in newspaper archives or newspaper libraries);

b) confirming the impact of Internet search engines on the dissemination of journalistic information (also the information that ends up being digitalized) and whether or not it is necessary to prevent this information from being indiscriminately, permanently and prejudicially disseminated online, if there are legitimate grounds relating to a particular personal situation;

c) suggesting the relevant media outlet to prevent the indexation of personal data contained in the news story.

2) Not guilty by reason of insanity in killing of 4-year-old son: *La Vanguardia*

In 1989, *La Vanguardia* published a news story regarding events that had occurred two years ago. A man suffocated his 4-year-old son with a pillow while he was sleeping. The Public Prosecutor charged him with murder, but he was finally acquitted by reason of insanity. Apparently, the father suffered from paranoid schizophrenia, and he was put in a mental institution.

Twenty years later, on 10 November 2009, the acquitted father filed a complaint before the AEPD exercising his right to object against *La Vanguardia* and Google Spain. The claimant made the following allegations: (a) when he entered his personal information in Google, despite the time elapsed since the events, the abovementioned news story popped up; (b) recalling the events undermined his recovery, as certified by his psychiatrist; (c) disseminating this information online caused him significant social and labor-related damage.

La Vanguardia contended, on the one hand, that it could not remove a story from a newspaper library without breaching other individual rights. Indeed, Article 20 of the Spanish Constitution (CE) proclaims the right to access documents stored in public records, including the obtainment of copies. On the other hand, *La Vanguardia* alleged that it had no control whatsoever over the search engines.[131]

Nevertheless, on 15 March 2010, *La Vanguardia* reported to the AEPD that it had finally accepted the data subject's request and that it would stop processing his data, following several technical modifications in the newspaper's indexation and publication system at www.lavanguardia.es.

La Vanguardia had effectively ensured the claimant's right to be forgotten when complying with the recommendation issued by the AEPD in Resolution no. 98/2010, of 24 May 2010: "if there is a legitimate interest relating to a personal situation, and keeping the information unaltered in its original form -since it would not be erased from historical records or files, it could be desirable for the webmaster to prevent indexation of the news story by Internet search engines. This would limit an indiscriminate, permanent and, where appropriate, prejudicial dissemination."

This is an innovative approach, evidencing the following aspects: 1′) there are numerous different stances amongst the media; 2′) the right to be forgotten can be effectively guaranteed in online media; 3′) the ability of the media to sacrifice the right to information for the benefit of the right to oblivion after weighing the interests at stake. In fact, lavanguardia.es removed the full digital version of the newspaper of the

---

[131] *La Vanguardia's* arguments were basically in line with the criteria laid down by the AEPD in Resolutions no. 85 and 94/2010: 1) the online publication of a news story is protected by the Constitution; 2) the right to receive truthful information has prevalence over the right to data protection in public affairs of general interest (having regard to the matter and the newsworthy individual); 3) the media are entitled to publish the information and to keep it unaltered; 4) the impact of Internet search engines in terms of dissemination of news stories encourages online media to assess whether, if there are compelling legitimate grounds relating to a particular personal situation, they must prevent indiscriminate, permanent and prejudicial online dissemination through the de-listing of the information by Internet search engines.

date when the disputed story was published (which inevitably prevented access to the remaining reports contained in that edition).[132]

The constitutional right to information would cover the intangibility of personal data in online media -the relevant online media outlet would then have to assess the compelling legitimate grounds relating to a personal situation and, where appropriate, prevent the indexation by Internet search engines. However, the right to information would not cover the intangibility of data in the search indexes online. Even if online media would did not actively prevent indexation, Google "should adopt any measures necessary to remove the data from its index and to prevent access to the data in the future" (R/98/2010).

The AEPD advocates for two different degrees in the scope of freedom of information in the Internet era given the expansive force of search engines: on the one hand, it espouses the inviolable right of media to assess whether or not it is convenient to limit access to information; on the other, it restricts search engines' ability to act, since it does not consider them the owners of the published and indexed information.

3) FRAP "terrorists": *ABC*

In 1975, the newspaper *ABC* published a news story, including names, last names and photographs, reporting the arrest of thirty-six members of the Marxist-Leninist Communist Party of Spain as well as of the so-called "*grupos de combate y autodefensa del FRAP*" ("FRAP combat and self-defense groups"). This report connected the arrested persons with the murder of two *Guardia Civil* officers (Military Police).

Almost thirty five years later, on 19 November 2009, one of the arrested

---

[132] Google Spain broadly restated the arguments held in the official gazette cases: the search engine's automatic nature; the neutral nature of the search engine vis-à-vis the webmaster's liability; the claim that Google Spain acts as a mere commercial representative of Google Inc. for the sale of advertising space, and the inapplicability of Spanish legislation, since the search engine services are provided by Google Inc. in the United States. The AEPD refuted these arguments using its usual line of reasoning: "Although the Spanish Constitution recognizes the freedom of expression and information as restrictions on the right to object against online media, no 'legal provision requires the claimant's personal data to be included in Google indexes to facilitate access to certain pages by users, and it neither provides that they must be included in the websites temporarily stored by Google in the cache memory' (...). Google should have implemented any measures necessary to withdraw the data from its index and to prevent access to the data in the future. Accordingly, the claimant's personal data had to be removed from Google search indexes.

persons, mentioned in the news story as a prominent member of the said terrorist group, exercised her right to object against Google Spain and *ABC* before the AEPD. She made the following allegations: the arrest took place when she was attending a college meeting without knowing what it was about; the proceedings initiated in the Public Order Court had been finally closed; the facts attributed to the claimant in the news story were uncertain, and they were private and past events; in spite of keeping it as reserved information, years later this news story led to dead threats to her family, a change of address and the need to conceal her telephone number.

The claimant exercised her right to object based on the following contentions: there were compelling legitimate grounds relating to a particular personal situation to prevent an unreasonable public dissemination of her data due to the nature of the news story; the information published by *ABC* could be anonymized in the newspaper library's virtual version; the prevalence of the right to "freely receive truthful information by any means of dissemination whatsoever" over other constitutional rights should not be construed in absolute terms, there must be a fair balance; the news report would not be deprived of its nature if her name and last name were replaced with her initials; the effects of the news story and the resulting personal prejudice were unreasonable, and the events had occurred in 1975, when data dissemination in print editions was limited. Nonetheless, within the information society, the media have digitalized their libraries and files, significantly affecting data protection.[133]

On 24 May 2010, the AEPD issued Resolution no. 962/2010 upholding the complaint against Google, yet rejecting the action brought against *ABC*. The Data Protection Agency ordered Google to remove the data from its index and to prevent future access. However, regarding *ABC*, it based its decision on the prevalence of the right to freedom of speech, although it issued the following recommendation to the newspaper: where there are compelling legitimate grounds relating to a particular personal situation, and provided that the published events are no longer relevant, it is advisable for the newspaper's webmaster to prevent indexation of the story through Internet search engines.

---

[133] Both Google and *ABC* rejected these claims. Google denied the request for deletion of information appearing in search results contained in third-party websites that could only be removed in cooperation with the webmaster.*ABC* alleged that the personal data were the result of digitalization of a news story published in *ABC* covered by the constitutional right to information.

Resolution no. 962/2010 refined the previous arguments:

1′) The right to object should be rejected, since the constitution gives prevalence to freedom of expression regarding truthful information of public relevance. Nonetheless, in view of the clash between fundamental rights, it is necessary to seek techniques that may allow for striking a fair balance between these rights in conflict.[134]

2′) Digitalization of newspaper archives and libraries -and their impact in terms of information thanks to Internet search engines- currently highlights the tremendous problems that could be posed by the permanent storage of personal information online (in spite of the initial protection granted by the right to information).[135]

3′) Without imposing a specific response on the media, reconciling or balancing conflicting rights (information and oblivion) would require the implementation of best practices which are currently offered by information society technologies.[136]

4′) The freedom of information does not require to maintain personal data in search indexes or in the pages temporarily stored in the cache memory. No legal or constitutional provision could be invoked against the right to erasure exercised vis-à-vis Google.

2.2.- News in online media: present information vs. future oblivion: a right to "rehabilitation from information"?

---

[134] "Nevertheless, the media should consider the need for encouraging a better balance between freedom of information and the enforcement of data protection principles. First, the public relevance of the identity of those persons affected by the newsworthy event should be carefully assessed. If such identity does not provide additional information, the identification should be avoided by removing the name and even the initials or any other ancillary reference which could identify them in a narow environment."

[135] "There is no doubt that Internet development and the widespread implementation of search engines entail an exponential and permanent update and dissemination of information in the media, including the personal data contained therein, such as personal identity. Therefore, the media should reflect on the significant effects of permanently providing total accessibility to data contained in news stories with probably no relevance nowadays. Consideration should also be given to the impact on privacy."

[136] "If there is a legitimate interest relating to a personal situation, and the event is no longer relevant, the media should use information technology to have their webmaster prevent the indexation of the relevant news story by Internet search engines. Accordingly, although keeping the information unaltered in its original form -it would not be erased from historical records or files- this would limit an indiscriminate, permanent and, as the case may be, prejudicial dissemination."

The digitalization of newspaper print editions faces us with a reality unknown to this date: due to Internet search engines, events that have occurred many decades ago ("dead news") become current again. The persons involved relive the events attributed to them as if they were taking place right now. When these events prejudiced their social image and undermined their dignity, they were relieved when they saw them fade away in dark newspaper libraries.

It is easy to predict that the impact of this new reality will be perceived by society with some degree of sensitivity, which will give rise to a right to "rehabilitation from information" when there are socially justifiable grounds to prevent reliving a distant past.

Nevertheless, it will be much harder to argue and justify an identical claim if the news are "alive." These are also truthful newsworthy events of general interest, yet without sufficient time having elapsed as to turn them into "dead news" (which lack the currency inherent to any newsworthy event).

The following AEPD resolutions have helped to illustrate these issues, as well as to show how hard it is to give general responses foreign to the analysis of each specific case.

1) The *Cibeles* Case: removal of criminal records and background information

The claimant in this case filed a complaint before the AEPD on 9 December 2009. He exercised his right to object against Google Spain. Apparently, there were personal data of the claimant in Google search indexes related to a 2004 judgment regarding events that had occurred that same year. These events had been reported by many digital newspapers (*El Mundo, ABC, El País*, etc.).

These digital media reported that the claimant had been sentenced for criminal damage to historical monuments for breaking a hand of the Cibeles monument in Madrid. He was sentenced to an 18-month penalty and to pay a fine to the City Council.

The claimant neither requested deletion nor objected to the processing of the data by digital media.[137] Some of the newspapers had anonymized, by using initials, the identity of the remaining persons involved. The complaint was filed against Google Spain, and the claimant put forward the following compelling legitimate grounds relating to a particular personal situation: he had already been held criminally and civilly liable, as he had already served the penalty imposed on him; his criminal and police records had already been expunged; the accessibility to this news story through Google Search caused him serious personal and professional damage, since he was of working age.

The AEPD Resolution (R/1509/2009), dated 11 September 2009, upheld the claimant's complaint and urged Google Spain to adopt any necessary measures to remove the data from its index and to prevent access to the data in the future. The Spanish Agency considered that that the constitutional right to freedom of expression did not entitle Google to include claimant's data in its indexes, and it also concluded that there were compelling legitimate grounds relating to a personal situation protected by the right to object.[138]

The claimant failed to fully identify the digital media involved, and the time elapsed from the publication until the date of the complaint cannot be considered particularly long. However, the case drew the attention to a couple of significant overlapping circumstances: on the one hand, the claimant's age when the newsworthy events occurred (twenty-one years old) in connection with the impact of information technology on his future work prospects; on the other, the contrast between the clearance of the criminal records (after the period of time that had elapsed) and the perpetuation of the social informational effects, i.e., the currency of information and its socially prejudicial effects vis-à-vis the expiration of criminal information.

2) The Case of the *Sociedad General de Autores Españoles* (SGAE, Spanish Authors and Publishers Association): elmundo.es. Inaccurate or obsolete data to justify the right to be forgotten?

On 29 July 2009, the Spanish Authors and Publishers Association

---

[137] In other cases, the claimant simply exercised his/her right to object against the online media outlet and not against Google, which led the AEPD to dismiss the complaint, not imposing specific obligations on Google. Regarding Resolution no. 1044/2010 issued by the AEPD in June 2010 (TD/487/2010), although the claim against *ABC* was dismissed, this newspaper reported the following: "if you consider it enough, we do intend to do our best in order to try to exclude the possibility of searching by your name and last name in our pages."
[138] R/801/2011, of 17 May 2011 (TD/1434/2010).

(SGAE) exercised its right to object by filing a complaint before the AEPD against Google Spain. The claim involved the processing of data collected in the online version of *El Mundo* in 2007. A news story reported the commission of crimes of fraud, embezzlement and misappropriation of subsidies through companies managed by certain members of SGAE. The Spanish Authors and Publishers Association alleged that the information was false, and it also founded its defense on the serious prejudice to the Association's honor, image, reputation, privacy and professional activity caused by this information.

On 17 February 2010, the AEPD (R/273/2010) dismissed the claim against Google on the view that the necessary requirements were not fulfilled (compelling legitimate grounds, connection with a particular personal situation and justification of the right to object on the alleged grounds). The Agency concluded that "it was an event of public significance where it has not been evidenced that the published data and information were inaccurate or obsolete."[139]

This AEPD Resolution provides two new elements to support the right to be forgotten vis-à-vis data processing in a digital news story: 1′) *inaccuracy* and 2′) *obsolescence*.

Although data protection law allows for the deletion of inaccurate data, challenging an inaccurate news story might clash with the distinct legal meaning attached to the truthfulness inherent to lawful information, and it also collides with certain specific legal remedies to this situation, such as the right to rectification.

The *obsolescence* of a piece of information links the news event with a hypothetical "life" of the news item based on "currency," whereas its "obsolescing dusk" revolves around "newsworthiness," which disappears with the course of time. On this basis, there is still a central question to be solved: how much time is it necessary to determine the obsolescence of a news story, thereby guaranteeing the right to be forgotten? When the AEPD confronted this complex matter, two years were deemed insufficient (R/273/2010), but five were considered enough (R/1509/2009). Identifying a personal situation cannot be based on a mere count, but it will require assessing other circumstances that can

---

[139] The AEPD has followed this same line of reasoning to deny the right to oblivion in numerous cases heard by the Agency: R/00599/2012, of 7 March 2012 (TD/413/2012); R/2010/2012 (TD/796/2012) -the data referred to a series of news stories published by *El País* in 1993 and 1994 regarding a prison sentence without parole and a subsequent acquittal by the Supreme Court.

qualify the course of time as a central element for the right to be forgotten.

3) The Case involving a Member of the Madrid Regional Legislature: the relevance of holding public office[140] as a limit to the right to oblivion in the news

There are many cases where the right to oblivion of the data published in online media cannot be recognized. Among them are specially relevant those where the person involved in the relevant newsworthy event is an elected public official, even if a long time has elapsed since the news item was published. The AEPD decided on a request for deletion of data (Resolution no. 2079/2011, dated 23 September 2011) contained in news items from 1985 and 1986 recorded in the digitalized newspaper archive of *ABC*. Those stories stated that the claimant was a Member of the Madrid Regional Legislature.

The claimant contended that the websites contained her name, last name, public positions held, her political affiliation, as well as additional data revealing her ideology and beliefs. She requested the blocking of these data in internal search engines or otherwise replacing them with initials not matching her name and last name. She also requested removing any other piece of information that could identify her, or make her identifiable, as well as preventing indexation by external search engines.[141]

However, in November 2010, the AEPD issued Resolution no. 2144/2010 (TD/610/2010). Through this decision, the AEPD upheld the right to object exercised against an Internet search engine in connection with personal data stored in local newspaper pages and in a legal journal regarding a candidate to a 2003 election.[142]

---

[140] The AEPD dismissed the complaint based on the right to object against Grupo Zeta for publishing personal data of a public official in a report released in interviu.es: AEPD Resolution no. 3106/2012 (TD/2029/2012).

[141] *ABC* opposed that claim on the grounds that its newspaper archive was a faithful record of old news items published in *ABC*. Having regard to its obligation to inform about historical events, the newspaper could not remove, neither fully nor partially, its contents under the constitutional right to inform enshrined in Article 20 of the Spanish Constitution (CE). The claimant did not provide evidence of compelling legitimate grounds relating to a particular personal situation, and she sought the removal solely of her personal data related to her duties as a Member of the Madrid Regional Legislature.

[142] The claimant did not bring an action against the websites that published the data (the AEPD urged him to do so in its decision), but only against the Internet search engine.

4) *La Vanguardia* Case: voluntary indexation of news stories by online media

AEPD's recommendation to online media (suggesting them to assess whether they should protect the right to be forgotten by preventing news story indexation by search engines on compelling legitimate grounds relating to a personal situation) has been fruitful, and it has been progressively complied with. In the abovementioned Resolution no. 1044/2010, the newspaper *ABC* showed its willingness to do as much as possible "in order to exclude the possibility of searching our websites by his name and last name, even if the search engines take some time to update our request."

Resolution no. 347/2011, of 23 February 2011, made it clear that this recommendation had been complied with. On 15 February 2010, the right to object was exercised against *La Vanguardia* and Google, by requesting the erasure of data contained in a news story from lavanguardia.es. This news item mentioned the claimant's health issues related to an accident where he was injured.

Google Spain argued against the right to object. However, the AEPD did not impose any obligation on Google, since *La Vanguardia* notified the AEPD that on 3 December 2010 it had told the claimant that it would de-list the news item containing his data. Although the AEPD believed that Google should have implemented any measures necessary to remove the data from its index and to prevent future access to such data, the right to object was entirely fulfilled, since the claimant's data could not be found online.

2.3.- The right to be forgotten in *Libro de estilo de El País* (*El País Manual of Style*) (2014)

AEPD resolutions on the right to be forgotten in the media have progressively reached an expansive scope which is greater than it can be inferred from their wordings.

The AEPD has taken a respectful stance toward the constitutional right to information held by the media, in spite of its blatant conflicts with another constitutional right, i.e., data protection. This right will only be ensured if the media acknowledge the need to guarantee this right as a deontological exercise. Media self-regulation is the only way to sufficiently protect personal data in journalism.

Journalistic practice and regulation limit the scope of personal data protection to the often erratic application of certain anonymization techniques for personal information. These techniques may entail replacing identifying data (name and last name) with the initials in certain cases: the victim's name in cases of rape, or children's names when they are arrested by the police or indicted.[143]

Surprisingly enough, the right to be forgotten has been included in the deontological guidelines of the 2014 *Libro de Estilo de El País* (*El País* Manual of Style) substantially in line with the AEPD doctrine:

1') *Update guarantee* of newspaper files on police and judicial information: "Any information that has been filed and remains accessible from *elpais.com* reporting investigations, charges, indictments, arrests, imprisonments or sentences that have been subsequently repealed by a police or court decision shall include a warning along with a link with the latest available information on the case. If the latter information is not timely published, the data subject may require that the actual news story include an explanatory note and a link with the relevant court notice or judicial decision."[144]

2') *Preserving the integrity* of news files: "*El País* digital files shall never be erased."[145]

3') *De-indexation* of the news story from the search results shown by *Internet search engines*: "One might consider the possibility of concealing this information from Internet search engines"[146] if the following requirements are met: a') "the information should have been published more than 15 years before the deletion is requested; b') the information must be prejudicial to the claimant's family or working life."[147]

4') The only *limit* to oblivion/de-listing: the facts contained in final judgments on violent acts.[148]

The exercise of the right to be forgotten against Internet search engines is acknowledged in the deontological document of the main Spanish media outlet: any news story can be de-listed from the newspaper's digital files

---

[143] These cases are expressly included in *Libro de Estilo de El País* (Aguilar, Madrid, 2014, pp. 33-34).
[144] *Libro de Estilo de El País*, Aguilar, Madrid, 2014, pp. 37-38.
[145] *Libro de Estilo de El País...*, p. 38.
[146] *Libro de Estilo de El País...*, p. 38.
[147] *Libro de Estilo de El País...*, p. 38.
[148] *Libro de Estilo de El País...*, p. 38.

if the data subject alleges that there is family or professional prejudice and a significant time period has elapsed (15 years). Setting a minimum time period is questionable -although there is a clear aim for legal certainty, and it would have been more reasonable to assess the time factor having regard to the remaining circumstances involved.

De-indexation of personal data by search engines is only excluded in case of information contained in "judgments on violent acts." Although this might be a vague and misleading reference, it significantly widens the scope of the right to oblivion.

3.- NO OBLIVION IN THE INTERNET SEARCH ENGINE WHEN NO CLAIM IS BROUGHT AGAINST THE SOURCE WEBSITE

The right to be forgotten seeks the removal of certain personal information from every Internet service or, depending on the circumstances, limiting access thereto or minimizing its dissemination.

This personal information is sometimes legally required to be stored in websites (as in official gazettes or online media, for instance), but its dissemination can be limited by removing it from online search results. That is how individuals see their quest for oblivion fulfilled, thereby striking a balance between rights and constitutional or legal requirements.

Nevertheless, it is inconsistent -and it would jeopardize the right to object against Internet search engines- that an individual may try to force search engines to prevent crawling of personal data hosted on a website whilst not urging webmasters to erase that personal information (when there is no legal obligation requiring its publication, and therefore it solely depends on the data subject's consent).

This discriminatory situation regarding the scope of the right to be forgotten would be inconsistent with the purpose of the right to object against the search engine, and it could render this purpose meaningless. That was the AEPD's understanding in Resolution no. 38/2013. The Agency rejected the complaint filed against Google, where the claimant (i.e., the author of a research paper appearing in certain websites) wanted Google to prevent indexation of data provided by the claimant himself. However, he failed to bring an action against those websites to require deletion of the said data. The AEPD found that it was contradictory and inconsistent to order a given search engine not to locate a research paper online without requiring at the same time to delete the paper from the websites where it appears.

4.- NEITHER PREVENTIVE OBLIVION NOR PREVIOUS CENSORSHIP ON THE INTERNET: THERE IS NO ROOM FOR A GENERAL AND PRECAUTIONARY OPPOSITION TO DATA INDEXATION

There is an insurmountable limit to the right to oblivion on the Internet: prior censorship online. The required weighing between data protection rights and freedom of information would clearly sacrifice the latter if we sought a precautionary and preventive ban on personal data dissemination on the Internet without previously assessing the specific risk inherent to such dissemination.

The current development of technology prevents monitoring Internet content to protect freedom of expression, the right to information, and the right to privacy. The AEPD drew this conclusion in proceedings no. TD/172/2009, which concluded on 20 July 2009 after the issuance of Resolution no. 1517/2009. In this decision, the Data Protection Agency rejected the generic and prior opposition to personal data indexation by search engines.

On 15 December 2008, a complaint was filed before the AEPD. Apparently, Google Spain (the respondent) had failed to fulfill the right to object exercised by an individual who, in her own behalf and on behalf of her four children, required their personal data not to appear in Google search indexes for "safety reasons." The claimant held that there was a ruling in Spain sentencing her former spouse for gender violence which also prohibited contact with the children.

The claimant had exercised the right to object regarding her personal data and those of her four children upon verifying that when she entered the data in Google Search she was able to access her personal information. This enabled her former spouse to locate her, thus posing a threat to her safety.

In spite of the various changes of residence, and although she had adopted the necessary preventive measures -for instance, not authorizing her children to appear in photographs, booklets and other school and extracurricular activity publications online, the efforts were futile, since the following references appeared in Google search indexes: 1') two of the children's names appeared on the list of participants for a local sports competition; 2') a daughter's information was included in the high school website along with her SAT scores. She appeared as the recipient of a college scholarship as well as on the list of college admissions; 3') another son's data were included on the list of participants for a soccer competition.

The claim was twofold: on the one hand, she required deletion of the existing Google search results; on the other, she asked for a general precautionary measure to prevent Google from indexing her and her children's future data, since her physical integrity was at stake.

The AEPD rejected this general non-indexation requirement regarding future data included in Internet search engines based on three arguments: a) the right to object requires a prior processing of the specific data to which the individual grounds for objection can be addressed. Thus, it is also necessary to identify the data not to be indexed; b) it is possible to exercise the right to object against the webmaster; c) it is technically unfeasible to prevent a potential indexation of personal data on a precautionary basis. This statement refers to the technological complexity of ensuring a general or precautionary right to oblivion. The foregoing does not exclude, however, that an advanced technical study might enable such an aseptic enforcement of the right to be forgotten online.[149]

5.- NEITHER BLIND OBLIVION NOR GENERAL ERASURE OF DATA IN INTERNET SEARCH ENGINES

Citizens sometimes exercise the right to oblivion vis-à-vis Internet search engines as a general opposition to any result obtained online by the said search engines. There is often the claim for a total deletion of personal data in search indexes on a general basis and without specifically identifying the links or memories temporarily stored by the search engines.

The AEPD has always supported such deletion only in the specific context of the right to object. Under Article 6(4) of the Spanish Data Protection Organic Act (LOPD), exercising the right to object requires assessing the compelling legitimate grounds relating to a particular personal situation, which is *a priori* incompatible with the "blind oblivion" of those who want to disappear entirely from the searches without justifying, on a case-by-case basis, the personal situation supporting this disappearance.

We should not overlook the claim that, given the current development of technology, it does not seem feasible to seek to prevent personal

---

[149] AEPD Resolution no. 516/2012, of 24 February 2012, was delivered in proceedings no. TD/1613/2011. The claimant sought "the withdrawal from the search engine of any personal data (name, last name, National ID number, etc.) or information pertaining to private life.

information from being crawled by search engines on a precautionary basis.

The AEPD did not hesitate to boldly dismiss these claims based on these two arguments: a) "We cannot uphold the **generic** request for non-indexation of data contained on the Internet, given the need to specify the data not to be indexed and the technical impossibility of provisionally avoiding any potential location of data. In order to avoid these crawling of data, data subjects must exercise the relevant right, specifying the particular data they request not to be indexed" (R/264/2013);[150] b) "[t]he so-called 'right to be forgotten' embodied in means for deletion and opposition granted by the LOPD cannot become an instrument to rewrite the past indiscriminately. Accordingly, the claim for the de-listing of 1,200 links collides with the justification requirement for the claim" (R/2884/2012).

---

[150] R/517/2012 (TD/1602/2011); R/520/2012 (TD/1616/2011); R/1512/2012 (TD/308/2012); R/264/2013 (TD/2196/2012); R/429/2013 (TD/283/2013).

CHAPTER III

THE RIGHT TO BE FORGOTTEN IN SPAIN (II): LEGAL GROUNDS OF THE GOOGLE V. AEPD DISPUTE

1.- GOOGLE[151] AND OTHERS: THE CLAIM FOR IMMUNITY[152] OF INTERNET SEARCH ENGINES

1.1.- The application of US legislation. Google Inc. as the sole responsible for the search engine: no establishment and no use of equipment in Spain

Google Search services are exclusively owned, provided and the sole responsibility of Google Inc. -a US company incorporated under the laws of Delaware and headquartered in California, and any dispute arising out of, or relating to, searches (crawling, storage, indexation or data

---

[151] The global success of services offered by Google (particularly of its search engine) and its constant conflicts regarding privacy protection have triggered many scholarly works in this regard: MATTHEW A. GOLDBERG: "The googling of online privacy: gmail, search-engine histories and the new frontier of protecting private information on the web," *Lewis and Clark Law Review*, vol. 9-1, 2005, pp. 249-272; OMER TENE: "What Google knows: privacy and Internet search engines," *Utah Law Review*, vol. 4, 2008, pp. 1433-1492; MUTH, K.T.: "Googlestroika: Privatizing Privacy," *Duquesne Law Review*, vol. 47, 2009, pp. 337-353; JEFFREY ROSEN: "'The Deciders: The Future of Privacy and Free Speech in the Age of Facebook and Google'," *Fordham Law Review*, vol. 80-4, 2012, pp. 1525-1538.

[152] As asserted by JOEL REIDEMBERG: "the initial wave of cases seeking to deny jurisdiction, choice of law, and enforcement to states where users and victims are located constitutes a type of "denial-of-service" attack against the legal system. Internet separatists use technology-based arguments to deny the existence of sufficient contacts for jurisdiction and the applicability of rules of law interdicting certain behavior. From this perspective, the attackers seek to disable states from protecting their citizens online" ("Technology and Internet Jurisdiction," *University of Pennsylvania Law Review*, vol. 153, 2005, p. 1953). A solid approach to this issue can be found in CHRISTOPHER KUNER: "Data Protection Law and International Jurisdiction on the Internet (Part 1)," *International Journal of Law and Information Technology*, vol. 18.2, 2010, pp. 176-193 y "Data Protection Law and International Jurisdiction on the Internet (Part 2)," *International Journal of Law and Information Technology,* vol. 18-3, 2010, pp. 227-247.

protection claims) will be exclusively subject to the laws of the US and the jurisdiction of the courts of California.[153]

Google Spain constitutes a mere subsidiary of Google Inc. devoted to promoting, facilitating and carrying out the sale of online advertising products and services to third parties and the marketing of that advertising in Spain. It does not provide any services related to the search engine, since it has no ability to do so.

Based on the two previous premises, and resorting to the arguments for[154]

---

[153] This is stated by the *Google Terms of Service* in their version from 1 March 2012: "The courts in some countries will not apply California law to some types of disputes. If you reside in one of those countries, then where California law is excluded from applying, your country's laws will apply to such disputes related to these terms. Otherwise, you agree that the laws of California, U.S.A., excluding California's choice of law rules, will apply to any disputes arising out of or relating to these terms or the Services. Similarly, if the courts in your country will not permit you to consent to the jurisdiction and venue of the courts in Santa Clara County, California, U.S.A., then your local jurisdiction and venue will apply to such disputes related to these terms. Otherwise, all claims arising out of or relating to these terms or the services will be litigated exclusively in the federal or state courts of Santa Clara County, California, USA, and you and Google consent to personal jurisdiction in those courts."
(*https://www.google.es/intl/es/policies/terms/regional.html*).
[154] Other domestic authorities, both administrative and judicial bodies, did consider that EU legislation was applicable to Google Search in disputes related to the "autocomplete" feature: 1) the Spanish Data Protection Agency (AEPD), through Resolution no. 2647/2012 (TD/1105/2012), upheld a complaint against Google Spain, where it ordered Google to adopt the measures necessary to prevent the association of the claimant's data with the term "gay" in the search suggestions provided by the autocomplete feature; 2) a Judgment delivered by the Paris Court of Appeal (*Cour d'Appel*) on 18 December 2011 in a dispute between Google and the insurance company Lyonnaise de Garantie concluded the following: since knowledge of the issue had been clearly evidenced by specific notifications, and provided that Google had failed to remove the suggestions -the insurance company name was associated to the French word "escroc" (fraud)- from the autocomplete feature, the Court decided to impose a penalty on Google and to order the removal of the automatic suggestion; 3) a court of justice in Milan, in a ruling dated 24 March 2011, ordered Google to remove from the autocomplete function the suggestion that associated the claimant with the Italian words "truffatore" (fraudster or scammer) and "truffa" (fraud or scam); 4) in April 2013, a Japanese tribunal entered judgment against Google for associating a citizen's name to a criminal group in its autocomplete feature suggestions; 5) finally, in May 2013, the German Supreme Court urged Google to withdraw from its search engine every automatic suggestion that connected a businessman's last name with the notions of "scientology" and "scam" (*El País,* 15 May 2013, p. 52).

and against[155] the applicability of EU legislation to the search engine, Google denies that Google Spain can be considered a company's establishment located in Spain. Accordingly, under the rules of territoriality laid down in Articles 4(1)(a) of Directive 95/46/EC and 2(1)(a) of the Spanish Data Protection Organic Act (LOPD), Google Inc. is fully responsible for search engine activities within the exclusive framework of US legislation.

Google neither accepts the "use of equipment situated in the territory of Spain" for the provision of search engine services. Google Inc. would provide such global service through data centers -none of them located in Spain- to which Spanish users would transfer their data. The "robots" or "web crawlers" would be located in such centers, from where they would crawl information on the Internet to locate and sweep up website content (if the responsible webmaster authorizes the referral) whilst automatically indexing the information. All processes related to search engine activities would be carried out in Google's equipment wherever it is located, yet without using technical means placed where the information is originally hosted.

Consequently, under the rules of territoriality, neither EU nor Spanish legislation would be applicable, since there is no "use of equipment situated" in Spain to process the data in the terms of Articles 4(1)(a) of Directive 95/46/EC and 2(1)(c) LOPD.

1.2.- The neutral nature of the automated means of search engines as the foundation for not holding search engines liable. The webmaster is directly and solely responsible

The neutral nature of the search service is one of the main arguments on which Google bases its lack of responsibility regarding the processing of

---

[155] In most of the proceedings heard by the AEPD, Google's stance was based on the approach of other domestic administrative and judicial authorities: 1′) A Resolution issued by the Italian Data Protection Agency dated 11 December 2008 dismissed a request for deletion of a data subject's data on the grounds that Google Inc. was not established in any EU Member State and the processing of data was carried out through servers located in the U.S.. 2′) A ruling delivered by the High Court of Paris (*Tribunal de grande instance de Paris*) on 14 April 2008 rejected the claims of a data subject against Google Inc. and Google France, on the view that the search service was exclusively provided by Google Inc. with no establishment in France and without using any equipment in France, whereas Google France solely acted as a commercial representative. 3′) A ruling handed down by a first instance court in Brussels on 2 June 2009 dismissed the complaint against Google Belgium, thereby preventing the claimant from deleting Google search results.

data entailed by/related to search engine activities. Conversely, the webmaster's ability to decide on the indexation of contents on its website would make it directly responsible, and thus it would have to ensure compliance with data protection law.

Google Search would obtain information in a similar way to Internet users: by means of its robots or web crawlers, it would issue an automatic request to servers hosting the information, and they would either allow total, partial access or none at all, according to the preconfigured instructions. Ultimately, the webmaster or whoever publishes the information would have to decide if the website hosting server sends the requested information. The search engine would never obtain information from the servers and would never access them if the webmaster does not allow it.[156]

Google would therefore avoid responsibility on the grounds that any decision on the purpose and destination of the personal information would exclusively lie with the webmasters that enable access to information and with third parties reproducing this information. Only webmasters could decide on "purposes and means of the processing of personal data" -Articles 2(d) Directive 95/46/EC and 3(d) LOPD.

To support its stance, Google resorts to Opinion 1/2008 on data protection issues related to search engines of Article 29 Data Protection Working Party, adopted on 4 April 2008. This Opinion differentiates between the webmaster's degree of responsibility and that of the search engine, excluding the primary responsibility of the latter for the processed data (i.e., not considering the search engine provider as the principal controller) whilst attributing that responsibility to the webmaster in

---

[156] Subsequently, Google acknowledged that the information collected from servers is stored in its servers -since it would be technically unfeasible to offer real-time search results to users- and it is processed through a mathematical algorithm which connects the search terms, the source website and other factors. The result of this processing is displayed to users by order of preference, as an index of links automatically generated in real time and without human intervention. Its contents would be subject to permanent updates, since the constant crawling of indexed websites would evidence content modifications. As opposed to the automatic nature of Google Search, third parties that published the information would have technological tools to control access to the information at all times, which would allow them to totally or partially exclude the information from the search engine indexes: by not accepting the information requests issued by search engines; by inserting instructions to prevent a website from being indexed, or by using the "robots.txt" exclusion protocol to limit or exclude search engine crawling of the whole website or of specific content, such as files or directories.

charge of the site where the personal information was originally published: "The principle of proportionality requires that to the extent that a search engine provider acts purely as an intermediary, it should not be considered to be the principal controller with regard to the content related processing of personal data that is taking place. In this case the principal controllers of personal data are the information providers."[157] Nevertheless, Google fails to notice that this statement also attributes the primary responsibility to search engine providers regarding the removal of personal data from their index: "The formal, legal and practical control the search engine has over the personal data involved is usually limited to the possibility of removing data from its servers. With regard to the removal of personal data from their index and search results, search engines have sufficient control to consider them as controllers (either alone or jointly with others)" insofar as there is an obligation to remove or block personal data stemming from Member State legislation.[158]

1.3.- The ineffectiveness of the right to be forgotten when exclusively exercised vis-à-vis Internet search engines and the principle of proportionality

Google notes that an administrative supervisory authority exclusively devoted to ordering search engine providers to remove personal information from their indexes would be ineffective as long as the webmaster that published the information does not delete it and/or provides for technical tools to prevent the indexation of the information. If such information remains on the website, it will still be accessible by any other search engine or Internet platform and thus it will be publicly accessible.

Google calls for the fulfilment of the principle of proportionality as the cornerstone of EU law to assess AEPD resolutions under EU legislation and case law, as well as under the freedom of expression and information and the freedom to conduct a business (Articles 11 and 16 CFREU): "Under the principle of proportionality, the content and form of Union

---

[157]http://ec.europa.eu/justice/data-protection/article-29/documentation/opinion-recommendation/index_en.htm

[158] Footnote 14 of Opinion 1/2008 refers to the Spanish case: "In some EU Member States data protection authorities have specifically regulated the responsibility of search engine providers to remove content data from the search index, based on the right of objection enshrined in Article 14 of the Data Protection Directive (95/46/EC) and on the e-Commerce Directive (2000/31/EC). According to such national legislation, search engines are obliged to follow a notice and takedown policy similar to hosting providers in order to prevent liability."

action shall not exceed what is necessary to achieve the objectives of the Treaties" (Article 5(4) TUE).

Google claims that the AEPD lacks legal capacity to decide on the right to object pursuant to which Google must erase information from its search engine by balancing the various rights at stake: the claimant's privacy and dignity, freedom of expression and information of whoever publishes the information and of third parties who may access such information, along with the freedom to conduct a business enjoyed by search engines.

Recent EU case law -regarding copyright protection vis-à-vis illegal downloading on the Internet- requires domestic authorities to weigh these rights in conflict: "Community law requires that, when transposing those directives, the Member States take care to rely on an interpretation of them which allows a fair balance to be struck between the various fundamental rights protected by the Community legal order. Further, when implementing the measures transposing those directives, the authorities and courts of the Member States must not only interpret their national law in a manner consistent with those directives but also make sure that they do not rely on an interpretation of them which would be in conflict with those fundamental rights or with the other general principles of Community law, such as the principle of proportionality."[159] The CJEU adds the following: "national authorities and courts must, in particular, strike a fair balance between the protection of the intellectual property right enjoyed by copyright holders and that of the freedom to conduct a business enjoyed by operators such as ISPs pursuant to Article 16 of the Charter."[160]

Obviously, the principle of proportionality plays a role in many preliminary rulings of the CJEU that have required a balance between the means used and the aim pursued to protect fundamental rights. None of these fundamental rights are absolute, as reiterated by the CJEU concerning the right to data protection (as well as many other fundamental rights in other cases). However, in Google's view, an appropriate application of the principle of proportionality in this dispute on the right to be forgotten vis-à-vis search engines should be based on the following premises: 1′) the accuracy of indexes regarding the content indexed on websites; 2′) the automatic and constant update of indexes to preserve the accuracy of this information; 3′) the excessively burdensome means (i.e., directly removing content from the search engine indexes) intended to prevent access to information lawfully published online.

---

[159] CJEU, 29 January 2008, *Case Promusicae v Telefónica*, C-275/06.
[160] CJEU, 24 November 2011, *Case SABAM*, C-70/2010.

Google draws a bold conclusion: being forced to remove links to websites in its indexes would be ineffective, inefficient, and disproportionate or unreasonable for the following reasons: 1′) in order to fulfill the right to be forgotten, it would be less expensive and more efficient for the webmaster to use the means it already has at its disposal to remove links, not only to a specific search engine, but also to any others and to the remaining applications on the Internet; 2′) the webmaster's restrictions would not force individuals to identify the various search engines, websites, networks, etc. hosting their information, and they could exercise their rights altogether; 3′) withdrawing links and references from the search engine indexes would not only entail deleting specific personal references, but also full Internet websites, thereby progressively subverting the search engine's utility and undermining its key role in the advancement of information and knowledge society; 4′) deleting search results would breach the right to information of publishers, as well as the fundamental right of users who are purportedly entitled to access such information.

1.4.- The stance of other Internet search engines toward the right to be forgotten: Bing-Microsoft and Yahoo

1°) The acceptance of EU jurisdiction and legislation by the search engine: Bing – Microsoft

The AEPD has heard very few cases involving Bing, but they show a different approach to the applicability of EU or Spanish data protection legislation (and jurisdiction) to Internet search engines.

Clause 12.1 of the Microsoft *Services Agreement* (applicable as of 14 May 2013) governing the use of Bing illustrates the differing stance with respect to other search engines (Google) that require users to abide by US legislation and to be subject to the jurisdiction of the courts of California.

Microsoft provides that users living in Europe contract with Microsoft Luxembourg, subject to the laws of Luxembourg. Nevertheless, for users living in Spain the Agreement shall be interpreted in accordance with Spanish legislation. All other claims shall be subject to the "laws of the country to which Microsoft directs your Services," and the parties will choose "the courts of the country to which we direct your Services [...] for all disputes arising out of or relating to these Terms" (alternatively, the user may choose the courts of Luxembourg).[161] The exercise of the right to be forgotten vis-à-vis Microsoft's search engine Bing should be covered by the legislation of each country -Spain, for instance- to which it specifically directs its services.

On 27 May 2010, a data subject exercised the right to erasure before the AEPD against Bing-Microsoft Ibérica (proceedings no. TD/848/2010). This company alleged that it was not responsible for Bing services or for the files attached thereto. Microsoft Ibérica clarified that Bing search engine services were not provided by a single entity worldwide. Apparently, there were various group companies within Microsoft that provided the services depending on the user's place of residence. In particular, users living in Spain contracted with Microsoft Luxembourg, which had sole responsibility for the files. Thus, on 26 November 2010, the AEPD dismissed the complaint against Bing-Microsoft Ibérica (R/2336/2010) on the grounds that the claim had not been filed against the right entity.

The previous criterion was modified in subsequent AEPD resolutions. The Spanish Data Protection Agency held Microsoft Ibérica liable and urged the company to adopt any measures necessary in order for Bing to prevent the indexation of personal data.

On 5 May 2011, the right to erasure was exercised regarding information on a pardon published in the Official State Gazette (BOE) which was accessible through Bing searches. The Resolution issued by the AEPD (R/2711/2011), dated 28 December 2011, upheld the complaint against Microsoft Ibérica. The AEPD ordered the company to adopt any measures necessary to prevent indexation of the data, applying the Google doctrine in the relevant decisions involving the territorial application of Spanish legislation, insofar as Bing used means located in

---

[161] "12.1. If you live in (or, if you are a business, your principal place of business is in) Europe, you are contracting with Microsoft Luxembourg S.à.r.l., 20 Rue Eugene Ruppert, Immeuble Laccolith, 1st Floor, L-2543 Luxembourg, and the laws of Luxembourg govern the interpretation of these terms, claims for breach of them, regardless of conflict of law principles, unless you live in (or, if you are a business, your principal place of business is in) Spain, in which case the laws of Spain govern the interpretation of these terms. All other claims (including consumer protection, unfair competition and tort claims), shall be subject to the laws of the country to which we direct your Services. With respect to jurisdiction, you and Microsoft agree to choose the courts of the country to which we direct your Services where you have your habitual residence for all disputes arising out of or relating to these Terms, or in the alternative, you may choose the responsible court in Luxembourg" (http://windows.microsoft.com/es-es/windows-live/microsoft-services-agreement).

Spain for data processing. This line of reasoning was unnecessary, having regard to Clause 13 of Microsoft *Services Agreement*, which stated the following: *"all claims shall be subject to the jurisdiction, and governed by the laws, of the user's place of residence,"* even if they were filed against Microsoft Luxembourg as the contracting party.

On 3 June 2011, the right to object was exercised before the AEPD (proceedings no. TD/1031/2011) against Microsoft Ibérica and Microsoft Luxembourg. The claim involved data displayed by Bing search results related to a criminal case that had been permanently stayed. Although Microsoft Ibérica denied responsibility for the search engine, the claimant held that Microsoft operated in Spain both through Microsoft Luxembourg and Microsoft Ibérica. The AEPD upheld the complaint against Microsoft Ibérica in Resolution no. 2655/2011, of 30 November 2011.

The AEPD insisted on holding Microsoft Ibérica entirely liable for the search results, and it did not attribute any liability to Microsoft Luxembourg. This prevented the search engine from defining its stance on the right to be forgotten regarding the indexed search results.[162]

2º) Yahoo: submission to EU and Spanish legislation and jurisdiction, and compliance with AEPD resolutions on the right to be forgotten

After an initial AEPD decision, where the Agency upheld a complaint against Yahoo for not replying to a request for deletion of data from its search engine,[163] this company has been exemplary in terms of submitting to the EU and Spanish legislation and jurisdiction. In addition, it has effectively ensured the right to be forgotten by fulfilling the right to object regarding personal information displayed in its search engine;

---

[162] In other cases where the right to object has been exercised against Bing, the AEPD has rejected the claims, on the view that there had been a lawful dissemination of information based on its relevance and public interest - R/1122/2012 (TD/70/2012) and R/1122/2012 (TD/70/2012)- or based on the general nature of the exercise of the right to oblivion -R/2884/2012 (TD/1255/2012)-.

[163] R/1076/2008 (TD/388/2008), of 13 August 2008)

Yahoo removed this information from its index and prevented future indexation thereof.[164]

In proceedings no. TD/191/2009, Yahoo admitted to "blocking its links and search results" after warning the claimant (who had exercised the right to object) that the search engine had no connection whatsoever with the linked websites nor was responsible for the material available therein. Accordingly, in Yahoo's view, the claimant had to address its request to those websites, so they could prevent that information from being accessible online.

Acting reasonably and with due care, as well as in compliance with Article 17 of the Act on Information Society Services and Electronic Commerce (LSSI), Yahoo acknowledged that it did not feel empowered to determine when a truthful piece of information could be prejudicial to legal interests or rights, or when certain linked data or information could be unlawful: "Neither Yahoo nor an individual, but the competent authority, must decide or determine when the content linked from Yahoo Search must be removed. The relevant resolution in this regard must be submitted to the entities responsible for the source websites, where the data or information were initially published, in order for these data to be deleted at source. This will prevent these data from being subsequently linked from any search engine or link service" (R/1639/2009, of 16 June 2009). This attempt to transfer to source website owners the responsibility for effectively ensuring the right to object did not prevent Yahoo from blocking the links and search results.

---

[164] It is worth noting the evolution of Yahoo's stance, evidenced by the cases heard by the AEPD and the background provided by J.R. REIDEMBERG: "While the days of Internet separatism have waned, many technology players continue to advocate in favor of legal immunity for online activities. Yahoo! exemplifies this view. As a proponent of technological immunity, Yahoo! believes that democratically chosen laws should not apply to its online activities. In the now famous French case, the U.S. company transmitted images of Nazi objects that were constitutionally protected in the United States, but illegal to display in France where the users were located and where Yahoo! targeted advertising. Yahoo! unsuccessfully argued that France did not have personal jurisdiction over the U.S. company because it was operating on the Internet from the United States and that French law did not apply to the images because they were stored on a server in the United States. Yahoo! also argued that the technology offered it no means to comply with French law. When the French courts rejected the technology-based defenses and ruled against Yahoo!, the company went forum shopping and sought to deny enforcement of the French order by suing for a declaratory judgment in federal court in California" (Technology and Internet Jurisdiction"..., p. 1952). On this issue, see REIDEMBERG, J.R.: "Yahoo and Democracy on the Internet," *Jurimetrics*, 2002, vol. 42, p. 261-280.

During proceedings no. TD/1022/2010, Yahoo's submission to the AEPD doctrine on the right to be forgotten was evidenced by the company's acceptance of the right to object.[165] Vis-à-vis the general exercise of this right, Yahoo urged the claimant to specify the compelling legitimate grounds relating to a particular personal situation founding the claimant's request under Article 6(4) of the Spanish Data Protection Organic Act (LOPD), as well as the specific search results to be erased.[166] Even without an upholding decision by the AEPD, the claimant confirmed that Yahoo Iberia had fulfilled its right to object by deleting the links from its search engine and subsequently sending a letter whereby the claimant's right to object was accepted" (R/2525/2010, of 20 December 2010).

In sum, Yahoo never challenged in any way the jurisdiction or the legislation applicable to the results indexed by its search engine. During Proceedings no. TD178/2011 (AEPD Resolution of 13 July 2011), Yahoo seized the opportunity to clarify the company's stance and the responsibility of the various entities toward the search engine:[167] 1´) both Yahoo Iberia and Yahoo Inc. belong to a multinational group of companies operating under the Yahoo brand; 2´) services are provided in each country through independent business entities with their own legal personality, adapting to each country's regulatory framework autonomously and independently: 3´) Yahoo Inc. customizes its services to the US market, it applies to users its own terms of service, and it submits to the laws of the country where it operates; 4´) Yahoo Iberia is an entity validly incorporated under the laws of Spain, and it is empowered to block and delete information in Yahoo Search. It suffices to examine Yahoo *Terms of Service* to confirm the submission to Spanish legislation and to the courts of Spain: "These Terms of Service shall be

---

[165] Yahoo was so keen on complying with the AEPD doctrine that, during proceedings no. TD/799/2010, the company even urged a claimant who was exercising his right to erasure of links to provide "compelling legitimate grounds relating to a particular personal situation founding his request." AEPD Resolution no. 1901/2010, dated October 2010, clarified that when data subjects exercised the right to erasure of their personal data, they were not required to provide any compelling legitimate grounds relating to a personal situation unless the data subjects deemed it convenient. These compelling legitimate grounds would only have to be provided if the data subjects had exercised the right to object to the processing of their personal data under Article 6(4) LOPD. However, during proceedings no. TD/400/2011, in spite of making the same allegations, the AEPD confirmed that Yahoo Search had fulfilled the right to erasure (R/1631/2011, of 22 July 2011).
[166] AEPD Resolutions no. 1835/2011 (TD/428/2011), of 23 August 2011; 1122/2012 (TD/70/2012), of 11 May 2012; and 2884/2012 (TD/1255/2012).
[167] AEPD Resolution dated 12 July 2011 (TD/249/2011).

governed by the laws of Spain. If the User lives outside of Spain, Yahoo! and the User hereby submit to the jurisdiction of the courts and tribunals of Villa de Madrid (Spain), expressly waiving any other jurisdiction."[168]

1.5.- Other global Internet services seeking impunity. YouTube: US legislation for Spanish videos?

Google Spain has rejected several requests for deletion and objections to videos hosted by YouTube on the grounds that it is not the owner of this video-sharing platform. In addition, and more importantly, Google Spain has also contended that Spanish data protection law was not applicable to YouTube, since the servers are not in Spain.[169]

Google puts forward its usual arguments against the application of EU data protection legislation to its search results: the technical complexity of capturing and hosting personal information through automated systems where the webmaster has the primary responsibility for allowing the search engine to access the data. Furthermore, Google argues that videos are ultimately hosted on servers located outside of Spain. In sum, Google seeks the same impunity for videos that breach data protection law directly shared by individuals in YouTube -owned by Google and with no intervention from third parties to be held liable.

The AEPD, in Resolution no. 02793/2011, of 13 December 2011, dismissed these claims, and it subsequently held Google Spain liable regarding the exercise of the right to erasure in view of YouTube privacy policy and its projection to Spain and Spanish users.

In the Case *Fraude* (TD/399/2012), Google yet again tried to bypass the application of data protection legislation to YouTube. However, the AEPD put forward a legal reasoning leading to the applicability of Spanish data protection law to YouTube:

1′) Google Inc. had designated Google Spain in the General Data Protection Registry as its representative in the territory of Spain and as the office where rights governed by the LOPD could be exercised.

2′) There was more than enough evidence that Google acted as YouTube's representative, having regard to statements made by managers of Google España in the media and considering that YouTube's privacy document refers to Google's privacy policy.

---

[168] http://info.yahoo.com/legal/es/yahoo/tos.html
[169] Case *Conferencista de Alicante* (TD/1226/2011).

3') The service provided by youtube.com specifically targets the Spanish territory, as evidenced by the following aspects: when the address is typed in from a computer located in Spain, the user is redirected to a website in Spanish customized for Spanish customers; youtube.com is in the Spanish language, and YouTube search results are directed to users living in Spain.

4') Personal data obtained by Google and displayed in YouTube can breach third party rights. Therefore, the AEPD, as the competent body, must seek compliance with data protection law.

5') YouTube liability regime is provided in Articles 14 to 17 of the Act on Information Society Services and Electronic Commerce (LSSI). Under these provisions, intermediary service providers are partially exempt from liability for the content hosted by websites. Intermediary service providers cannot be generally required to monitor stored or transmitted personal data, let alone to actively search for facts or circumstances regarding unlawful activities. YouTube is not a content provider, and therefore it is not required to verify *ex ante* the lawfulness of the content it hosts. Its only -yet very significant- obligation is to cooperate with data subjects, in order to immediately withdraw the content following a breach. Ultimately, YouTube will not be liable until it actually becomes aware of the unlawful video (for breaching data protection law) and fails to remove it.

Google's stance toward the inapplicability of Spanish data protection legislation to YouTube service raises some concerns stemming from the poor transparency of the information provided to users.[170]

2.- THE AEPD: THE RIGHT TO OBJECT AS THE RIGHT TO BE FORGOTTEN IN THE CURRENT TECHNOLOGICAL STATUS OF INTERNET SEARCH ENGINES

2.1.- The application of Spanish legislation to the Internet search engine (I): Google Spain as an "establishment" of Google Inc. in Spain.

Google Spain denied all responsibility for the provision of search engine services, on the grounds that these services are offered by Google Inc. and thus neither EU Directive 95/46/EC nor Spanish data protection legislation apply to them, since itis a company intended to sell advertising space associated with the internet users' search terms. The AEPD asserted just the opposite.

Article 2(1)(a) of the LOPD covers any processing of personal data "when the processing is carried out in the context of the activities of an

---

[170] A Spanish High Court Judgment, of 20 October 2011, mentioned a request for information issued to Google by the AEPD regarding YouTube service to which Google's legal team replied the following: "provided that Google is a U.S. company (...), the request for information will be addressed to Google Inc. (...). [E]ven considering that Google Spain could be held liable for the actions of YouTube LLC, Spanish data protection law would not be applicable to video hosting in YouTube. Video hosting services are provided in full from servers located outside the territory of Spain. YouTube does not have any equipment in Spain, and it neither uses Google Spain or any other natural person or legal entity established in Spain to provide its services. Therefore, both the EU Data Protection Directive and Spanish legislation are inapplicable." Nevertheless, YouTube *Terms of Service*, in their version of 9 June 2010 (http://www.youtube.com/t/terms (last accessed on 21 May 2013) referred to Google's privacy policy, and they confirmed that any users of YouTube website would be subject to the terms and conditions of a legal agreement with YouTube LLC (a company headquartered at 901 Cherry Avenue, San Bruno, CA 94066, United States). However, they accepted the application of Spanish legislation and they submitted to the jurisdiction of the courts of Spain. This was stated in Clause 14.7: "The Terms and Conditions and your relationship with YouTube under these provisions shall be governed by the laws of Spain."

establishment of the controller on Spanish territory."[171] In other words, this provision transposes Directive 95/46/EC on data protection. Regarding the applicable domestic law, this Directive provides that Member States shall apply the national provisions they have enacted pursuant to this Directive to the processing of personal data where: "the processing is carried out in the context of the activities of an establishment of the controller in the territory of the Member State; when the same controller is established in the territory of several Member States, he must take the necessary measures to ensure that each of these establishments complies with the obligations laid down by the national law applicable" (Article 4(1)(a)).

Under Article 4(1)(a) of Directive 95/46/EC, Spanish legislation would be applied to Google Spain if it was considered the "establishment" in the context of whose activities the processing is carried out by the search engine in Spain. Put differently, is Google Spain the "establishment" responsible in Spain for data processing carried out by the search engine?

Answering the previous question requires interpreting the texts that enable an adequate understanding of Directive 95/46/EC: the Recitals preceding the Directive provisions, along with the Opinions adopted by Article 29 Data Protection Working Party -made up of all Data Protection Authorities and created under the Directive for consultation purposes.

In order to determine the actual purpose of the EU legislature regarding the scope of the territorial applicability of domestic law, it is essential to assess whether we are confronted with an "establishment" within the meaning of Article 4(1)(a) of the Directive. For these purposes, we are compelled to review Recital (18): "in order to ensure that individuals are not deprived of the protection to which they are entitled under this Directive, any processing of personal data in the Community must be carried out in accordance with the law of one of the Member States; whereas, in this connection, processing carried out under the responsibility of a controller who is established in a Member State should be governed by the law of that State."

Recital (19) is also decisive to determine whether in Google v. Spain

---

[171] Article 3(1) of the Implementing Regulation of the LOPD (RLOPD) adds the following: "This Regulation shall govern any processing of personal data: a) When the processing is carried out as part of the activities of an establishment pertaining to the data controller, whenever the establishment is in Spanish territory. When the previous subsection is not applicable, but the data processor is located in Spain, the rules contained in Title VIII hereof shall be applicable thereto."

there is an "establishment" within the meaning of Article 4(1)(a) of the Directive: "establishment in the territory of a Member State implies the effective and real exercise of activity through stable arrangements; whereas the legal form of such an establishment, whether simply a branch or a subsidiary with a legal personality, is not the determining factor in this respect; whereas, when a single controller is established in the territory of several Member States, particularly by means of subsidiaries, he must ensure, in order to avoid any circumvention of national rules, that each of the establishments fulfils the obligations imposed by the national law applicable to its activities."

The purpose of both Recitals is to effectively guarantee the right to data protection: on the one hand, by confirming the indispensable requirement that any processing of personal data carried out in the territory of the EU is subject to Member State law; on the other, avoiding formalistic approaches aimed at circumventing the application of domestic legislation to whoever is making decisions on the processing of data.

The anti-formalist approach of Recital (19) of Directive 95/46/EC leads to conceive an "establishment" as any entity which, by means of a stable arrangement, actually and effectively exercises an activity, regardless of its legal form: whether simply a branch or a subsidiary with a legal personality. This understanding of "establishment" is necessary in the complex and heterogeneous world of the information and knowledge society: multinational companies operating online use a wide array of legal forms to reach local domains. Mostly, they attempt to bypass their globalizing scope by submitting to U.S. legislation, which seeks to circumvent the national laws of the countries where they operate.[172]

Search engine providers are a paradigmatic example of these risks. In order to unravel the legal-formal complexity underlying Recital 19 of the Directive, one must resort to Opinion 1/2008 on data protection issues related to search engines, of 4 April 2008, where Article 29 Working Party laid down certain <u>criteria</u> that allow to determine when there is an "establishment," regardless of its legal form:

1´) when a search engine provider establishes an office in a Member State (EEA) that is involved in the selling of targeted advertisements to the inhabitants of that state;

---

[172] On the approach of U.S. and EU protection regimes, see, DAVID VLADECK: "Separated by common goals: A U.S. perspective on narrowing the U.S.-EU privacy divide," *Hacia un nuevo derecho europeo de protección de datos. Towards a new European Data Protection Regime* (eds.) A. Rallo & R. García, Tirant lo Blanch, Valencia, 2015, pp. 207-243.

$2'$) when an establishment is responsible for relations with users of the search engine in a particular jurisdiction;

$3'$) when the establishment of a search engine provider complies with court orders and/or law enforcement requests by the competent authorities of a Member State with regard to user data.

The AEPD has come up with evidence that Google Spain meets these three criteria as to conclude that it is indeed an establishment located in Spain responsible for the search engine.

Obviously, advertising is Google Search's source of financing, and users cannot avoid it if they want to use the search engine. The processing of data performed by Google is aimed at providing personalized advertising services.[173] Advertising linked to search engine services and specifically addressed to Spain is based on Google Spain's activities. Therefore, given that the economic activity performed in Spanish territory by Google Inc. is the generation of advertising inserted in the free search service, it must be concluded that for such activity it uses local promoters, such as Google Spain, encouraging the purchase of advertising space.

Google Spain usually claims that it simply intends to sell advertising space, and that it has no responsibility in terms of compliance with data protection law. In many of its resolutions, the AEPD includes data evidencing how Google Inc. is represented by Google Spain in various cases heard by the AEPD. Google Spain has fulfilled many requirements addressed by the AEPD Oversight Sub-Directorate in the context of complaints filed by Spanish individuals against the search service.[174]

Far from simply trying to sell advertising space, Google Spain further represents Google Inc. in Spain in terms of promotion, and even settlement, of disputes on data protection involving other Google services. A good example are the allegations made by Google Spain in proceedings E/01544/2007, following a complaint filed by a Spanish user organization with respect to the free email service "Gmail." It is also worth noting Google Spain's intervention acting as YouTube's

---

[173] The AdWords system offers advertising based on users' search results, mainly considering their location. In fact, advertisers are requested to define their potential consumers depending on the country they are targeting. The AdSense advertising service automatically crawls the content of websites and publishes relevant advertising for users located in Spain.

[174] TD/299/2007, TD/463/2007, TD/814/2007, TD/155/2008, TD/387/2008, TD/420/2008, TD/444/2008, TD/569/2008 and TD/580/2008.

representative in light of the promotional statements by its managers in the media.

Both Google Inc. and Google Ireland have designated Google Spain as the entity responsible for fulfilling the rights of access, rectification, erasure or blocking provided in the LOPD before the AEPD General Data Protection Registry.

In sum, the AEPD clearly confirmed that Google Spain was Google Inc.'s representative in Spain, acting as the establishment of the search engine provider.

2.2.- The application of Spanish legislation to the Internet search engine (II): Google uses "equipment" located in Spain

The application of Spanish data protection law, either alternatively or cumulatively, can stem from a second criterion. Article 2(1)(c) of the LOPD enforces this provision on data processing "when the person responsible for the processing is not established in the territory of the European Union and is using for the processing equipment situated on Spanish territory, unless such equipment is used solely for transit purposes."[175] This provision transposes Directive 95/46/EC on data protection, which also requires the application of domestic law to any processing of personal data when: "1 (c) the controller is not established on Community territory and, for purposes of processing personal data makes use of equipment, automated or otherwise, situated in the territory of the said Member State, unless such equipment is used only for purposes of transit through the territory of the Community. (2) In the circumstances referred to in paragraph 1 (c), the controller must designate a representative established in the territory of that Member State, without prejudice to legal actions which could be initiated against the controller himself (Article 4)."[176]

---

[175] Article 3(1) of the Implementing Regulation of the LOPD (RLOPD) reproduces the content of the LOPD: "This Regulation shall govern any processing of personal data: c) when the data controller is not established on European Union territory and uses equipment located on Spanish territory for the processing of data, unless such equipment are only used for transit purposes. In this case, the data controller must designate a representative established in Spanish territory."

[176] A comprehensive analysis of this provision, and particularly on its drafting process, can be found in LOKKE MOEREL: "The long arm of EU data protection law: Does the Data Protection Directive apply to processing of personal data of EU citizens by websites worldwide?" *International Data Privacy Law*, vol. 1-1, 2011, pp. 28-46.

In order to determine the purpose of EU legislation regarding the territorial applicability of Spanish law to search engine activities due to the use of means or equipment located in a Member State, we must examine Recital (20) in connection with Articles 4(1)(c) and 4(2): "the fact that the processing of data is carried out by a person established in a third country must not stand in the way of the protection of individuals provided for in this Directive; whereas in these cases, the processing should be governed by the law of the Member State in which the means used are located, and there should be guarantees to ensure that the rights and obligations provided for in this Directive are respected in practice."

Directive 95/46/EC supplements the anti-formalist construction of "establishment" with a teleological approach that underscores the purposes of Directive 95/46/EC. These purposes cannot fade away nor be disregarded due to the transnational nature of many Internet services. Recital (20) confirms that, within the Internet, there are usually persons responsible for services established in third countries (mainly the United States), and puts forward that such practice "must not stand in the way" of the protection of individual rights. This Recital also asserts the applicability of the law of Member States in which the means used for the processing of personal data are located, and it urges to implement the guarantees laid down in data protection law to ensure that the rights and obligations provided for in the Directive are respected "in practice." Ultimately, the normative-formalist approach, rooted in traditional categories regarding transnational relations and responsibilities, gives way to a realistic-material understanding which, in practice, prioritizes the effective guarantee of the rights at stake vis-à-vis hindering behaviors.

It cannot be expressly inferred from Directive 95/46/EC exactly when one should consider that search engines use "means" located in a Member State. Thus, the Opinions, along with the Working document of Article 29 Working Party, are essential.

On 30 May 2002, Article 29 Working Party adopted "Working Document 56 on determining the international application of EU data protection law to personal data processing on the Internet by non-EU based web sites" where the wide array of means or "equipment" located in the territory of Member States to which Article 4(1)(c) of Directive 95/46/EC applies was illustrated: "Examples of equipment are personal computers, terminals and servers, which may be used for nearly all kind of processing operations (...). A typical case where equipment is used for transit only are the telecommunications networks (back bones, cables etc.), which form part of the Internet and over which Internet communications are travelling from the expedition point to the destination point (...) it is not necessary that the controller exercise full control over the equipment. The extent, to which it is at the disposal of the controller, can vary. The necessary degree of disposal is given if the controller, by determining the way how the equipment works, is making the relevant decisions concerning the substance of the data and the procedure of their processing. In other words, the controller determines, which data are collected, stored, transferred, altered etc., in which way and for which purpose (...) the concept of "making use" presupposes two elements: some kind of activity undertaken by the controller and the intention of the controller to process personal data (...). The power of disposal of the controller should, however, not be confused with property or ownership of the equipment, either of the controller or of the individual. In fact, the directive does not attach any relevance to the ownership of any equipment."[177]

A twofold analysis is required at this point: on the one hand, regarding the technological elements that make up the notion of equipment used for the processing of data by the controller; on the other, regarding the legal-formal nature of the equipment, evidencing the necessary relativism to assess the degree of "property or ownership" that the controller may exercise over such equipment.

Opinion 1/2008 on data protection issues related to search engines will provide specific conclusions on the applicability of domestic legislation to Internet search engines for the use of means located in Member States.

When search engine services are provided from outside of the EU, the following shall be considered as means:

1′) data centers situated on the territory of a Member State used for the storage and remote processing of personal data;
2′) the use of personal computers, terminals and servers;
3′) cookies and similar software devices.[178]

---

[177]http://ec.europa.eu/justice/data-protection/article-29/documentation/opinion-recommendation/index_en.htm
[178] Working Document 56 of Art. 29 WP concluded the following: "the user's PC can be viewed as equipment in the sense of Article 4 (1) c of Directive 95/46/EC. It is located on the territory of a Member State. The controller decided to use this equipment for the purpose of processing personal data and, as it has been explained in the previous paragraphs, several technical operations take place without the control of the data subject. The controller disposes over the user's equipment and this equipment is not used only for purposes of transit through Community territory. The Working Party is therefore of the opinion that the national law of the Member State where this user's personal computer is located applies to the question under what conditions his personal data may be collected by placing cookies on his hard disk."

The AEPD has further examined how Google Search specifically targets Spain with its services[179] as well as the circumstances illustrating the use of means or equipment located in Spain by Google Search.

The search engine service is provided worldwide through www.google.com, but there are many national versions using the local language (or even various local languages) accessed by default considering the user's location.

In Spain, this search engine service is offered at google.es. Web servers located in Spain are visited by Google Search to retrieve information to be stored and subsequently offer its results, particularly to Spanish users. The information that has been crawled, stored and indexed by the search engine from servers located in Spain will relate both to users' and third parties' data.

The language used in the documents, or in the web servers hosting them, is essential for the search engine crawling, since users decide if their search results are referred to sites located in Spain. The search engine needs to access Spanish web servers and to store the results of the crawling to offer them to the user based in Spain. Self-evidently, all of the foregoing requires the use of equipment situated on the territory of Spain.

The AEPD emphasizes that Google search services, provided through

---

[179] The CJEU Judgment, of 7 December 2010 (C-585/08 and C-144/09), *Pammer v Reederei Karl Schlüter GmbH & Co KG and Hotel Alpenhof GesmbH v Oliver Heller,* elaborates on elements which, among others, may provide evidence that a given activity is targeting the Member State of the consumer's domicile: "the international nature of the activity, mention of itineraries from other Member States for going to the place where the trader is established, use of a language or a currency other than the language or currency generally used in the Member State in which the trader is established with the possibility of making and confirming the reservation in that other language, mention of telephone numbers with an international code, outlay of expenditure on an internet referencing service in order to facilitate access to the trader's site or that of its intermediary by consumers domiciled in other Member States, use of a top-level domain name other than that of the Member State in which the trader is established, and mention of an international clientele composed of customers domiciled in various Member States. It is for the national courts to ascertain whether such evidence exists. On the other hand, the mere accessibility of the trader's or the intermediary's website in the Member State in which the consumer is domiciled is insufficient. The same is true of mention of an email address and of other contact details, or of use of a language or a currency which are the language and/or currency generally used in the Member State in which the trader is established."

google.es, specifically target the Spanish territory having regard to the following elements:

1') The language used in google.es is Spanish, although there are versions in Catalan, Basque and Galician.

2') The domain used by Google's search engine in Spain (google.es) is a country code domain corresponding to Spain.

3') The search results indexed in google.es are directed to users located in Spain.

4') Google's financing comes from advertising annexed to search results that evidence its specific link to the Spanish territory.

2.3.- The application of Spanish law to Google Search (III): Directive 2000/31 and Act on Information Society Services and Electronic Commerce (LSSI)

The usual debate on the application of data protection law to Internet search engine services provided by companies from outside the EU sometimes disregards the existence of specific pieces of national legislation governing these information society services. These pieces of legislation leave no room to doubt that the said information society services are subject to national law, and particularly Spanish law.

Act 34/2002, of 11 July, on Information Society Services and Electronic Commerce (LSSI) (LSSI) transposes Directive 2000/31 on certain legal aspects of information society services, in particular electronic commerce, in the Internal Market. Article 4 LSSI sets out that "providers who address their services specifically towards Spain -i.e., Google's search engine in the view of the AEPD- shall furthermore be subject to the obligations set down herein, provided that the terms of the applicable international treaties and conventions are not thus breached." Additionally, Article 8(1)(c) LSSI adds the following: "If a given information society service[180] violates, or could somehow violate, *human*

---

[180] The Annex to the LSSI defines "intermediary services" as "those information society services facilitating the provision or use of other information society services or access to information." Additionally, it provides a list of intermediary services including "the provision of search, access and storage tools for data or links to other Internet sites."

dignity,[181] those bodies responsible for the protection thereof, in the exercise of the functions legally vested upon them, may adopt any measures necessary to discontinue the provision of those services or to remove the data violating human dignity. Regarding the adoption and enforcement of the restrictive measures mentioned herein, the guarantees, as well as the rules and procedures of the legal system aimed at safeguarding the rights to private and family life, the right to data protection, freedom of speech or freedom of information, shall be preserved in any event in case they could be affected."

Under the LSSI, Internet search engines are subject to the obligations laid down in this piece of legislation when they address their services towards the territory of Spain. The LSSI also empowers competent authorities to discontinue the search engine services as well as to remove any unlawful data in breach of the principles set out in the LSSI, such as human dignity.

The AEPD claims for itself the condition of national authority empowered by Spanish legislation to order information society services to be discontinued or to order the removal of data violating human dignity and thus any fundamental rights inherent to human dignity (Article 10(1) of the Spanish Constitution, CE). Amongst those fundamental rights, the right to personal data protection is particularly affected.

The AEPD has issued numerous resolutions aimed at protecting the right to be forgotten vis-à-vis Internet search engines. In those resolutions, the AEPD puts forward significant constitutional case law asserting the link between *human dignity* and data protection: "Article 18(4) of the Spanish Constitution establishes (...) a fundamental right or freedom, i.e., the right to be free from potential injuries to dignity and personal freedom stemming from an unlawful use of the automatic processing of data, designated by the Constitution as 'information technology' (...); the fundamental right to data protection seeks to guarantee that the right holder controls his/her personal data, particularly the use and destination thereof, in order to prevent an unlawful traffic that could undermine

---

[181] The principles whose violation could trigger that competent bodies, exercising the duties legally vested upon them, may adopt the measures necessary to discontinue the provision of services, or to remove the data breaching those principles, are the following: "a) The preservation of public order, criminal inquiries, public safety and national security. b) The protection of public health or of natural or legal persons considered as consumers or users, even when they act as investors. c) Respect for human dignity and non-discrimination on the basis of race, sex, religion, opinion, nationality, disabilities or any other personal or social circumstance. d) The protection of youth and childhood. e) The safeguard of intellectual property rights."

human dignity and the data subject's individual rights" (STC 292/2000).

2.4.- Google's liability: Supreme Court Judgment (STS) no. 144/2013, of 4 March, on the "effective knowledge" of unlawful searches

The main question refers to the scope of Google's liability for potentially unlawful indexing of personal information.

Article 15(1) of Directive 2000/31, of 8 June, on electronic commerce, provides that there is no general obligation to monitor: "Member States shall not impose a general obligation on providers, (...) to monitor the information which they transmit or store, nor a general obligation actively to seek facts or circumstances indicating illegal activity."

Article 17 LSSI regulates the "liability of service providers facilitating hyperlinks or location tools:"[182] a) As a general rule, Article 17 LSSI excludes liability for data supplied to "information society service providers facilitating links to other content or including search directories or tools in their own content" (Internet search engines and, particularly, Google Search). b) However, search engines will be held liable if two conditions are met: 1) the provider has actual knowledge of the unlawful activity or personal information that it references, or is aware that it breaches indemnifiable third-party rights or legal interests; 2) and, upon gaining such knowledge, it fails to act diligently to remove the link.

Internet search engines, as intermediary service providers that do not offer own content but simply provide external content, are not liable *in*

---

[182] In almost identical terms to Article 14 of Directive 2000/31, it established the following: "1. Where an information society service is provided that consists of the storage of information provided by a recipient of the service, Member States shall ensure that the service provider is not liable for the information stored at the request of a recipient of the service, on condition that: (a) the provider does not have actual knowledge of illegal activity or information and, as regards claims for damages, is not aware of facts or circumstances from which the illegal activity or information is apparent; or (b) the provider, upon obtaining such knowledge or awareness, acts expeditiously to remove or to disable access to the information."

principle[183] for the content they crawl, store, index and disseminate on the Internet.

The automatic processing carried out by search engines does not give rise to liability *per se* unless knowledge of its unlawfulness is proved, thus overturning the neutral nature of this automatic processing. In this case, they can be held liable for breaching legal obligations regarding the protection of fundamental rights.[184]

Therefore, search engines are held liable when three cumulative requirements are met: 1) "declared unlawfulness of the information;" 2) "actual knowledge;" 3) and "lack of diligence" in its removal.

Article 17 LSSI adds two additional elements to clarify the scope of these requirements: 1′) the "actual knowledge" occurs when the service provider becomes aware of the competent body's resolution declaring the unlawfulness of the data, or when it orders the removal or the prohibition to access such data, or declares that there has been an injury; 2′) the

---

[183] It is worth noting that in the *SABAM* Case, the CJEU (C-70/2010, 24 November 2011) refused to impose on information society services an "indiscriminate and preventive" system for filtering the content hosted by them following a joint analysis of Directives 2000/31, 2001/29 and 2004/48. The Directives, read together and construed in the light of the requirements stemming from the protection of the applicable fundamental rights, must be interpreted as precluding an injunction made against an Internet service provider which requires it to install a system for filtering (1) the information stored in its servers by the recipients of their services; (2) which applies indiscriminately to all its customers; (3) as a preventive measure; (4) exclusively at its expense; and (5) for an unlimited period.

[184] The CJEU (C-236/08 and C-238/08, Case *Google France v Louis Vuitton*, 23-3-10) illustrates this conclusion: "in order to establish whether the liability of a referencing service provider may be limited under Article 14 of Directive 2000/31, it is necessary to examine whether the role played by that service provider is neutral, in the sense that its conduct is merely technical, automatic and passive, pointing to a lack of knowledge or control of the data which it stores (...) the national court, which is best placed to be aware of the actual terms on which the service in the cases in the main proceedings is supplied, must assess whether the role thus played by Google corresponds to that described in paragraph 114 of the present judgment (...). Article 14 of Directive 2000/31 must be interpreted as meaning that the rule laid down therein applies to an internet referencing service provider in the case where that service provider has not played an active role of such a kind as to give it knowledge of, or control over, the data stored. If it has not played such a role, that service provider cannot be held liable for the data which it has stored at the request of an advertiser, unless, having obtained knowledge of the unlawful nature of those data or of that advertiser's activities, it failed to act expeditiously to remove or to disable access to the data concerned."

service provider may gain "actual knowledge" by applying its voluntary content detection and removal protocols.

It is worth underlining that the resolution issued by the competent body providing this actual knowledge cannot be limited (a´) to declare the unlawfulness of the data or the infringement of rights; it must also include: (b´) the order to remove, or the prohibition to access, the unlawful data.

The legal requirements to hold Google Search liable (whether civilly, criminally or administratively) for the indexation and dissemination of unlawful data seem clear. Supreme Court Judgment (STS) no. 144/2013, of 4 March, sheds more light on this issue.[185]

There are two core aspects clarified by this tremendously significant ruling (STS no. 144/2013): 1) When is the LSSI applied in Spain, based on rules of territoriality, to a search engine provider like Google?, and; 2) when does the actual knowledge of unlawfulness of data occur? STS no. 144/2013 upheld the ruling delivered by the Madrid Provincial Court, which had declared that the LSSI applied to Google Inc., which operates in Spain through a permanent branch based in Torre Picasso (Madrid), with a sole shareholder, Google Inc., and through which it carried out all its activities targeting the Spanish market. STS no. 144/2013 upheld the application of the LSSI upon verifying that Google Inc. has a sales office in Spain, according to its own corporate information: "this notion falls within the case of an office outside of Spain, yet with 'regular or steady' availability of 'premises or workplaces where it carries out all or part of its activities.'" The Supreme Court applied the straightforward terms of Article 2(2) LSSI by imposing its application to information society services provided by entities residing or domiciled in third countries "through a permanent establishment located in Spain." Ultimately, STS no. 144/2013 confirms that Google Spain constitutes the permanent establishment of Google Inc. in Spain to carry out part of its activities on a regular and steady basis.

---

[185] STS no. 144/2013 dismissed a complaint against Google Inc. for an infringement of the right to honor for disseminating information published in various websites ("Aquí Hay Tomate," "PRNoticias" and "Lobby per la Independencia") and linked by the search engine, thereby implicating the claimant in the Marbella corruption scheme known as *Operación Malaya.*

The Supreme Court defines more precisely the notion of "actual knowledge," which it had already framed in previous rulings.[186] Nevertheless, STS no. 144/2013 deals with a new case: it does not involve unlawful content hosted on a website, but the linking and indexation of information by Google as a search engine. This STS is very rigorous when it comes to applying the formal requirements laid down in Article 17 LSSI to prove the actual knowledge of unlawfulness regarding Internet search engines.

Although the Provincial Court judgment had acknowledged that the claimant addressed notices to Google reporting the existence of ongoing proceedings, as well as of a judicial decision declaring that the information was false, the Supreme Court concluded in STS no. 144/2013 that actual knowledge would only occur as soon as a copy of the judicial decision was submitted to Google. According to the Supreme Court, "from the facts of the case it cannot be reasonably inferred that the information was false, nor that its content evidenced that it was unlawful," having regard to the following aspects: 1´) It would not suffice that the injured party brought an action against Google urging it to withdraw the information on grounds of unlawfulness; 2´) the information itself would not clearly reveal its unlawful nature; 3´) it neither suffices to provide notice that civil action has been brought or that there is a judicial decision, nor that a court order has been issued; 4´) these documents must be submitted to Google, without the party

---

[186] STS no. 72/2011, of 10 February 2011, is particularly interesting. It considers that assimilating to actual knowledge the existence of a decision declaring the unlawfulness of the stored data and ordering their removal is not in line with Directive 2000/31, since it "unreasonably narrows the possibilities of gaining such 'actual knowledge' of unlawfulness regarding the content stored, whilst widening the scope of the liability exemption with respect to the harmonizing provision, which requires actual knowledge, but does not limit the means to acquire it (...). Act 34/2002 allows for this favorable interpretation of the Directive when it leaves the door open for other means to gain actual knowledge. However, it is also worth noting that this Act gives equal weight to 'actual knowledge' and to the knowledge gained by the service provider from facts or circumstances that may lead to an actual understanding of reality, even in an indirect manner or through logical inferences within the power of any person." In fact, this STS grants such "capacity to reveal of the stored or link content insofar as its unlawful nature is blatant and self-evident, not dependent on data or information unavailable to the intermediary." This doctrine had already been advanced by STS no. 773/2009, of 9 November, where the Supreme Court accepted as actual knowledge of unlawfulness a domain name (www.putasgae.org), on the grounds that "this name, given its insulting character, constituted adequate means to reveal, alongside the existing circumstances, the offensive nature of the hosted data."

concerned being the only one aware of them. Accordingly, STS no. 144/2013 denied that Article 17 LSSI had been breached, and excluded Google's liability on the grounds that it lacked actual knowledge of unlawfulness regarding the information.

2.5.- Google's liability, shared with the webmaster, as the inevitable consequence of the impact of Internet search engines

Allocating liability to websites or search engines regarding indexed information is not as easy as it could appear at first when it comes to verifying compliance with data protection law.

There are no specific references in Directive 95/46/EC or the LOPD about the impact of search engines on the rights and obligations stemming from data protection law. Therefore, it is essential to rely on the general principles governing the application of data protection provisions.

Opinion 1/2008 of Article 29 Working Party differentiates between the main or primary liability (of search engines) and secondary liability (of information providers), but always as concurrent liabilities.

Too often, in this regard, there seems to be a biased view that liability on the Internet lies exclusively with information providers, whereas search engines are somehow held harmless due to their purported neutrality.

This is far from reality, having regard to the sound judgment of Article 29 WP expressed in Opinion 1/2008. An appropriate application of the principle of proportionality necessarily leads to the consideration that search engines act exclusively as intermediaries, and thus they cannot be considered primarily responsible for the processing or publication of information online. This is particularly so if we take into account that webmasters are able to prevent search engines from capturing this information through *robots.txt* and *Noindex/Noarchive* tags.

However, the search engine's liability arises *a posteriori*, when certain questions arise regarding the lawfulness of the data processed in terms of potential breaches of data protection law: "The formal, legal and practical control the search engine has over the personal data involved is usually limited to the possibility of removing data from its servers. With regard to the removal of personal data from their index and search results, search engines have sufficient control to consider them as controllers (either alone or jointly with others)."[187]

Google carries "sufficient liability," which will force it to act when the removal of personal data from its index and from its search results may be required under data protection law. Search engines will incur "full responsibility" when they do not act as mere intermediaries, but also (a´) store in their servers personal data retrieved from the Internet, or; (b) orient the search, analysis and indexation through personally identifiable information (as could happen regarding facial recognition).

Within the information society, services provided through the Internet become so complex and have such a heterogeneous impact on data protection that it is reasonable to imagine different degrees of responsibility: "primary liability," "shared liability," "full liability" or "sufficient liability."

As pointed out by Opinion 1/2008, the obligation to remove personal data from search indexes is incumbent upon Internet search engines insofar as the obligation to withdraw or to block personal data may be subject to the Member State's tort law provisions.[188]

2.6.- The right to object as a proportionate/balanced instrument for a responsive exercise -neither preventive nor censoring- of the right to be forgotten

Data protection rights are applicable to search engine activities. The apparent neutrality stemming from the automatic intermediary role of search engines did not prevent Opinion 1/2008 from asserting the enforceability of data protection rights vis-à-vis search engine providers.

Opinion 1/2008 refers to the right to request the erasure of data by Internet search engines as follows: 1´) search engines should respect the right to delete data -particularly from authenticated users, including their personal profiles, but also from non-registered users; 2´) this same right to delete information also applies to cache data held by search engine

---

[187]http://ec.europa.eu/justice/data-protection/article-29/documentation/opinion-recommendation/index_en.htm

[188] Opinion 1/2008 expressly refers to the Spanish case: "In some EU Member States data protection authorities have specifically regulated the responsibility of search engine providers to remove content data from the search index, based on the right of objection enshrined in Article 14 of the Data Protection Directive (95/46/EC) and on the e-Commerce Directive (2000/31/EC). According to such national legislation, search engines are obliged to follow a notice and takedown policy similar to hosting providers in order to prevent liability."

providers, who must promptly remove any "incomplete or outdated information," i.e., "once these data no longer match the actual contents published on the Web by the controllers of the website(s) publishing this information;" 3′) search engine providers must update the cache by means of an automatic instant revisit of the original publication; 4′) website editors should come up with measures to automatically inform search engines of any request they receive to delete personal data.

The right to be forgotten on the Internet can be exercised through two legal instruments. Although these remedies resemble each other and lead to identical results, they have a different scope on the Internet, and particularly regarding search engine activities: the "right to erasure" and the "right to object."

The right to erasure enshrined in Article 16 LOPD provides that "erasure shall apply to data whose processing is not in accordance with the provisions of this Act and, in particular, when such data are inaccurate or incomplete. Erasure shall lead to the data being blocked and maintained solely at the disposal of public authorities, judges and courts, for the purpose of determining any liability arising from the processing, and for the duration of such liability. On expiry of such liability, they shall be deleted."[189] Generally transferring this right to the Internet, and particularly to search engine activities, can lead to serious trouble. The inaccuracy or incompleteness of information, or the lack of consent to data processing, could empower any users to challenge the nature and use of search engines as key tools within the information society.

However, the right to object makes it possible to achieve the same results (the deletion of indexed personal data), yet through more proportionate means: the erasure of data requires to weigh the grounds on a case-by-case basis, and it does not entitle data subjects to claim for the general deletion of information online on a general basis. It is worth recalling that Article 6(4) LOPD provides that in the cases where the consent of the data subject is not required for processing personal data, and unless provided otherwise by law, the data subject may object to such processing

---

[189] This provision transposes Article 12 of Directive 95/46: "Member States shall guarantee every data subject the right to obtain from the controller (...) erasure or blocking of data the processing of which does not comply with the provisions of this Directive, in particular because of the incomplete or inaccurate nature of the data."

when there are compelling and legitimate grounds relating to a particular personal situation.[190]

According to the AEPD, the right to object to personal information indexed by search engines is the most suitable remedy to ensure the right to be forgotten. The legal and sociological reasons are clear:

a) the lack of preventive filtering of personal data through technical instruments that might resemble previous censorship;
b) the absence of a legal provision forcing individuals to have their hosted personal data indexed and/or temporarily stored in the cache memories of search engines;
c) the allegation of compelling legitimate grounds relating to a particular personal situation through a responsive procedure;
d) the lack of public interest of personal data published online (the data subject does not play a role in public life or the event is not newsworthy).

In the AEPD's view, the tremendous multiplier effect of search engines in terms of dissemination of personal data and their permanent storage call for effective and enforceable remedies to preserve the right to be forgotten. The right to object is the proportionate legal remedy to preserve human dignity vis-à-vis the impact of information society. Implementing a legal remedy that allows individuals to bring action against personal data hosted in search engine indexes, on compelling legitimate grounds relating to a particular personal situation, is neither disproportionate nor deprives Internet search engines from the role they undisputedly play within society.

---

[190] Article 14 of Directive 95/46 provides the following: "The data subject's right to object: Member States shall grant the data subject the right: (a) at least in the cases referred to in Article 7 (e) and (f), to object at any time on compelling legitimate grounds relating to his particular situation to the processing of data relating to him, save where otherwise provided by national legislation. Where there is a justified objection, the processing instigated by the controller may no longer involve those data." As to clarify the scope of this right, Recital (45) of Directive 95/46 establishes that "in cases where data might lawfully be processed on grounds of public interest, official authority or the legitimate interests of a natural or legal person, any data subject should nevertheless be entitled, on legitimate and compelling grounds relating to his particular situation, to object to the processing of any data relating to himself; whereas Member States may nevertheless lay down national provisions to the contrary."

2.7.- The right to be forgotten vis-à-vis search engines given the current technological development: technical limitations

The downside of the AEPD's approach is the series of technical difficulties relating to the compliance with its resolutions aimed at ensuring the right to be forgotten vis-à-vis search engines, ordering them to "adopt any measures necessary to remove the data from their index and to prevent access to the data in the future."

Removing a link from search indexes on compelling legitimate grounds relating to a particular personal situation should not entail any technical difficulties for the search engine. The first part of the AEPD decisions does not pose any additional problem.

The AEPD also urges search engines to "adopt any measures necessary to prevent *access to the data* [contained in the links vis-à-vis which the right to be forgotten is exercised] *in the future.*" At this point, Google's claims are definitely worth highlighting: in the absence of the webmaster's intervention (through *robots.txt* or *Noindex/Noarchive* tags) limiting access to the content by search engines, search engines will yet again crawl, store, index and disseminate personal data which had been removed from the index based on the right to object.

The purported technical difficulties to prevent future access by search engines to data hosted online (without the webmaster's cooperation) is a recurrent claim in the Internet industry. There are no reasons to believe (in light of the extraordinary development of Internet services) that technological evolution does not allow to implement technical mechanisms to guarantee the right to be forgotten in these terms. If an administrative provision or decision requires preventing "access in the future" and the search engine fails to prove the alleged technical unfeasibility, what will the legal effects of those administrative acts be? Will the impossibility to fulfill the decision lead to the impunity of the search engine? Or will the search engine still be held liable and subject to a penalty?[191]

The AEPD has consistently ordered Google to adopt any measures necessary to prevent future access to the data removed from search indexes. The sole responsible for withdrawing the data from search indexes is Google. Nevertheless, adopting the "measures necessary to prevent access to the data in the future" does not necessarily and

---

[191] VICTOR MAYER-SCHÖNBERGER's analysis on the already existing possibility of applying his proposal to adopt expiration dates on data is extremely interesting (*Delete: The Virtue of Forgetting in the Digital Age...*, pp. 179-180).

exclusively mean that Google -and only Google- must technically prevent subsequent data crawling.

The AEPD's approach is sufficiently broad to strike a fair balance between legal requirements and technological development: a) when AEPD resolutions urge Google to "adopt any measures necessary to prevent access to personal data in the future," the AEPD is actually *ordering* Google to directly prevent its search engine (without any cooperation from the webmaster) to access these links given the possibilities provided by current technology. Furthermore, it *urges* Google to perfect any technological tools that allow for these actions;[192] b) however, insofar as there are no technical instruments enabling the search engine to directly prevent the crawling of already removed links, the "any measures necessary" demand will be met by means of the technology already offered by Google to webmasters to limit access to website content.

Google's claim that it is technically unfeasible to prevent future access to search results is hardly acceptable given the provisions of its *Privacy Policy* relating to *content removal in another user's website*[193] when the webmaster neither deletes the content nor prevents crawling: "We remove very little content from the search results on a discretionary basis. In addition to *spam*, we only act with regard to certain personal data (specified below) and 'adult spam.' Upon a user's request, we will remove personal information if we believe it can somehow be prejudicial, such as identity theft or financial fraud. This kind of information includes confidential national identification numbers, such as social security numbers, bank accounts or credit cards, as well as images of signatures. We usually do not remove information such as dates of birth, addresses or telephone numbers (...). In order to determine whether certain identification information must be considered confidential, we apply the following criteria, among others: Is it a government-issued identification number? Is it confidential, or is it publicly available information? Can it be used for common financial transactions? Can it be used to obtain more information about an individual? We apply this content removal policy on

---

[192] This criterion shows the approach of JOEL REIDEMBERG that the response to the jurisdiction issues and protection of rights on the Internet must stem from "innovation" in the field of information technologies: "the assertion of sovereign jurisdiction to protect citizens is likely to advance the fundamental public policy that the rule of law should be supreme to technological determinism. At the same time, the multiplicity of states with jurisdiction over Internet activities is likely to stimulate creativity and new Internet services such as more accurate and selective filtering technologies, stronger security zones and more robust, customized compliance capabilities" ("Technology and Internet Jurisdiction."., p. 1974).
[193] http://support.google.com/webmasters/bin/answer.py?hl=es&answer=1663688

a case-by-case basis. We usually do not remove information that can be found on official government websites because the information is publicly available. If we believe that a removal request is being used to try and remove other, non-personal information from search results, we will deny the request. We will remove any website containing sexually explicit spam and a user's or his/her business full name upon a user's request."[194]

If the user requesting the removal has contacted the webmaster and has received no reply, Google admits that it "may help" the requesting user[195] when the data to be removed relate to bank account or credit card numbers, images of handwritten signatures, pornographic content including a full name, etc. In other words, Google explicitly acknowledges its technical possibilities to remove links from the search engine index.

2.8.- Specific criteria for two distinct domains: online media and digital versions of official gazettes

1) Online media: striking a balance between the prevailing right to information and the lawful demand for oblivion

Any legal analysis on the clash between the rights to information and data protection must necessarily depart from the specific significance of the right to information in democratic societies, as well as from the need to solve this conflict based on the following legal reasoning.

1) There is no democracy without free elections, and there will not be free elections if citizens are not able to freely shape their opinions. Along these lines, citizens will never be able to shape their free opinions without freedom of expression and freedom of information. Beyond their nature as individual rights, these freedoms have an essential institutional value in democratic systems. All constitutional declarations of rights over the last centuries have proclaimed these freedoms in similar terms to Article 20(1) of the Spanish Constitution (CE): "The following rights are recognized and protected: a) the right to freely express and spread thoughts, ideas and opinions through words, in writing or by any other means (...) d) to freely communicate or receive truthful information by any means of dissemination whatsoever."

2) There are no absolute rights and freedoms within the constitutional

---

[194] https://support.google.com/websearch/answer/2744324?
[195]https://support.google.com/websearch/troubleshooter/1209905#ts=1231445,28 89054,2889099,2889064

system. Article 20(4) CE establishes that information rights are limited by compliance with constitutional rights, "and particularly by the right to honor, to privacy, to the own image (...)." In other words, certain constitutional rights are *enhanced* or *strengthened* when they collide with information freedoms, since they affect the most personal sphere of the individual, and because their most dangerous threat can be posed by freedoms of information and expression. This enhanced group of "borderline rights" should also include the right to data protection, given the unequivocal stance taken by constitutional case law, which has established this right as a fundamental right (STC no. 292/2000). Nevertheless, this recent constitutional recognition of the right to data protection will not make up for centuries of protection of the right to honor or privacy. Additionally, in practice, its enforceability will be significantly weakened when it clashes with information freedoms.

3) How can we solve the inevitable conflicts that will arise when information freedoms and the said fundamental rights (particularly data protection) collide? Constitutional case law has given prevalence to information freedoms:[196] the fundamental right to data protection will be superseded by truthful information about events of public interest, having regard to the subject and the persons involved.

4) This traditional response to the abovementioned clash of rights is still fully applicable to the media. However, the unprecedented impact of information and knowledge society makes it more complex to solve these conflicts, considering the effects of online media,[197] and particularly considering the existence of Internet services, such as search engines, which exponentially increase the disseminating effects of any piece of information.

Spanish constitutional drafters were concerned with the effects of information technologies, as shown by Article 18(4) CE. They sensed the

---

[196] "On a general basis, given its institutional role, when freedom of information and the rights to honor and privacy collide, the first should prevail. Additionally, any restrictions imposed on freedom of expression as a result of this clash must be construed so that the core content of the right to information retains its essence and significance (...). When these rights collide, freedom of information must generally prevail, insofar as the information is truthful and relates to public affairs of general interest having regard to the events and the persons involved, thus helping to shape public opinion" (STC no. 171/1990).

[197] A specific dimension of this conflict can be seen in ARTEMI RALLO & RICARD MARTINEZ: "Data Protection, Social Networks, and Online Mass Media," *European Data Protection: Coming of Age*, Serge Gutwirth, Ronald Leenes, Paul De Hert and Yves Poullet Editors, ed. Springer, London-New York, 2013, pp. 407-430.

risks of a technology whose current significance was unthinkable in 1978. However, at this point, there is no doubt that updating this constitutional provision to match social reality requires "enhancing" or "strengthening" the right to data protection as the most suitable specific safeguard (STC 292/2000) in the context of the Internet information society.

5) AEPD Resolution no. 266/2007 already put forward a basic criterion to solve the clash between data protection online and information freedoms: "Individuals who are neither public figures nor have been involved in newsworthy events of public interest shall never be forced to have their personal data circulating online without any legal actions at hand to remedy the unlawful inclusion of such data in a universal communication system such as the Internet. Requesting everyone's individual consent to the inclusion of their personal data on the Internet, or implementing technical mechanisms that could prevent or filter the unauthorized inclusion of personal data, could entail an untenable barrier to the free exercise of freedoms of expression and information, i.e., it would be some sort of censorship, which is proscribed by the Constitution. Nevertheless, the fact remains that individuals who are not subject to the said freedoms (because their personal data are not of public interest and they do not shape public opinion, as a cornerstone of the rule of law) must be undisputedly entitled to legal remedies (such as the right to delete personal data) preventing their personal information from being held online."

If the enforceability of the right to be forgotten online requires personal data related to a natural person involved in an event of public interest: when is this requirement actually met? Does an event (and the personal data attached) become information (truthful and of public interest) only if such conditions are evidenced prior to being published? Or do these conditions apply following the publication of this information?

These are not trivial issues considering that the Constitution protects freedom of information "by any means of dissemination" (Article 20(1)(d) CE), and the Internet is definitely a paradigmatic example. Consideration should also be given to the fact that, according to constitutional case law, any privilege or "enhanced fundamental right" must be superseded by the freedoms of expression and information granted to journalists or the media (STC no. 225/2002).

It is essential to weigh the social interest or public relevance of personal information depending on the context of dissemination: websites, search engines, online media, etc.

6) Directive 95/46/EC on data protection empowers Member States to

provide for exemptions or derogations from provisions on the processing of personal data carried out solely for journalistic purposes or the purpose of artistic or literary expression only if they are necessary to reconcile the right to privacy with the rules governing freedom of expression (Article 9). Recital (37) emphasizes the need to provide for exceptions or restrictions if deemed necessary to strike a balance between the fundamental rights of individuals with freedom of information, "and notably the right to receive and impart information, as guaranteed in particular in Article 10 of the European Convention for the Protection of Human Rights and Fundamental Freedoms." Therefore, the requirement is clear: there is not only a need for striking a fair balance -and, in its absence, for setting aside the right to data protection in the interest of the prevailing right to information, but there must also be a quest for "reconciling" both rights to the extent possible or, at least, the prevalence of one over the other must be minimized.

7) When confronted with this challenge to strike a balance between these rights without downplaying freedom of information, the AEPD asserts that "Internet development and the widespread implementation of search engines entail an exponential and permanent update and dissemination of information."

Accordingly, the AEPD (in Resolution no. 2010/2012) suggests the following techniques and procedures to all online media involved in disputes on the right to be forgotten: 1′) assessing the need for their actions to reconcile the right to freedom of information with the application of data protection principles; 2′) carefully assessing the public relevance of the identity of persons involved in the newsworthy event; 3′) avoiding identification by deleting the name and, where appropriate, by erasing the initials and any other reference that can lead to identifying the persons involved insofar as the persons' identity does not provide any additional information; 4′) reflecting on the significance of permanently allowing access to data contained in news items which are probably irrelevant at this point; 5′) using software ("robots.txt" files, for instance) to prevent indexation of news reports containing personal data, thereby avoiding indiscriminate, permanent and potentially prejudicial dissemination (yet without altering documentary records or newspaper libraries).

8) Internet search engines are not specifically entitled to gather personal information or to include it in their search indexes or to temporarily store it in their cache memories. Freedom of information can only be invoked by those who publish news including personal data, but not by search engines, which are required to prevent indexation and future capturing of data.

9) Any restrictions on information activities carried out by online media, or the capturing of data by search engines, should only be based on compelling legitimate grounds relating to a particular personal situation on which the right to object could be founded. Indeed, these restrictions could never lead to any general preventive or *ex post facto* censorship,[198] or to the claim for general oblivion. In particular, the AEPD has considered that these grounds could be: 1´) inaccuracy of information; 2´) loss of journalistic interest of the news item after a significant period of time that has rendered it outdated or obsolete.

2) Official gazettes: publicly accessible sources responsible for the processing of published data

The right to be forgotten vis-à-vis official gazettes poses distinct legal challenges, given the specific legal framework applicable to official gazettes:

1) Official gazettes are publicly accessible sources "available for consultation by any person" (Article 3(j) LOPD).

2) Official gazettes are legally required to include certain decisions and resolutions (Article 6(1) of Act 5/2002, of 4 April; Articles 58 and 59 of Act 30/1992, of 26 November; or Article 30 of Act 1/1988, of 14 January).

3) Official gazettes must comply with data protection law: "Any

---

[198] As can be noticed, the previous criteria are fully in line with the standards suggested by FRANK LA RUE to consider that a restriction imposed on online content is legitimate: "As with offline content, when a restriction is imposed as an exceptional measure on online content, it must pass a three-part, cumulative test: (1) it must be provided by law, which is clear and accessible to everyone (principles of predictability and transparency); (2) it must pursue one of the purposes set out in article 19, paragraph 3, of the International Covenant on Civil and Political Rights , namely: (i) to protect the rights or reputations of others; (ii) to protect national security or public order, or public health or morals (principle of legitimacy); and (3) it must be proven as necessary and the least restrictive means required to achieve the purported aim (principles of necessity and proportionality). In addition, any legislation restricting the right to freedom of expression must be applied by a body which is independent of any political, commercial, or other unwarranted influences in a manner that is neither arbitrary nor discriminatory. There should also be adequate safeguards against abuse, including the possibility of challenge and remedy against its abusive application" (*Report of the Special Rapporteur on the promotion and protection of the right to freedom of opinion and expression*, United Nations General Assembly, 16 May 2011, p. 19).

reference on a website to persons, identifying them by their names or otherwise (...) amounts to the processing of personal data wholly or partly by automatic means as provided by Article 3(1) of Directive 95/46/EC" (High Court Judgment of 20 April 2009). In other words, when official gazettes publish personal data on their websites, a processing of personal data wholly or partly by automatic means subject to data protection law is taking place.

4) When official gazettes use their digital versions to publish, they are required to "adopt any measures necessary to prevent indiscriminate dissemination of third party personal data, who shall be able to enforce their rights when prejudiced by this general and universal access to information that may be captured through Internet search engines" (R/02553/2010).

5) The right to delete exercised vis-à-vis official gazettes, with the aim of erasing or anonymizing data, is hardly compatible with the legal obligation imposed on official gazettes to keep unaltered a specific content stemming from the public body that decided to include it in the gazette.

6) Recognizing the right to object, on compelling legitimate grounds relating to a particular personal situation, enables a subjective and individualized assessment, which fulfills the main legal interest at stake: preventing indexation by search engines with no need for deletion or removal.

7) The effectiveness of the right to object requires official gazettes to adopt any necessary and appropriate measures to prevent indexation of websites by search engines, having regard to the "current state of technology." Otherwise, the law would be at odds with reality, and the fundamental right would be deprived of its effectiveness.

8) The complexity of the Internet environment requires identifying as a "necessary and appropriate measure to prevent indexation" by search engines the measure that currently fulfills the alleged interest: the so-called "robots.txt" protocol, that allows the webmaster to create a "negative file" with content that cannot be crawled or indexed by search engines (Google). In spite of its reluctance towards the AEPD's views, the Official State Gazette (BOE) had already used these "robots.txt" files

to prevent indexation of certain content by search engines.[199] Given the "current state of technology -aside from the technical improvements that could be subsequently implemented, adopting the 'robots.txt' protocol is a valid response to citizens' requests exercising their right to delete or their right to object against an official gazette. These claims are based on the view that there are justified grounds to put an end to the indexation of personal data published in a given edition" (R/1777/2012).[200]

---

[199] In Official Provincial Gazettes, the use of the "robots.txt" protocol to prevent indexation of certain content by search engines became widespread: AEPD Resolution (R/2283/2011), dated 14 October 2011, issued in proceedings no. TD/637/2011. The claimant requested the deletion of his personal data published in the Balearic Islands Official Gazette in 2000, included in two court notices issued when the claimant's whereabouts were unknown. The Gazette rejected the requested deletion. However, it conceded to implement any necessary measures to prevent the indexation of his data and their capture by search engines. The AEPD considered that, "given the time elapsed since the publication in the Gazette, and provided that there was no interest in indiscriminately disseminating the data subject's information," there were compelling legitimate grounds to preserve the claimant's privacy and to limit access to information on him. The AEPD settled the dispute as soon as the Balearic Islands Gazette evidenced that it had implemented the measures necessary to prevent indexation.

[200] AEPD Resolution (R/688/2012), of 15 March 2012, issued in proceedings no. TD/1768/2011 is based on the same doctrine. In this case, the claimant exercised her right to deletion against BOE regarding the personal data provided in a resolution published by the Student Advancement Agency (*Instituto Nacional de Asistencia y Promoción del Estudiante*), which settled sanctioning proceedings that had been initiated against her.

CHAPTER IV

THE RIGHT TO BE FORGOTTEN IN EUROPE

1.- EUROPEAN AND AMERICAN COMPARATIVE LAW

a) France

France can be regarded as a reference in the attempt to guarantee the right to be forgotten on the Internet.

On 27 May 2009, Senators Mr. Yves Détraigne and Ms. Anne-Marie Escoffier presented the *Rapport sur la vie privée à l'heure des mémoires numériques. Pour une confiance renforcée entre citoyens et société de l'information.* Its Recommendation no. 14 urged to consider setting up a right to be forgotten (*"réfléchir à la création d'un droit à l'oubli"*).

Admittedly, the proposals would be imperfect and incomplete, and the main challenge would be to find a balance between the right to be forgotten and the freedom of expression and information. On that basis, the Report raised some questions: "Ne devrait-il pas exister un 'droit à l'oubli' pour les internautes, quand bien même ceux-ci auraient souhaité, à un moment donné de leur vie, se 'mettre à nu' sur le web? ... Ce droit à l'oubli pourrait s'exercer devant le juge à tout moment. Le demandeur démontrerait par exemple que les faits ou les propos rapportés ne correspondent plus à son mode de vie ou à ses opinions et qu'ils lui causent un préjudice dans sa vie familiale ou professionnelle. Il appartiendrait au juge d'apprécier si la demande de retrait porte atteinte à la liberté d'expression. L'intérêt de l'information pour le public, son ancienneté et la notoriété de la personne seraient des critères."[201]

However, the Report[202] warned that the effective fulfillment of such right would require the removal of information from websites (with difficulties associated with their being hosted abroad or the potential duplication and reappearance of information). At the same time, search engines should be prevented from indexing unwanted information. According to the Report, the advantages of this proposal are clear: "Cette solution a pour avantage d'être plus respectueuse de la liberté d'expression. L'information n'est pas retirée, mais les conditions pour y accéder sont rendues plus difficiles. Elles se rapprochent de celles du monde physique. Elle est aussi plus

---

[201] http://www.senat.fr/rap/r08-441/r08-441.html
[202] For more information, see PETER WALDKIRCH: "France and the Right to Forget," (http://www.iposgoode.ca/2010/01/france-and-the-right-to-forget).

aisée à mettre en œuvre. Certes, il existe plusieurs moteurs ou méta-moteurs de recherche, mais les principaux ne sont pas si nombreux. En outre, par le biais des moteurs de recherche, en cas de résurgence de l'information, quelle que soit la page, celle-ci ne sera pas indexée. Les moteurs de recherche pourraient mettre à disposition des utilisateurs identifiés des outils qui leur permettraient, même d'une manière imparfaite, de « nettoyer leur passé » en coupant certains liens issus du référencement."[203]

On 6 November 2009, the Senators who authored the Report presented a draft law to the French Senate,[204] the *Proposition de Loi visant à mieux garantir le droit à la vie privée à l'heure du numérique.*[205] It significantly lowered the guarantees for the right to be forgotten envisaged in the Report. Far from enshrining the right to be forgotten, the draft law only justified itself by explaining in its preamble that some measures could make it more effective.[206] In parallel, other public initiatives advocated reinforcing the right to be forgotten. On 13 October 2010, the *Secrétariat d'Etat chargée de la prospective et du développement de l'économie numérique* published the *Charte du droit à l'oubli dans les sites*

---

[203] http://www.senat.fr/rap/r08-441/r08-441.html. Notice the parallelism between these proposals and the path followed by the Spanish Data Protection Agency (AEPD) to guarantee the right to be forgotten.

[204] The draft law was approved by the French Senate on 23 March 2010.

[205] http://www.senat.fr/leg/ppl09-093.html

[206] Among them, the following were listed: "-l'information spécifique, claire et accessible donnée aux personnes, avant tout traitement, mais également de manière permanente, sur le site Internet du responsable du traitement, de la durée de conservation des données; -la possibilité de demander à la CNIL la durée de conservation des données ; -l'exercice plus facile du droit d'opposition; -la possibilité de saisir plus facilement et plus efficacement qu'aujourd'hui les juridictions civiles pour la suppression des données ; une meilleure traçabilité des transferts de données et permettent de lutter contre leur dissémination." (http://www.senat.fr/leg/ppl09-093.html).

collaboratifs et les moteurs de recherche,[207] signed by a dozen organizations committed to the development of best practices.[208]

The French political debate has been accompanied by several judicial decisions, specifically on the right to be forgotten. In March 2011, a court in Montpellier recognized a teacher's right to be forgotten against Google. In 2008 she had discovered that, when the term "Laetitia school" was entered in the search engine, there were links to an amateur porn video she had made when she was 18, and she was listed as a "porn actress." The teacher claimed that this was a violation of her private life and an unlawful processing of her personal data which would cause significant damage to her image if her family, friends and students were to have access to that episode of her past. The court considered that the association of her name to the search engine links constituted an invasion of privacy and ordered Google to delete them.[209]

On 15 February 2012, the Paris Court of First Instance (*Tribunal de Grande Instance*) ordered Google to delete some links from its search engine.[210] After establishing the existence of pornographic links

---

[207] http://www.aufeminin.com/aide/files/charteno.pdf

[208] This Charter advocated the following: "1.3 Donner aux internautes dès la collecte des données une information claire, transparente, complète, et facile à retrouver sur le site, sur les points suivants: la durée de conservation des données à caractère personnel; les modalités d'exercice du droit d'opposition; les conditions d'indexation par les moteurs de recherche... 2. Protéger les données personnelles de l'indexation automatique par les moteurs de recherche... Les moteurs de recherche signataires s'engagent à : 2.1 Collaborer avec les sites de publication pour faciliter la non-indexation de certains contenus. 2.2 Procéder dans les meilleurs délais à la mise à jour des caches quand une modification leur est signalée, et à leur vidage lorsqu'un contenu est désindexé. 3. Faciliter la gestion des données publiées par l'internaute lui-même. Objectif : Permettre aux internautes de localiser les informations qu'ils ont communiquées ou publiées. Eviter que des données personnelles mises en ligne sur un profil ne demeurent accessibles et ne soient conservées indéfiniment. Il s'agit de faciliter la mise en œuvre du droit d'opposition tel que prévu par la loi Informatique et Libertés, pour les données publiées par l'internaute. Les signataires considèrent que toute demande d'opposition portant sur une telle donnée est légitime. La donnée doit alors être supprimée du traitement, sauf en cas d'obligation légale ou de nécessité d'exécution d'un contrat ; dans ces cas elle ne doit plus être accessible publiquement."

[209] "Google, condenada en Francia a retirar enlaces a un vídeo pornográfico de una profesora," *El País*, 16 March 2011.

[210] http://www.legalis.net/spip.php?page=jurisprudence-decision&id_article=3362

139

associated to a certain name and last name[211] in Google search engine, the court held: 1) that such indexing was a breach of privacy; 2) that it could be prejudicial to the claimant's professional life; and 3) that it violated the legally recognized right to object. In addition to imposing a penalty on Google for the damage caused to the claimant, the court ordered the de-indexing of her name and last name from all pornographic links of the search engine and to delete all search results.

On 6 November 2013, the Paris Court of First Instance ordered Google to stop publication and remove from its search engine nine pictures from 2008 where Max Mosley, former president of the International Automobile Federation, appeared wearing a Nazi uniform and engaging in sadomasochistic games with five prostitutes.[212]

In connection with the debate prompted by the inclusion of the right to be forgotten in the GDPR Proposal, on 1 August 2013 the French Data Protection Authority (CNIL) launched a public consultation on the right to be forgotten.[213] The questions raised in this context suggested future

---

[211] The claimant, who in the past had recorded certain pornographic scenes under the pseudonym "L," found that her name and last name were linked by the Google search engine to the website www.sexe...com. After unsuccessfully requesting the producer of the film, the website editor and Google Inc. to delete such links, she went to court to seek their de-indexing.

[212] ANTOINE CHÉRON: "Affaire MOSLEY/GOOGLE : liberté d'expression, atteinte à la vie privée et droit à l'oubli numérique," 12 February 2014 (http://www.dalloz-actualite.fr/chronique/affaire-mosleygoogle-liberte-d-expression-atteinte-vie-privee-et-droit-l-oubli-numerique#.UvuYB_GYb4g).

[213] The major Internet companies were reluctant towards this initiative: "L'Association des Services Internet Communautaires (ASIC), fondée en 2007 et qui regroupe les grands acteurs de l'Internet (notamment Deezer, eBay, Facebook, Google, Microsoft, Skype, PriceMinister, AOL, Yahoo...)... s'oppose à l'obligation systématique de suppression des données par les hébergeurs. 'Le projet de la CNIL d'imposer aux hébergeurs une obligation de suppression de contenus, sans passage préalable par le juge, semble attentatoire à la liberté d'expression'" (http://www.journaldunet.com/ebusiness/le-net/droit-a-l-oubli-asic-tacle-cnil-0913.shtml); "L'AFDEL (Association française des éditeurs de logiciels et solutions internet), qui réunit notamment Microsoft France et Google parmi plus de 300 membres livre une série d'arguments: 'Un droit à l'oubli général pourrait en effet résulter en une forme de censure d'Internet, qui mettrait en cause le modèle libre et ouvert sur lequel s'est construit ce dernier ... Il serait contreproductif de donner à l'internaute le sentiment d'évoluer dans un environnement autorisant quasiment sans condition l'oubli, libérant dès lors tous les comportements, même les plus irresponsables ... Aussi, sur les propositions de la CNIL aboutissant à limiter la liberté de la presse au nom du droit à l'oubli (anonymisation des personnes citées, désindexation des articles, mise sous archives payantes des articles plus anciens), l'AFDEL se montre résolument

---

developments[214]: 1) the CNIL, aware of the lack of a non-controversial concept of the right to be forgotten, asked whether such right should include "la possibilité offerte à chacun de maîtriser ses traces numériques et sa vie - privée comme publique - en ligne avec un équilibre entre le droit à l'oubli et le devoir de mémoire et la liberté d'expression;" 2′) the CNIL raised the possibility of setting up a European reference standard on maximum data retention periods; 3′) the CNIL asked about the possibility of entitling users to set an "expiration date" (by default or freely) regarding their publications, allowing them to directly modify or erase them; 4′) as for the application of the right to be forgotten to online media, the CNIL asked about the possibility of anonymizing identities (and deleting identifying elements) and/or de-indexing news articles, and/or establishing a maximum online dissemination period (after which the articles would be stored for member access); 5′) the CNIL raised the possibility of laying down a legal obligation for search engines to immediately de-index any information deleted by users; and 6′) the CNIL considered the possibility of providing Internet users with tools to directly manage de-indexing of data contained on social networks from search engines, both public and internal.

b) Italy

Il diritto all'oblio (the right to be forgotten) has a long theoretical and scholarly tradition. However, like in many other countries, its implementation on the Internet has been difficult and chaotic. The following are only a sample of the many decisions issued by the *Garante per la Protezione dei Dati Personali* (the Italian Data Protection Authority) that illustrate this reality.

---

opposée" (http://www.numerama.com/magazine/27126-droit-a-l-oubli-de-bonnes-raisons-de-l-oublier.html).
[214]http://www.numerama.com/magazine/27126-droit-a-l-oubli-de-bonnes-raisons-de-l-oublier.html

On 15 January 2009, the *Garante* issued Resolution no. 1589209, partially granting the application to delete the data included in newspaper archives available online through Internet search engines.[215] On 17 November 2008, an application had been filed against *Il Corriere della Sera* seeking the erasure of personal data contained in an article filed in the newspaper's online archive, as well as its deletion from Google's and other search engines' indexes. The article, published fifteen years ago, referred to some threatening phone calls made by the applicant to prevent the staging of a play. The applicant claimed that *republishing* this article would undermine his honor, reputation and dignity, since it did not take into account his current social, professional and emotional life. The *Garante* rejected the request to erase the personal data on the view that it was unfounded, but it partially upheld the action by granting the right to object in order to protect the data, thereby requiring the publishing company to adopt the necessary technical measures to prevent their indexing by external search engines. The *Garante* held the online media exclusively responsible for preventing external access by Internet search engines, but it exempted the latter from any obligation or liability.[216]

---

[215] http://www.garanteprivacy.it/web/guest/home/docweb/-/docweb-display/docweb/1589209

[216] The *Garante* adopted the same position in Resolution no. 1617673, of 8 April 2009, ruling on an application for deletion against *Il Corriere della Sera* with regard to personal data included in a newspaper article hosted in its online archive and referred to the victim of a crime (http://www.garanteprivacy.it/web/guest/home/docweb/-/docweb-display/docweb/1617673). On the contrary, in its Resolution no. 1635938, of 22 May 2009, the *Garante* rejected as unfounded the appeal against *Il Corriere della Sera* requesting the deletion of data regarding the appellant's professional activity. The *Garante* held that "il trattamento di dati personali relativi all'interessato effettuato mediante la riproposizione *on-line*, sul sito Internet dell'editore resistente, dell'articolo che li contiene quale parte integrante dell'archivio storico del quotidiano, non risulta in termini generali illecito, essendo riferito a notizie relative a fatti di interesse pubblico e ciò, tanto al tempo della sua pubblicazione, quanto attualmente, per chi opera una ricerca relativa alle vicende in esso narrate, vicende che hanno interessato il ricorrente con riferimento all'attività politica locale e nazionale che lo stesso ha svolto negli anni, anche nel corso delle più recenti legislatura ... contrariamente a quanto sostenuto dal ricorrente, le notizie pubblicate rimangono di interesse pubblico in quanto fanno riferimento a vicende direttamente connesse alla sfera di un personaggio pubblico protagonista nell'ambito della vita politica nazionale (lo stesso, infatti, è stato candidato alle ultime elezioni politiche ed è attualmente in lista per le prossime elezioni del Parlamento europeo)" (http://www.garanteprivacy.it/web/guest/home/docweb/-/docweb-display/docweb/1635938).

Italian Court of Cassation Judgment no. 5525/2012, of 5 April 2012, held that hosting an article in the newspaper's online archive, and making it available, traceable and indexable by Internet search engines, required establishing an appropriate system to identify (in the body or the margin of the article) a relevant result. That is, it imposed on the online media -but not on the search engines- the obligation and responsibility to allow updates to the articles included in the online historical archives.[217]

However, the Italian case[218] with greatest international impact did not

---

[217] The facts that gave rise to this judicial decision date back to the *Tangentopoli* years, when arrests for alleged corruption piled up and a local Milanese politician, former city councilman and president of a municipal company, was arrested for corruption and subsequently acquitted. The news of his arrest was widely disseminated by the media, while his acquittal had little visibility. The data subject brought an action before the *Garante* and the Court of Milan to block any personal references contained in the *Corriere della Sera*, but both of them dismissed his claim (G. GUERCILENA: "Lungo la linea della vita," 18 April 2012, http://www.ilsole24ore.com/pdf2010/SoleOnLine5/_Oggetti_Correlati/Document i/Norme%20e%20Tributi/2012/04/corte-cassazione-sentenza-5525-2012.pdf?uuid=11fb990c-7fc2-11e1-a8f6-20908e87732a). The Judgment is available at: http://www.ilsole24ore.com/pdf2010/SoleOnLine5/_Oggetti_Correlati/Document i/Norme%20e%20Tributi/2012/04/corte-cassazione-sentenza-5525-2012.pdf?uuid=11fb990c-7fc2-11e1-a8f6-20908e87732a?uuid=Ab5asrJF. In this Judgment, the Italian Court of Cassation reviewed a resolution from the Garante to ensure greater protection of the individual right, holding that: a) the original publication of the arrest for alleged corruption was lawful, since it served a public information purpose, and it was not defamation because at the time the information was a true news story; b) the original article could remain on the Internet for historical research purposes, but only if it was accompanied by the subsequent judgment in order to ensure compliance with the principles of completeness, accuracy and timeliness enshrined in the Privacy Code. As recalled by R. IMPERIALI, "trattandosi del perseguimento di una finalità di ricerca storica operata tramite l'archivio online dell'editore, non si parlare – in senso stretto – di esercizio del diritto all'oblio, in quanto quest'ultimo non si applica nei riguardi degli archivi storici che, per loro natura, non soffrono di obsolescenza" ("Difficile l'update degli archivi online," 7 April 2012, http://www.ilsole24ore.com/art/norme-e-tributi/2012-04-07/difficile-update-archivi-online-081727.shtml?uuid=AbK3wMKF&fromSearch).

[218] A thorough analysis of the first stage of such case can be found in GIOVANNI SARTOR & MARIO VIOLA DE AZAVEDO CUNHA: "The Italian Google-Case: Privacy, Freedom of Speech and Responsibility of Providers for User-Generated Contents," *International Journal of Law and Information Technology*, vol. 18-4, 2010, pp. 356-378.

specifically address the right to be forgotten on the Internet, but it dealt with other relevant issues, such as the liability of Internet intermediary services for the contents hosted in them by third parties. In particular, it assessed the potential criminal liability (!) of some Google senior executives (including Peter Fleischer, Google's Global Privacy Counsel) for an alleged violation of Italian legislation on data protection, as a result of hosting a video of a disabled person being insulted and harassed. In November 2006, a video hosted in Google Videos showed a disabled student (autistic) being bullied and insulted by three of his colleagues, which was recorded by another student. It remained as one of the most popular videos in Google Videos. Despite repeated requests for the video to be removed, Google did not take it down until required by the Police two months later. The Milan Public Prosecutor initiated criminal proceedings against four Google executives (with responsibilities in Italy but also at a global scale). They were accused of aggravated defamation of a disabled teenager and violation of data protection law, on the basis that Google was processing health data to make a profit. In February 2010, the four Google executives were acquitted by a Judge of the defamation charges, but they were sentenced to six months in prison for violating data protection legislation.[219]

c) **Canadá**

It is worth taking a look at the Canadian experience. Although geographically far from Europe, it is very close in terms of data protection law.[220]

---

[219] The conviction was overturned by a later judgment.

[220] As recalled by PIERRE TRUDEL, "Il y est prévu d'instaurer un «droit à l'oubli» sur Internet. Cela se passe en Europe, mais l'importance des liens de toute nature que nous avons avec l'Europe fait en sorte que la question va forcément se poser ici. En particulier, le Canada et le Québec ont toujours tenu à harmoniser leur législation avec les règles européennes en matière de protection des données personnelles" ("La menace du 'droit à l'oublie," 5 October 2013 (http://blogues.journaldemontreal.com/pierretrudel/droit/la-menace-du-droit-a-loubli/).

Under the Canadian legal system, the *right to be forgotten*[221] does not provide a specific position on the guarantees against Internet search engines. Surveillance of Internet services by the Privacy Commissioner Office offers a wide array of actions aimed at effectively ensuring the right to delete data on the Internet, which would broadly protect the right to be forgotten.[222]

On 30 May 2008, representatives of the Canadian Internet Policy and Public Interest Clinic (CIPPIC) filed a complaint against Facebook, giving rise to the *Report of Findings into the Complaint Filed by the Canadian Internet Policy and Public Interest Clinic (CIPPIC) against Facebook Inc. under the Personal Information Protection and Electronic Documents Act* presented on 16 July 2009.[223] This investigation by the Canadian authority addressed, among other things, the right to delete data. The information provided by Facebook was especially confusing with regard to the difference between *deactivating an account* -which implied leaving the account without activity, but keeping the personal data in a digital memory without definitely deleting them, which made it possible to retrieve them in the event the user wanted to recover the account- and *cancelling the account* -which, instead of being temporary, like deactivation, meant that personal data would be effectively and

---

[221] The relevance of such category in Canadian civil law is reflected by several judicial decisions on the publication of relatively old data by current media. A paradigmatic example is the case of *Ouellet contre Pigeon* (1997, RRA, 1168) ruled by the Civil Chamber of the Court of Québec. In 1986, the claimant's wife killed her four children and then committed suicide, which received wide coverage in the media. In 1996, a newspaper article was published which described the facts and included some pictures under the title "Cas femmes qui ont tué ... à vous de juger." The claimant was informed by some colleagues and considered to be morally affected. The Court held that such in-depth and sensationalist publication 10 years later was not a reasonable or legitimate manifestation of the right to information, since such retrieval of past events served no public interest. Even if there were no inaccuracies, exaggerations, or malicious intent, the Tribunal considered that it constituted an invasion of privacy. The claimant was the survivor of a tragedy that had taken place 10 years ago; he had been able to rebuild his life and to forget this nightmare. He had the right to respect for his private life, and he had not been informed by the journalists. Other Judgments by the Courts of Québec on the right to be forgotten against the media are those delivered in the cases of *Bouchard contre Bombardier* (1996, RRA, 321) and *Mathieu contre La Presse* (24 November 1998).

[222] ARTEMI RALLO: "La protección de la privacidad en las redes sociales de Internet: la experiencia canadiense con facebook, google y otros," *Derecho y Redes Sociales*, A. Rallo and R. Martínez (Eds.), 2nd edition, Civitas-Thomson Reuters, Pamplona, 2013, pp. 257-284.

[223] http://www.priv.gc.ca/cf-dc/2009/2009_008_0716_e.asp

---

definitely deleted from Facebook's servers, without any possibility of subsequent recovery.

As a result of the exchange between the Canadian Privacy Commissioner Office and Facebook, it was concluded that Facebook would implement a data retention policy according to which the personal data of users who had deactivated their accounts would be definitely erased from the servers after a reasonable period of time. Also, in the deactivation process users would be specifically informed of the possibility to delete and erase their accounts in a definite manner.

On 29 February 2012, the Canadian Privacy Commissioner Office concluded that Nexopia, a youth-oriented social network, had violated Canadian privacy laws.[224] This resolution stemmed from a complaint filed in 2010 by representatives of the Public Interest Advocacy Centre (PIAC) against Nexopia for violation of numerous legal obligations: personal information was stored indefinitely without the users' knowledge or consent, and without any possibility to delete it permanently. The investigation by the Privacy Commissioner Office concluded with a wide set of Recommendations among which it is worth mentioning those referred to *data retention*: Nexopia was required to implement appropriate policies and practices regarding personal data retention and destruction, including retention periods established for non-users and for users' personal data. The social network had to offer a real option to delete the users' accounts and personal data, and also a clear option, explained in plain language, between (a) temporarily deactivating the account; or (b) permanently deleting them from the website's database.[225]

---

[224] *Report of Findings under the* PERSONAL INFORMATION PROTECTION AND ELECTRONIC DOCUMENTS ACT *(PIPEDA): Social networking site for youth, Nexopia, breached Canadian privacy law* (http://www.priv.gc.ca/cf-dc/2012/2012_001_0229_e.asp).

[225] On 29 May 2012, the Canadian Privacy Commissioner Office appeared before the House of Commons Standing Committee on Access to Information, Privacy and Ethics on Privacy and Social Media to assess the main challenges facing the social media in order to better protect the citizens' privacy. Express reference was made to data retention as an issue of concern: "organizations failing to establish retention schedules of personal information and true deletion options for individuals. Social media companies need to be clear about how long they retain the personal information they are collecting ... firms are obliged to keep data only as long as is necessary for a specific purpose and then they must destroy it" (http://www.priv.gc.ca/parl/2012/parl_20120529_e.asp).

d) Argentina

The demand for recognition of the right to be forgotten on the Internet has also reached the Southern part of the American continent.

In Argentina, in 2009, the name of the singer and Model Virginia Da Cunha appeared in Internet search engine result pages associated with various websites containing pornographic montages. Google and Yahoo! were ordered by a Court of First Instance to pay a compensation of 100,000 pesos.[226] However, the Argentinian Federal Court of Appeals on Civil and Commercial Matters (*Cámara Nacional de Apelaciones en lo Civil y Comercial Federal*) reversed such ruling, exempting them from any liability on the grounds of their intermediary nature, unless they were negligent in blocking clearly unlawful results.[227]

In turn, on 16 April 2013, the Argentinian Supreme Court ordered Yahoo! to indemnify the model Priscila Prete for failing to remove from search results the contents linked to pornographic sites, considering that Yahoo! had been negligent (although exempting them from the obligation to previously filter the content).[228]

e) Nicaragua

For the first time in history, a national piece of legislation acknowledged the right to be forgotten on the Internet. Unambiguously, Article 10 of Nicaraguan Act no. 787, of 21 March 2012, on Personal Data Protection, under the heading *Right to digital oblivion* (*Derecho al olvido digital*), established that: "the data subject is entitled to request social networks, Internet browsers and servers to delete and erase personal data contained in their files."[229] It is a bold affirmation of the right to delete data on the

---

[226] CARLOS CORTÉS: "Derecho al olvido: entre la protección de datos, la memoria y la vida personal en la era digital," http://www.palermo.edu/cele/pdf/DerechoalolvidoiLEI.pdf.

[227] RICARDO BRAGINSKI: "Google y Yahoo! dan vuelta un fallo contra una ex Bandana," *Clarín*, 16 August 2010, https://www.clarin.com/internet/Google-Yahoo-vuelta-fallo-Bandana_0_B1546SR6wXl.html

[228] ROMINA FLORENCIA CABRERA: "Sentencia sobre privacidad, derecho al olvido y buscadores," 16 May 2013, http://oiprodat.com/2013/05/16/sentencia-sobre-privacidad-derecho-al-olvido-y-buscadores/. También, http://censorshipcases.wordpress.com/2013/07/30/argentina-prete-priscila-cyahoo-de-argentina-s-r-l-sdanos-y-perjuicios-6-9-2012/

[229] *La Gaceta-Diario Oficial*, 29-3-2012, vol. 61, p. 2404. In its original Spanish version: "El titular de los datos tiene derecho a solicitar de las redes sociales, navegadores y servidores que se supriman y cancelen los datos personales que se encuentren en sus ficheros."

Internet with respect to leading online services (social networks and search engines), thus responding to a growing social demand.

2.- JUDICIAL PRECEDENTS

2.1.- Deletion of personal data (and its impact on the Internet) in the case law of the European Court of Human Rights (ECtHR)

The ECtHR has developed an interpretative doctrine of the "right to respect for private and family life" enshrined in Article 8 of the European Convention on Human Rights (ECHR). Based on that provision, the ECtHR has affirmed the existence of an evolving right to personal data protection which has gained remarkable relevance and significance[230] in the context of a technological revolution -and, of course, with the ubiquity of the Internet.[231]

ECtHR's case law doctrine has dealt with the impact of new technologies and the Internet on the protection of individuals' privacy and, in particular, their personal data. Some judgments are especially useful to assess the potential scope of protection the ECtHR may grant to the right to be forgotten on the Internet.

1) The duty of the press to ensure the accuracy of historical information published online includes attaching a "qualification" or "notice" to the relevant articles: *Case Times Newspapers v. UK* (10 March 2009).

In 1999, The Times published in its print and online versions two articles on a money-laundering case involving an alleged Russian mafia boss whose name appeared in the original article. Proceedings for libel were

---

[230] Given the "dialogue" that informs the relation between both Courts, it is worth recalling the importance of this case law before the CJEU. See, in this regard, MÓNICA ARENAS RAMIRO, M.: "El derecho a la protección de datos personales: de la Jurisprudencia del TEDH a la del TJCE," *Constitución y Democracia. 25 años de Constitución democrática en España*, vol. I, Universidad del País Vasco, 2006, pp. 575-589.

[231] For an overall summary of the ECtHR's case law on data protection, see the lecture given by the President of the ECtHR, DEAN SPIELMANN: "La protection des données dans la jurisprudence de la Cour européenne des droits de l'homme," Commission Nationale pour la Protection des Données, Luxembourg, 28 January 2013 (http://hub.coe.int/google-search/?q=data+protection&sitesearch=coe.int&x=0&y=0). As for the case law regarding data protection on the Internet, see the Report by the ECtHR's Research Division of June 2011 entitled "Internet: la jurisprudence de la Cour européenne des droits de l'homme," (http://www.echr.coe.int/Documents/Research_report_internet_FRA.pdf).

brought against the editor of The Times and the two journalists who signed the articles. The defendants did not dispute that these articles were potentially defamatory, but they claimed to be under a duty to publish the information given the seriousness of the alleged facts.

During the libel proceedings, both articles remained published on The Times' website available to users as part of the newspaper's archives. In 2000, a second action for libel was brought on the grounds of the continuing Internet publication of the articles. The defendants added a notice to the online articles informing that they were subject to libel litigation and that they should not be reproduced without consulting The Times Legal Department. The Times contended that only the first publication on the Internet could give rise to liability for libel, but not the subsequent downloads. The British judge considered the opposite, declaring that each access to a defamatory article gave rise to a separate cause of action. The ECtHR concluded that there had been no violation of Article 10 ECHR, since the finding by the domestic courts was not a disproportionate restriction on the freedom of expression.[232]

Particular attention should be paid to the reasoning of the ECtHR regarding the potential impact on the freedom of expression resulting from altering newspaper articles online: 1) The ECtHR acknowledged the substantial contribution made by Internet archives to preserving and making available news and information as an important source for education and historical research; 2) The ECtHR held that, while the primary function of the press in a democracy is to act as a "public watchdog," it has a "valuable secondary role in maintaining and making available to the public archives containing news which have previously been reported. However, the margin of appreciation afforded to States in striking the balance between the competing rights is likely to be greater where news archives of past events, rather than news reporting of current affairs, are concerned. In particular, the duty of the press to act in accordance with the principles of responsible journalism by ensuring the accuracy of historical, rather than perishable, information published is likely to be more stringent in the absence of any urgency in publishing the material;" 3) The ECtHR found it significant that The Times had not added any qualification to the online version of the articles until 2000, and that the archives had been kept posted without any removal order from the domestic courts. The British Court of Appeal had concluded that the attachment to the archive copies of a notice informing of the ongoing

---

[232] In *Case Renaud v. France* (25 February 10) the ECtHR considered a conviction for defamation on the Internet to be disproportionate in relation to the objective pursued of protecting the right to honor, which amounted to a violation of Article 10 ECHR.

libel proceedings "would normally remove any sting from the material" (although The Times considered such measure excessive). In any case, the British Court of Appeal had never indicated that potentially defamatory articles should be removed from the archives altogether: "the Court, like the Court of Appeal, does not consider that the requirement to publish an appropriate qualification to an article contained in an Internet archive, where it has been brought to the notice of a newspaper that a libel action has been initiated in respect of that same article published in the written press, constitutes a disproportionate interference with the right to freedom of expression."[233]

2) The vital function of the press covers the use of inaccurate personal information obtained from the Internet: *Case Pravoye Delo and Shtekel v. Ukraine (5.5.11)*.

In 2003, the Ukrainian newspaper Pravoye Delo published an anonymous letter, purportedly written by an employee of the Security Service of Ukraine, which had been downloaded from a news website. It accused senior officials of the Odessa Regional Department of Security of corruption and other crimes. The newspaper cited the source and warned that the letter could contain false information. Subsequently, the President of the Ukraine National Thai Boxing Federation, who was referred to in the letter as a member of a criminal group, filed a defamation lawsuit. The Ukrainian courts ruled against the editorial board and the editor-in-chief, ordering them to publish a retraction.

The ECtHR noted that the reproduction of material downloaded from a publicly accessible newspaper was covered by the Ukrainian Press Act, which exempted journalists from civil liability for disseminating statements made by others. However, the Ukrainian courts considered that such immunity did not exist when such material was reproduced from Internet sources "not registered" pursuant to the Ukrainian Press Act.

ECtHR recalled the relevant role played by the Internet with respect to media activities and the freedom of expression. On these grounds, the ECtHR held that the absence of a legal framework allowing journalists to use information obtained from the Internet without fear of being

---

[233] The ECtHR stressed that the content of the brief notice attached to the article archived on the Internet rebutted The Times' argument that such qualification was difficult to formulate. The notice read as follows: "This article is subject to High Court libel litigation between [G.L.] and Times Newspapers. It should not be reproduced or relied on without reference to Times Newspapers Legal Department."

sanctioned hampered the exercise of the vital function of the press as a "public watchdog." The lack of clarity of the domestic legislation on the use of information obtained from the Internet was contrary to the requirement that any interference with the freedom of expression should be based on a clear, accessible and foreseeable law. The ECtHR therefore concluded that there had been a violation of Article 10 ECHR.

3) Absence of a requirement to notify public subjects prior to publication of their personal data on Internet media: *Case Mosley v. UK (10 May 2011).*

In 2008, News of the World published in both its print and online versions an article featuring a British citizen headed "F1 boss has sick Nazi orgy with 5 hookers," including some video footage and photographs. Mr. Mosley claimed damages and sought an injunction against further dissemination of the video on the Internet. The UK High Court denied the injunction, considering that the data were no longer private, since they had already been widely disseminated in print and on the Internet. However, taking into account that the images had no public interest, the court concluded that there had been a violation of the applicant's right to privacy and ordered News of the World to pay damages.

Nevertheless, Mr. Mosley claimed that he remained a victim of a violation of Article 8 ECHR by reason of there not being a legal obligation of pre-notification ahead publication, so that an injunction could be sought.

The ECtHR considered that the publication constituted a flagrant and unjustified invasion of privacy, and recalled that the British authorities were required to adopt positive measures to ensure the enjoyment of such right.[234]

---

[234] In *Case K.U. v. Finland* (2 December 2008), the ECtHR also referred to the State's positive obligation to protect the right to privacy against the publication of pictures of a minor on an Internet portal. The ECtHR took into account the physical and moral risk for children, and their vulnerability, to conclude that publishing an advertisement of a minor online was a criminal act which made the minor a target for pedophiles on the Internet. This conduct should be criminally punished in the form of effective deterrence. The ECtHR argued that in 1999 it was already well-known that the Internet, because of its anonymous nature, could be used for criminal purposes, especially with regard to sexual abuse of minors. On that basis, the State's failure to establish effective criminal-law provisions and sanctions to protect children from pedophiles on the Internet constituted a violation of Article 8 ECHR.

The ECtHR examined the viability of the applicant's claim regarding a legal obligation to pre-notify, concluding that there was no such requirement under Article 8 ECHR for the following reasons: 1) In spite of its potential effectiveness, the impact of a pre-notification rule would not be limited to sensationalist publications but would extend to political reporting and serious investigative journalism; 2) any restriction on journalistic activities requires careful scrutiny; 3) a precautionary measure such as an interim injunction could be sought to prohibit dissemination of information threatening individual privacy; 4) no international standards or comparative legislation provide for that measure. In the ECtHR's view, despite the potential deterrent effect of a pre-notification requirement, it raised significant doubts over its effectiveness.

It is worth noting, however, that at a later moment, on 6 November 2013, the Paris Court of First Instance ordered Google to remove and stop publication in its search engine of the images where Max Mosley appeared dressed in a Nazi uniform and engaging in sadomasochistic games with five prostitutes.[235]

4) Restriction of Internet access without specific legal support violates the freedom of expression: *Case Ahmet Yildirim v. Turkey* (18 December 2012).[236]

In 2009, the applicant published an academic work on a website created using Google Sites. As a result, a criminal court accused him of insulting the memory of Atatürk and ordered the temporary blocking of his website and a wholesale blocking of Google Sites.

The ECtHR considered that the limited effect of the restriction did not diminish its significance, "since the Internet has now become one of the

---

[235] ANTOINE CHÉRON: "Affaire MOSLEY/GOOGLE : liberté d'expression, atteinte à la vie privée et droit à l'oubli numérique," 12 February 2014 (http://www.dalloz-actualite.fr/chronique/affaire-mosleygoogle-liberte-d-expression-atteinte-vie-privee-et-droit-l-oubli-numerique#.UvuYB_GYb4g).

[236] On the State's limitations to ensure respect for privacy on the Internet, see *Case Muscio v. Italy* (ECtHR, Decision on inadmissibility of 2 December 2008), where the president of a Catholic parents' association complained about receiving pornographic spam messages. The ECtHR considered that such unwanted communications constituted an interference with the right to respect for his private life, but once connected to the Internet, e-mail users expose themselves to these unwanted messages. The applicant's claim had no chance of success, and both national authorities and Internet service providers encountered objective difficulties to combat "spam." Therefore, the ECtHR "could not find that the State should have made additional efforts."

principal means by which individuals exercise their right to freedom of expression and information." The Turkish law entitled the judge to block access to the Internet (although not a wholesale blocking) where there were sufficient grounds to suspect that such publications constituted crimes. Nothing suggested that "Google Sites" was aware of the illegal nature of certain contents or that it refused to comply with an interim measure.

The ECtHR concluded that there had been a violation of Article 8 ECHR.[237] The ECtHR argued that "such prior restraints are not necessarily incompatible with the Convention as a matter of principle," but "a legal framework is required, ensuring both tight control over the scope of bans and effective judicial review to prevent any abuse of power." The wholesale blocking of Google Sites ordered by the Turkish courts was only based on the opinion issued by an administrative body, the Telecommunications and Information Technology Directorate (TIB), without looking for less intrusive measures to block exclusively the affected website: "they should have taken into consideration, among other elements, the fact that such a measure, by rendering large quantities of information inaccessible, substantially restricted the rights of Internet users and had a significant collateral effect."

5) Internet news portals are liable for the offensive online comments of their readers: *Case Delfi AS v. Estonia* (10 October 2013)

In 2006, Delfi AS, one of the leading Internet news portals in Estonia, published an article on the change of routes of a shipping company which attracted many offensive and threatening comments. In 2008, the Estonian courts found Delfi liable for such defamatory comments, on the grounds that Directive 2000/31/EC on Electronic Commerce did not exclude liability arising from the comments posted by readers.[238]

---

[237] In the case of *Copland v. UK* (3 March 2007), the ECtHR held that an employer had breached Article 8 ECHR by obtaining and retaining personal data regarding e-mail and Internet usage when this type of access was not legally admitted to monitor employees.

[238] As recalled by the ECtHR, "the Court of Appeal rejected the applicant company's argument that its responsibility was excluded on the basis of the Information Society Services Act. It noted that the applicant company was not a technical intermediary in respect of the comments, and that its activity was not of a merely technical, automatic and passive nature; instead, it invited users to add comments. Thus, the applicant company was a provider of content services rather than of technical services ... The Supreme Court approved the lower courts' interpretation of the Information Society Services Act, and reiterated that an information society service provider, falling under that Act and the Directive on Electronic Commerce, had neither knowledge of nor control over information

In assessing the attribution of liability to the Internet news portal by domestic courts, the ECtHR weighed the proportionality of such interference with the portal's freedom of expression: 1′) The nature of the article allowed the portal to anticipate that it would attract insulting, threatening and defamatory comments, so it should have been more careful considering the potential reputational damage; 2′) the portal attributed liability to its readers,[239] it prohibited threatening or insulting comments and it had adopted some mechanisms to remove comments reported by third parties; however, a great number of insulting comments were actually not removed; 3′) the news portal preserved the anonymity of the authors of the comments, thus preventing the shipping company from taking legal actions against them.

The ECtHR ruled that there had been no violation of the freedom of expression protected by Article 10 ECHR as a result of the domestic courts' imposition of liability on the Internet news portal. This was considered a justified and proportionate restriction on the freedom of expression, taking into account: the extreme nature of the comments, the insufficiency of the measures taken to remove them without delay, and the preservation of the authors' anonymity. For future interpretative

---

which was transmitted or stored. By contrast, a provider of content services governed the content of information that was being stored. In the present case, the applicant company had integrated the comment environment into its news portal and invited users to post comments. The number of comments had an effect on the number of visits to the portal and on the applicant company's revenue from advertisements published on the portal. Thus, the applicant company had an economic interest in the comments. The fact that the applicant company did not write the comments itself did not imply that it had no control over the comment environment. It enacted the rules of comment and removed comments if the rules were breached. The users, on the contrary, could not change or delete the comments they had posted; they could merely report obscene comments. Thus, the applicant company could determine which comments were published and which not. The fact that it made no use of this possibility did not mean that it had no control over the publishing of the comments. Furthermore, the Supreme Court considered that in the present case both the applicant company and the authors of the comments were to be considered publishers of the comments."

[239] Delfi's *Rules of comment* established the following: "The Delfi message board is a technical medium allowing users to publish comments. Delfi does not edit comments. An author of a comment is liable for his/her comment. It is worth noting that there have been cases in the Estonian courts where authors have been punished for the contents of a comment ... Delfi prohibits comments the content of which does not comply with good practice. These are comments that: - contain threats; - contain insults; - incite hostility and violence; - incite illegal activities ... - contain obscene expressions and vulgarities ... Delfi has the right to remove such comments and restrict their authors' access to the writing of comments ...."

purposes, the following statement by the ECtHR merits particular emphasis: "the spread of the Internet and the possibility -or for some purposes the danger- that information once made public will remain public and circulate forever, calls for caution. The ease of disclosure of information on the Internet and the substantial amount of information there means that it is a difficult task to detect defamatory statements and remove them. This is so for an Internet news portal operator, as in the present case, but this is an even more onerous task for a potentially injured person, who would be less likely to possess resources for continual monitoring of the Internet. The Court considers the latter element an important factor in balancing the rights and interests at stake."

2.2.- The Court of Justice of the European Union (CJEU) as a driving force for data protection on the Internet

If the ECtHR's case law is relevant to know the basic criteria governing personal data protection under the ECHR, the analysis of the CJEU's case law on the right to data protection[240] on the Internet provides an essential framework to understand the protection of the right to be forgotten on the Internet.

1) First application of the Data Protection Directive to the Internet: *Lindqvist* (Case C-101/01, 6 November 2003[241])

---

[240] For an overview of the first judgments of the CJEU, see PIÑAR MAÑAS, J.L.: "El derecho a la protección de datos de carácter personal en la jurisprudencia del Tribunal de Justicia de las Comunidades Europeas," *Cuadernos de Derecho Público*, vols. 19-20, *2003*, pp. 45 to 90; ARENAS RAMIRO, M.: "El derecho a la protección de datos personales en la jurisprudencia del TJCE," *Revista Aranzadi de Derecho y Nuevas Tecnologías*, vol. 4, 2006, pp. 95 to 119.

[241] On 20 May 2003 (C-465/00, C-138/01 and C-139/01, *Case Österreichischer Rundfunk,*) the CJEU had already noted the extraordinary impact arising from the Directive's wide scope.

Lindqvist[242] is the reference case where the CJEU confirmed the full applicability of the Data Protection Directive to the Internet in the following terms: 1´) Referring, on an Internet page, to various persons and identifying them by name or by other means, for instance by giving their telephone number or information regarding their working conditions and hobbies, constitutes *the processing of personal data wholly or partly by automatic means* (Article 3(1) of Directive 95/46/EC); 2´) Processing of personal data consisting in publication on the internet so that those data are made accessible to an indefinite number of people cannot be interpreted as relying only to activities which are carried out in the course of *private* or *family* life. Therefore, that activity is not exempted from the application of Directive 95/46/EC pursuant to its Article 3(2).

The CJEU also contributed decisively to define the scope of the Directive in relation to the Internet in terms of implementation reasonability. In this regard, it denied the existence of a *transfer of personal data to a third country* (hence not applying Article 25 of Directive 95/46/EC[243]) when an individual in a Member State loads data on a website hosted in that or

---

[242] Mrs. Lindqvist had been accused of violating the Swedish legislation on personal data protection for publishing on her internet site personal data of a number of people working with her on a voluntary basis in parish of the Swedish Protestant Church. Mrs. Lindqvist worked as a catechist in the parish of Alseda (Sweden) and, after taking a data processing course, she set up several internet pages from her home and on her personal computer, so that parishioners could easily obtain any information they might need for their confirmation. Such pages contained information about Mrs. Lindqvist and eighteen colleagues in the parish: full or first names, humorous comments, hobbies, family circumstances, telephone numbers, information on sick leaves, etc. Mrs. Lindqvist was fined for processing personal data by automatic means (included in some cases sensitive data) without authorization, for not giving prior written notification to the Data Protection Authority (the *Datainspektionen*), and for transferring personal data to a third country without authorization.

[243] For a critical approach, see YVES POULLET: "Flujos de datos transfronterizos y extraterritorialidad: la postura europea," *Revista Española de Protección de Datos*, vol. 1, July-December 2006, p. 99.

another Member State, even if those data are made available to anyone connected to the Internet in third countries.[244]

The *Lindqvist* case allowed the CJEU to consider whether the protection of personal data on the Internet could encroach on other fundamental rights, such as the freedom of expression, protected by the European Union and the ECHR. According to the CJEU, 1′) fundamental rights have *particular importance* so it is necessary to weigh the freedom of expression (in Mrs. Lindqvist's case, also the religious freedom) against the protection of the private life of the individuals whose data are loaded on the Internet; 2′) it is for the *national authorities* to carry out this weighting by interpreting their national law in a manner consistent with Directive 95/46/EC, as well as by preventing conflicts with fundamental rights protected by the EU legal order or with other general principles of EU law such as the principle of proportionality; 3′) the protection of private life requires the application of effective sanctions which must respect the *principle of proportionality* by taking into account circumstances such as the duration of the breach or the importance of the data disclosed.

The CJEU considered that Directive 95/46/EC did not in itself conflict with the freedom of expression or with other rights and freedoms, reaching the following conclusion: "It is for the national authorities and courts responsible for applying the national legislation implementing Directive 95/46 to ensure a fair balance between the rights and interests in question, including the fundamental rights protected by the Community legal order."

Three core ideas should be highlighted from this judgment, which was a groundbreaking decision issued at a time when the Internet and services like search engines were in full upswing:
1) Any publication of data on the Internet constitutes automatic processing necessarily affecting the right to data protection;
2) Any conflicts that may arise between the protection of personal data and other freedoms and rights should be weighed by the

---

[244] The CJEU held that: 1) given the state of development of the Internet at the time Directive 95/46 was drawn up and the absence of criteria applicable to use of the Internet regarding transfers to third countries, it could not be presumed that the *will of the European legislature* was to include, within the expression "transfer of data to a third country," the loading, by an individual like Mrs. Lindqvist, of data onto an internet page, even if such data were thereby made accessible to persons in third countries; 2) a contrary interpretation would imply that every time that personal data are loaded onto an Internet page, Member States would be required to prevent their dissemination on the Internet whenever it was found that a third country did not provide an appropriate level of protection.

national authorities to prevent the sacrifice of either, taking into account, in accordance with the principle of proportionality, all relevant circumstances;

3) The Directive should not be applied unreasonably (for instance, by assimilating the dissemination of data on the Internet to a transfer of personal data to third countries). A disproportionate interpretation of the Directive could distort its purpose by imposing an unbearable preventive censorship.

2) The interpretation most favorable to a fair balance between fundamental rights, legitimate interests, and principles in conflict on the Internet: *Promusicae* (Case C-275/06, 29 January 2008)

The *Promusicae* case[245] focuses mainly on data protection on the Internet and the resolution of conflicts with other fundamental rights and legitimate interests.

The CJEU advocates reconciling the protection of fundamental rights (data protection and respect for privacy) with the rights to protection of intellectual property and to an effective remedy, in the following terms: 1`) The directives provide the mechanisms which allow for a fair balance between rights and interests by determining in what circumstances and to what extent the processing of personal data is lawful, as well as the safeguards that must be provided; 2´) these mechanisms require the adoption by the Member States of *national provisions* ensuring transposition of those directives and their application by the national authorities; 3´) the directives that affect data protection are *relatively general* in nature, since they are applied to many different situations

---

[245] The *Promusicae* case arose from a question referred for a preliminary ruling by Madrid Commercial Court no. 5 (*Juzgado de lo Mercantil*) in the proceedings between Promusicae, an intellectual property rights management organization (*Productores de Música de España* or Promusicae) and *Telefónica de España* arising from the latter's refusal to disclose to Promusicae personal data relating to use of the Internet by means of connections provided by Telefónica. Promusicae had asked for Telefónica to be ordered to disclose the identities and physical addresses of certain persons whom it provided with Internet access services, whose IP address and date and time of connection were known. According to Promusicae, those persons used a file exchange program (peer-to-peer or P2P) and provided access in shared files of personal computers to musical content, thereby infringing intellectual property rights. It therefore requested such information to bring civil proceedings. Telefónica opposed the application on the grounds that, under Act 34/2002 on information society services and electronic commerce (LSSI), the communication of these data is authorized only in a criminal investigation or for the purpose of safeguarding public security and national defense, not in civil proceedings.

which may arise in any of the Member States; therefore, these directives leave the Member States the necessary *discretion* to define transposition measures which may be adapted to the various possible situations; 4´) when *transposing the directives*, the Member States should rely on an interpretation which allows a *fair balance* to be struck between the various fundamental rights protected by the EU legal order; 5´) it is for the authorities and courts of the Member States: 1´´) to interpret their national in a manner consistent with those directives; and 2´´) to make sure that such interpretation is not in conflict with the fundamental rights or general principles of EU law such as the principle of *proportionality*.

In the *Promusicae* case, the CJEU considered: a) that the relevant directives (2000/31, 2001/29, 2004/48 and 2002/58) *did not specifically require* the Member States to lay down an obligation to communicate personal data in order to ensure effective protection of copyright in the context of civil proceedings; b) that EU law *did require* that the transposition of the directives should achieve a *fair balance* between the various fundamental rights; and c) that national authorities should interpret their national law in a manner which would not be in conflict with those fundamental rights or with other general principles of EU law. The *Promusicae* case dealt with a conflict between the right to protection of personal on the Internet and intellectual property rights. The CJEU avoided a definitive ruling on the prevalence of a fundamental right over the other under EU law. Instead, it referred such assessment to the national authorities in order to seek a balanced solution, in accordance with the principle of proportionality, so that neither of those rights had to be sacrificed.

3) Internet Search engines are not liable unless they play an *active* role not just technical, automatic and passive: *Google France v. Louis Vuitton* (Cases C-236/08 to C-238/08, 23-3-2010)[246]

In *Google France v. Louis Vuitton*, the CJEU addressed the questions referred for a preliminary ruling by the French Court of Cassation (*Cour de Cassation*) in the proceedings between Google and Louis Vuitton, concerning the display on the Internet of advertising links on the basis of keywords corresponding to trade marks.

In 2003, Louis Vuitton became aware that the entry of its trade marks into Google's search engine triggered the display, under the heading "sponsored links," of links to sites offering imitations of Vuitton's

---

[246] Subsequently, the CJEU decided on similar cases following exactly the same approach: 8 July 2010 (Case C-558/08, *Primakabin*); 12 July 2011 (Case C-324/09, *L'Oréal*), 22 September 2011 (Case C-323/09, *Interflora*).

products. Also, Google offered advertisers the possibility of combining Vuitton's trade marks with expressions such as "imitation" and "copy." Vuitton brought proceedings against Google for infringement of its trade marks and, after a number of rulings favorable to Vuitton, the Court of Cassation referred several questions to the CJEU for a preliminary ruling. These questions concerned the liability of Internet search engines offering "referencing services."

The CJEU recalled that the restriction on liability set out in Article 14(1) of Directive 2000/31[247] applied to information society services consisting in the storage of data provided by the recipient of the service. This meant that the provider of such service could not be held liable for the data stored at the request of the recipient, unless it failed to act expeditiously to remove or disable access to those data after gaining knowledge of unlawfulness.

According to the CJEU, search engines that offered internet referencing were "information society service providers," which covered "services which are provided at a distance, by means of electronic equipment for the processing and storage of data, at the individual request of a recipient of services, and normally in return for remuneration." These are exempted from liability when their "activity is of a mere technical, automatic and passive nature, which implies that the information society service provider has neither knowledge of nor control over the information which is transmitted or stored." The service provider may only be exempted from liability if its role is *neutral* in the above sense.

In *Google France v. Louis Vuitton*, Google processed the data entered by advertisers, triggering the display. Google controlled the conditions giving rise to the resulting display of the ads, determining the order of

---

[247] Article 14 of Directive 2000/31: "Hosting 1. Where an information society service is provided that consists of the storage of information provided by a recipient of the service, Member States shall ensure that the service provider is not liable for the information stored at the request of a recipient of the service, on condition that: (a) the provider does not have actual knowledge of illegal activity or information and, as regards claims for damages, is not aware of facts or circumstances from which the illegal activity or information is apparent; or (b) the provider, upon obtaining such knowledge or awareness, acts expeditiously to remove or to disable access to the information. 2. Paragraph 1 shall not apply when the recipient of the service is acting under the authority or the control of the provider. 3. This Article shall not affect the possibility for a court or administrative authority, in accordance with Member States' legal systems, of requiring the service provider to terminate or prevent an infringement, nor does it affect the possibility for Member States of establishing procedures governing the removal or disabling of access to information."

160

display according to the price paid by the advertisers. However, the CJEU did not hold Google liable by reason of the control over the data or the remunerated nature of the service, nor based on the concordance between the keyword selected and the search term entered by an internet user: Google's liability arose from the drafting of the commercial message that accompanied the advertising link or from the selection of keywords. It is for the national judge to assess in each case whether the foregoing circumstances are fulfilled.

Finally, the CJEU concluded that Google could be held liable for the activity of its search engine (under Article 14 of Directive 2000/31) only when it played an "active role of such a kind as to give it knowledge of, or control over, the data stored." Otherwise, liability for the data stored at the request of an advertiser could only arise if, upon becoming aware of such unlawfulness, it failed to act expeditiously to remove o to disable access to the information.

4) Violations of fundamental rights on the Internet are to be assessed by the courts of the Member State where the victim has his/her "center of interests": *Date Advertising v. Olivier and Martínez* (Case C-509/09 and C-161/10, 25 October 2011)

The case of *Date Advertising v. Olivier and Martínez* is of great interest because it addresses the complex issue of the national courts competent to hear disputes concerning the Internet. In this case, the references for a preliminary ruling concerned Regulation 44/2001 on jurisdiction and Directive 2000/31 on electronic commerce, in the proceedings between the company eDate Advertising and Olivier and Robert Martínez, on the one hand, and MGN Limited, on the other hand, in respect of the civil liability arising from the publication of personal data and photographs on the Internet.[248]

This case raised the question of whether the German courts had jurisdiction over a dispute in which a citizen domiciled in Germany had requested the removal of personal information from an Austrian

---

[248] In 1993, two brothers domiciled in Germany had been sentenced to life imprisonment for the murder of an actor. In 2008, they were released on parole. eDate Advertising, a company established in Austria, operated an internet portal which informed on the names and the appeal filed against their conviction with the German Federal Constitutional Court. The company removed the information from its website. One of the brothers brought an action before the German courts against eDate Advertising, requesting that it should desist from reporting such information. The company challenged the jurisdiction of the German courts, but they granted the application at each successive level.

company's website. If so, then it had to be determined whether German or Austrian law was applicable.

This special jurisdiction rule -an exception to the principle of the defendant's domicile as the general ground for jurisdiction- is based on a close connecting factor between the dispute and the courts of the place where the damage occurs, seeking a sound administration of justice. The CJEU recalled that, on *Shevill* (Case C-68/93, 7 March 1995), the attribution of jurisdiction to the courts of "the place where the harmful event occurred" was particularly helpful in relation to the evidence and the conduct of the proceedings. In such case, the CJEU had held that defamation by means of a newspaper article distributed in several Contracting States entitled the victim to bring an action for damages against the publisher (1) either before the courts of the Contracting State where the publisher was established; or (2) before the courts of each Contracting State in which the publication had been distributed and where the victim claimed to have suffered injury to his/her reputation.

The CJEU was well aware of the difficulties of applying the *Shevill* criteria (place of the harm) to the Internet: unlike for print media, publication of content on a website intends to ensure its ubiquity, so that it may be consulted instantly by an unlimited number of users worldwide. Therefore, the jurisdiction criterion relating to distribution is of little use for content placed online, where the scope of the distribution "is in principle universal." Paradoxically, the difficulties in applying the criterion of "the place where the harmful event occurred" contrast with the "serious nature of the harm" which may be suffered by the holder of a personality right.

The CJEU adapted the rule of jurisdiction on the basis of two premises:

1') Victims of personality rights violations on the Internet should be entitled to bring an action in one forum in respect of *all* the damage caused;

2') The huge potential impact that content placed online can have on the *personality rights* of an individual "might best be assessed by the court of the place where the alleged victim has his *center of interests*," thereby pursuing a double objective: 1) a sound administration of justice; 2) the predictability of the rules governing jurisdiction with regard to publishers of harmful or prejudicial content on the Internet;

3') The *center of interests* of a person corresponds in general to his/her habitual residence.

According to the interpretation most favorable to the rights of the injured party, the CJEU concluded that, in the event of an alleged infringement of personality rights by means of content placed online on an internet website, the person who has suffered the right may claim compensation for all the damage caused: 1) before the courts of the State in which the publisher is established; 2) before the courts of the State where such person's center of interests is based; or 3) before the courts of each State where the content published online has been accessible, if compensation for all the damage is not sought.

5) Jurisdiction over Internet search engines: *Wintersteiger* (Case C-523/10, 19 April 2012)

The *Wintersteiger* case dealt with the jurisdiction over a dispute between Wintersteiger (an Austrian company) and Products 4U Sondermaschinenbau (a German Company): the former applied to prevent the latter from using the Austrian trade mark Wintersteiger as a keyword on the website of a paid referencing service provider (Internet search engine).

The CJEU recalled that, according to its own case law laid down in *eDate Advertising*, in the event of an alleged infringement of personality rights, the party injured by the publication of content on a website may bring an action before the courts of the State in which the *center of his/her interests* is based.

However, in the *Wintersteiger* case, the CJEU considered that such criterion relating to the "center of interests" could not apply to the determination of jurisdiction in respect of infringements of intellectual property rights, for the following reasons:

1) Unlike the infringement (and protection) of personality rights, which extends to all Member States, the protection of national trade marks is limited to the territory of the Member State in which they are registered. The courts of such Member State are best suited to assess whether the protected trade mark has been infringed. Consequently, the CJEU considered them competent to decide on the dispute caused by the use by an advertiser of a keyword identical to that trade mark *on a search engine website operating under a country-specific* top-level domain of another Member State.

2) The territorial limitation of the protection of a national mark is not such as to exclude the international jurisdiction of courts other than the courts of the Member State. The display on a search engine of an advertisement using a keyword identical to that trade mark does not give rise, in itself, to the infringement. The violation results from the

activation by the advertiser of the technical process displaying, according to pre-defined parameters, the advertisement: it is the advertiser choosing a keyword identical to the trade mark who uses it in the course of trade. Therefore, it is the *advertiser* and not the *search engine* (which limits itself to conveying the commercial communication) who gives rise to the infringement of rights (of the trade mark).

3) It is true that the technical display process is ultimately activated on a server of the search engine, but its location is uncertain, which defeats the objective of foreseeability of jurisdiction rules: "since it is a definite and identifiable place, both for the applicant and for the defendant, and is therefore likely to facilitate the taking of evidence and the conduct of the proceedings, it must be held that the place of establishment of the advertiser is the place where the activation of the display process is decided."

The CJEU concluded that this type of disputes -where an advertiser used a keyword identical to a trade mark on a country-specific top-level Internet search engine of another State- could be brought before either the courts of the Member State in which the trade mark is registered or the courts of the Member State of the place of establishment of the advertiser.

3.- QUESTION REFERRED BY THE SPANISH NATIONAL HIGH COURT TO THE CJEU FOR A PRELIMINARY RULING (C-131/12[249])

On 2 March 2012,[250] the first section of the administrative chamber of Spain's National High Court (AN) referred several questions to the CJEU for a preliminary ruling. These questions concerned the appeals filed by Google against the AEPD's resolutions upholding the rights of citizens to object and to erasure against Google.

---

[249]http://curia.europa.eu/juris/document/document.jsf?docid=123131&mode=req &pageIndex=1&dir=&occ=first&part=1&text=cancelacion%2Bde%2Bdatos%2B en%2Binternet&doclang=ES&cid=373248

[250] On 17 January 2012, the AN notified the parties of the issues it intended to refer for a preliminary ruling: 1′) applicability to the case of Directives 95/46/EC and/or 2000/31/EC; 2′) Consideration of Google's activity as provider of third parties' content as falling within the concept of "processing of data" under Article 2(b) of Directive 95/46. If so, Google's obligations with regard to the rights to object and to erasure referred to in Articles 12(b) and 14(a) of the Directive, and appellant's rights arising from Article 14(a) in relation to Article 7(e) and (f) of Directive 95/46; 3′) powers of the AEPD, under Article 28(3) of Directive 95/46 and Article 13(1)(e) of Directive 2000/31 to directly require Google to erase or block data even if such information is lawfully kept on the source website.

As the AN submitted, this issue affected the interpretative scope of Directive 95/46/EC for all EU Member States. It justified the referral to the CJEU on the basis of "difficulties in interpretation and implementation of Directive 95/46/EC with respect to technologies developed after its publication, and the need for a uniform interpretation thereof." The preliminary ruling of the CJEU constituted a significant case law precedent to determine the scope of protection of the right to data protection on the Internet.

3.1.- The case of an administrative announcement of an auction resulting from a seizure published in *La Vanguardia*: ¿a bad *leading case*?

Among the hundred or so cases the AN could have referred to the CJEU for a preliminary ruling, it chose Google's appeal against Resolution 1680/2010 of the AEPD, of 30 July 2010 (TD/650/2010).

On 19 January 1998, the print edition of *La Vanguardia* published the announcement of a real estate auction placed by the Barcelona provincial office of the Social Security Treasury (an administrative body under the Secretary of State for Social Security of the Ministry of Labor and Social Affairs), including personal data of Mario Costeja and his wife (postal address and a debt of 8.5 million pesetas -the former Spanish currency).

Between 1998 and 2010, Mario Costeja had paid his debt, he had divorced, but... "according to Google, am I still a debtor and married?."[251] Fifteen years later, the print edition of *La Vanguardia* had been digitized and, when his name and surnames were entered into Google, the seizure for the default of a small business appeared again as the digitized announcement of the auction was indexed by the search engine.

On 5 March 2010, Costeja exercised his right to object against Google Spain and Google Inc., as well as against *La Vanguardia* for the publication of the announcement of the auction upon the request of the Barcelona provincial office of the Social Security Treasury. The newspaper opposed the application on the grounds that it was not journalistic information in the strict sense, given that the publication had been ordered by the Ministry of Labor and Social Affairs.

AEPD's Resolution 1680/2010 contained two distinct decisions: a') it rejected the claim against *La Vanguardia*, considering that the publication

---

[251] Interview published in *El País*, 22 March 2013.

of information about these real estate auctions is lawful, since the widest possible publicity seeks the greatest participation of bidders; b') it upheld the right to object against Google Spain and Google Inc., ordering them to adopt any measures necessary to remove the data from their index and to prevent further access.

Resolution 1680/2010 has some particularities. That is why referring precisely this resolution for a preliminary ruling might be questionable if the intention was for the CJEU to clarify the scope of the right to be forgotten in the European system of data protection. It might have been better to choose any of the many resolutions with identical legal grounds relating to the right to be forgotten and online media.

This case does not reflect a direct conflict between the right to be forgotten and the freedom of information. Although the information is conveyed through a newspaper, the disputed personal data are not a piece of news produced by the media. The publication of these personal data does not seek to shape a free public opinion in a democratic society. Rather, its purpose is merely to provide the widest possible dissemination of a real estate auction. Consequently, the day after the auction, the dissemination of this information will be meaningless. In this regard, the choice of this case might seem a good one, since there is no risk of news censorship (given that the information in question is not of such nature). Also, this case shows the wide variety of situations that can be covered by the right to be forgotten against Internet search engines when there is no legal or constitutional mandate requiring the dissemination of the information.

Nevertheless, Resolution 1680/2010 rejected the application against *La Vanguardia* considering that the publication was justified by the legal obligation to ensure maximum dissemination of the auctions, so that they could have the best possible outcome. It seems difficult to refute that the dissemination objective no longer exists once the auction is held. After that moment, the announcement does not serve any purpose and it ceases to be required by any legal or constitutional provision. An administrative decision notified through an official gazette could be covered by the legal obligation to ensure the intangibility of its content -even after the legal effects of the notification are fulfilled. However, this does not apply to an administrative announcement disseminated through a newspaper. There should have been no obstacle to withdrawing it from the digitized version of the newspaper and to blocking its indexing by search engines.[252]

---

[252] In line with the recommendations given by the AEPD to online media, which *La Vanguardia* itself had followed in other occasions by voluntarily de-indexing true journalistic information (Resolution no. 347/2011, of 23 February 2011).

Therefore, there are reasonable doubts as to the choice of this *leading case* to exemplify before the CJEU the issues raised in Spain with regard to the right to be forgotten: are Internet search engines the only ones responsible for compliance with the right to be forgotten, by preventing the indexing of web pages, but without there being a similar obligation upon the websites? This is not the approach followed by dozens of resolutions issued by the AEPD over more than five years.

3.2.- The questions referred by the Spanish National High Court (*Audiencia Nacional*): Decision of 27 February 2013

It should be noted that, by referring the questions for a preliminary ruling, the AN showed that it had a complete, comprehensive and accurate knowledge of the legal issues raised by the appeals filed by Google against the AEPD's resolutions. According to these resolutions, Internet search engines were subject to data protection regulations, their activities amounted to data processing for which they were liable, and they were required to ensure compliance with the right to erasure and to object. That extensive knowledge came from the large number of appeals filed since 2008, as well as from an oral hearing held on 19 January 2011 which focused on six issues:

1) The absence of specific legislation on data protection in Internet search engines. The AN verified that there was no specific legislation governing the activity of Internet search engines. Hence, this issue had to be analyzed in the light of Directive 95/46/EC. It had been adopted well before the expansion of the Internet and the indiscriminate use of search engines, but many subsequent regulations referred to this Directive.[253]

2) The territorial application of Directive 95/46/EC and the Spanish data protection legislation to Internet search engines: is Google Spain an "establishment" of Google Inc. in Spain? The AN submitted its doubts as to the interpretation of Article 4(1)(a) of Directive 95/46/EC regarding the application of the Directive to the processing of personal data carried out in the context of the activities of an establishment of the controller on the territory of the Member State. The AN intended to determine whether

---

[253] That was the case of Directive 2000/31, which limited the liability of information society services in certain cases related to Internet search engines – when their activity was "of a mere technical, automatic and passive nature," and the service provider had "neither knowledge of nor control over the information which is transmitted or stored," which did not prevent the competent authorities from requiring the removal of data in breach of certain principles (for instance, human dignity) when these service providers became aware of such circumstance (Articles 8 and 17 LSSI).

both Google Inc. and Google Spain fell within that concept: *must it be considered that an "establishment," within the meaning of Article 4(1)(a) of [the Directive], exists when any one or more of the following circumstances arise: when the undertaking providing the search engine sets up in a Member State an office or subsidiary for the purpose of promoting and selling advertising space on the search engine, which orientates its activity towards the inhabitants of that State; or when the parent company designates a subsidiary located in that Member State as its representative and controller for two specific filing systems which relate to the data of customers who have contracted for advertising with that undertaking; or when the office or subsidiary established in a Member State forwards to the parent company, located outside the European Union, requests and requirements addressed to it both by data subjects and by the authorities with responsibility for ensuring observation of the right to data protection, even where such collaboration is engaged in voluntarily?*

The AN considered it proven that: 1´) Google's search engine -with global reach and several local versions geographically adapted- was managed by Google Inc. (parent company of the group with registered office in California); 2´) the search engine indexes web pages from all over the world and stores them temporarily on unknown servers for business reasons; 3) Google Spain, a subsidiary, acts as commercial representative for the advertising functions of the search engine, but it does not carry out in Spain any activities directly linked to the indexing or storage of information or data contained in third parties' web pages.

Based on these elements, the AN could have clearly concluded that Google Spain was not responsible for the search engine. However, the AN explored a new argument: "promotional and sales activities regarding these advertising spaces are an integral part of Google's business, and they can be considered closely linked to the activity of its search engine in Spain, since the advertisements are displayed alongside the search results and are normally related to the search criteria entered by the user."[254]

3) The territorial application of Directive 95/46/EC and of the Spanish data protection legislation to Internet search engines: use of "equipment"

---

[254] Of course, AN's doubts were fed by the fact that Google Spain represented Google Inc. before the AEPD, that it forwarded to the parent company the requests and requirements addressed to it, that its designated address was that of the law firm shared by both of them, and that it was designated as the controller for filing systems which relate to the data of customers who have contracted for advertising.

in Spain? Regardless of the consideration of Google Spain as "establishment," Article 4(1)(c) of the Directive provides for the application of European and national legislation when the controller makes use of equipment, automated or otherwise, situated on the territory of the said Member State.

The AN noted that the Directive contained no definition of the term "equipment." However, recital 20 made it clear that the processing of data carried out by controllers established in a third country (USA) must not stand in the way of the protection of individuals. In these cases, the processing should be governed by the law of the Member State in which the means or equipment used are located, and there should be guarantees to ensure that the rights and obligations provided for in the Directive are respected in practice.

The AN pointed to the difficulty of identifying the equipment used by search engines to provide their services, and of determining when they are on Spanish territory. To overcome this difficulty, the AN distinguished between two activities that could be potentially considered "equipment" and referred the following question to the CJEU: *1') is there "use of equipment situated on the territory of that Member State" when a search engine uses crawlers or robots to locate and index information contained in web pages located on servers in that Member State or when it uses a domain name pertaining to a Member State and arranges for searches and the results thereof to be based on the language of that Member State?; 2') is it possible to regard as a "use of equipment" the temporary storage of the information indexed by internet search engines?*

If the answer to the first question is affirmative, Internet search engines would be required to comply with the laws and regulations of all countries to which they had access, and to provide the most effective protection of individual rights.

However, an affirmative answer to the second question would conflict with Google's refusal to provide information on the location of the servers that temporarily store the indexed information, thus rendering the data protection legislation ineffective and useless. The AN added the following question: *can it be considered that that connecting factor is present when the undertaking refuses to disclose the place where it stores those indexes, invoking reasons of competition?* Either the undertaking is required to specify the location of the data centers and servers, or, otherwise, other connecting factors are needed, such as the origin of the web or the complaints made by citizens in a Member State. Finally, the AN asked the CJEU about "one of the main battlegrounds for the struggle to establish the rule of law in the Information Society":[255] jurisdiction over Internet activities.

4) The effectiveness of the protection of the rights enshrined in Article 8 of the Charter of Fundamental Rights of the European Union (CFREU). The AN's doubts on Internet search engines (Google) and the European and Spanish data protection legislation was not limited to the interpretation of Directive 9/46/EC.

The AN boldly referred to the *constitutional nature* of the CFREU. It highlighted that Internet search engines, even when managed from a third State without establishment or equipment in a Member State, could undermine fundamental rights of European citizens. The Data Protection Directive had been adopted well before Internet search engines had reached their current expansion. The rules on the territorial applicability of the Directive could give rise to impunity in an extraordinarily complex technological field. Furthermore, Article 6 of the Treaty on European Union (TEU) had granted constitutional status to the fundamental right to data protection (Article 8 CFREU) and called for an interpretation of the EU legal system that would effectively guarantee it.

The rules on the territorial applicability of Directive 95/46/EC should be interpreted in the manner most favorable to the protection of the fundamental right to data protection. Consequently, it should prevent strategic business decisions in a technologically globalized world from infringing the relevant guarantees of these rights. The AN's decision of 27 February of 2013 added that: "an effective protection of this fundamental right cannot depend on the place where the undertaking decides to have its technical equipment. The use of non-material technical devices, which enables the provision of services from a different territory and, in many cases, without any equipment on the territory where the services are addressed, makes it more difficult to effectively protect personality rights against potential violations in cyberspace, especially regarding data protection."[256] The AN referred the following question to the CJEU: *must the Directive be applied, in the light of Article 8 of the [Charter], in the Member State where the center of gravity of the conflict is located and more effective protection of the rights of European Union citizens is possible?* Underlying this question was the clear position adopted by the AN with respect to the applicability of the Spanish

---

[255] JOEL REIDEMBERG: "Technology and Internet Jurisdiction…," p. 1951.
[256] On the difficulties to file individual complaints for violations of rights arising from the online world, see LISA COLLINGWOOD: "Privacy in Cyberworld: Why Lock the Gate After the Horse Has Bolted?," *European Journal of Law and Technology*, vol. 3-1, 2012, pp. 1-11.

---

legislation to Internet search engines: "we are faced with a case of indexing of data from web pages hosted in Spain, regarding information published in Spain, under Spanish legislation, concerning a Spanish citizen and which may adversely affect his personal and social environment in Spain (center of interests). In these circumstances, requiring the affected party to exercise his right to data protection in the USA (because it is where the controller has its technical means) would place the affected party in a situation of particular vulnerability and would prevent or hamper the effective protection of such right. This, in turn, could be incompatible with the object and purpose of the Directive and, especially, with the effective protection of a fundamental right enshrined in the European Charter of Fundamental Rights."

5) The activity of search engines as "processing" of data and the position of Google as "controller" before the national authority

In order to apply the Spanish and European data protection legislation, and to determine the responsibilities and obligations, it was essential to know whether the activity of Internet search engines constituted processing of data in the sense of Article 2(b) of Directive 95/46/EC. The AN defined such activity carried out by search engines: "locating information published or included on the net by third parties, indexing it automatically, storing it temporarily and finally making it available to internet users according to a particular order of preference." The AN asked the following to the CJEU: *must an activity like the one described be interpreted as falling within the concept of "processing of data" used in Article 2(b) of the Directive? Must Article 2(d) of the Directive be interpreted as meaning that the undertaking managing the "Google" search engine is to be regarded as the "controller" of the personal data contained in the web pages that it indexes?*

The AN expressed doubts as to whether the search engine should be considered "controller" because of its activity of indexing information already published online with personal data, for two reasons: the fact that the information was gathered automatically and the lack of effective control over its correctness and accuracy. The AN acknowledged that the obligations imposed by the data protection legislation upon controllers would be hardly compatible with the activity of search engines. However, it admitted that the protection of the relevant rights (to rectification, erasure, blocking and to object) could be subject to national legislation.

According to the AN, the main difficulty of holding the search engines liable (as "controllers") was the double set of responsibilities: on the one hand, the owners of the web could remove data from the automatic indexes of search engines by preventing indexing or storage of copies;

and, on the other hand, the search engines locate, store and disseminate information published on the Internet and index it according to a particular order. Consequently, the AN referred the following question: *may the AEPD, protecting the rights embodied in Articles 12(b) and 14(a) of Directive 95/46/EC, directly impose on the search engine of the "Google" undertaking a requirement that it withdraw from its indexes an item of information published by third parties, without addressing itself in advance or simultaneously to the owner of the web page on which that information is located? Would the obligation of search engines to protect those rights be excluded when the information that contains the personal data has been lawfully published by third parties and is kept on the web page from which it originates?*

The AN clearly identified the problems of holding the search engines directly (instead of subsidiarily) responsible for complying with the right to erasure or to object to indexing of personal data: only the owner of the web has knowledge and control over the lawfulness or accuracy of the information, since no one else has the technological means to prevent indexing; prevalence of other rights (to information or freedom of expression) or necessary compliance with legal obligations; proportionality in the processing of data; infringement of third party rights arising from erasure; limited effectiveness of keeping the information on the originating web page or its replication on other websites; removal of all data regarding the data subject (even those he/she would like to keep) and any coinciding third parties.

In view of all these difficulties and faced with the undeniable risks arising from the activity of Internet search engines, the AN suggested an approach that gave priority to the principle of interpretation most favorable to the right to data protection: "there is an unquestionable need to effectively protect the rights of the data subject. It is very easy to replicate the information on other web pages, to change the name and location of the page replicating the same information, and it is difficult to act against websites hosted on other States. All this can render ineffective or excessively burdensome the protection of the data subject if he/she has to go principally against all the websites containing such information. Holding the search engine directly responsible has the advantage that it prevents, or at least significantly hampers, the location and widespread dissemination of the relevant data. It also neutralizes the risks associated to the access that search engines provide to all the data of an individual, even creating personal profiles. Also, it should not be forgotten that it is the data subject who must determine the scope of the protection of his/her rights in accordance with the applicable legislation" (AN, 27 February 2013).

6) The rights to erasure, blocking and to object as part of the right to be forgotten. The AN entered headlong into the debate about the recognition of the right to be forgotten on the Internet, and referred the following question to the CJEU: *must it be considered that the rights to erasure and blocking of data, provided for in Article 12(b), and the right to object, provided for by Article 14(a), of Directive 95/46/EC, extend to enabling the data subject to address himself to search engines in order to prevent indexing of the information relating to him personally, published on third parties' web pages, invoking his wish that such information should not be known to internet users when he considers that it might be prejudicial to him or he wishes it to be consigned to oblivion, even though the information in question has been lawfully published by third parties?*

AN's question refers strictly to the interpretation of Directive 95/46/EC. In particular, to the scope of protection of the rights to erasure, blocking and to object with respect to data crawled by Internet search engines. The AN invokes to possible reasons that could trigger the exercise of these rights: the wish to prevent access to certain information by Internet users when it might be prejudicial, and the wish that it be forgotten, even it was lawfully published by third parties. Ultimately, the AN pointed, on the one hand, to the principle of individual consent (wish to prevent knowledge), and, on the other, to the less well settled right to be forgotten.

With almost 130 cases pending resolution, the AN had perfectly identified the relevant legal and social debates underlying the dispute between Google and the AEPD. The classical categories of the right to data protection were hardly useful: "The Internet transcends geographical boundaries and temporal limits. Search engines multiply this effect by providing global dissemination and making it possible to locate the information. This entails significant risks for an adequate protection of personal data of citizens, since it is now easy to search all the information available online about a person. Chances are thus increased that any user may have access to personal data and information that were previously difficult to locate, thereby enabling the creation of personal profiles and "histories" of the life and activities, or economic and professional trajectories. This risk does not only affect people subject to public exposure or media coverage, but any citizen. A huge amount of personal data and information are now publicly available on the Internet, referring to everyday aspects of their lives, and not necessarily linked to events of public or general interest" (27 February 2013).

The classic approach of Directive 95/46/EC, pursuant to which the data must be adequate, relevant and not excessive in relation to the purposes for which they are processed, is undermined by the effect of Internet search engines. They bring the past to the present and foster an accumulation of data that can hardly be considered adequate, relevant and not excessive. As the AN points out, the right to be forgotten not only refers to the past, but also to the future: 1′) "Before the emergence of these new technologies, the dissemination of such information was limited geographically and temporally, and it fell into oblivion after some time. Now, this information can be easily located and globally disseminated, and it is never forgotten because it stays on the web forever. This poses an added risk, potentially fatal, for the protection of personal data. Some information, even if originally accurate and lawfully published, may become outdated by subsequent events. However, every time the name of a person is entered into a search engine, that piece of information is retrieved and linked to that person;" 2′) "Even when the information is recent, the citizens, aware that any information published online will be available throughout their whole life, may wish that it not be disseminated, haunting them and their descendants." Furthermore, human dignity can be affected: "current technological equipment, particularly search engines, subject the affected parties to constant public exposure about a fact or an event, even if it is true, of which he/she might not want to be constantly reminded, and whose knowledge might cause social or professional damage."

The purpose of traditional data protection rights (to erasure, blocking and to object) is to protect the quality of personal data and the individual right to consent to their processing. However, they are hardly effective when it comes to prevent search engines from indexing lawful and accurate personal information considered prejudicial by the data subject.

The AN encouraged the CJEU to update its catalogue of rights, based on the existing EU legal system, and to acknowledge a new right to be forgotten. Nevertheless, the AN was not oblivious to the difficulties hampering a further recognition of this right to be forgotten: 1') any measures imposed on search engines to protect this right must be necessary, adequate, proportional and effective, taking into account the function of search engines in today's society and the rights and freedoms of the owners of websites and other Internet users; 2') the right of every person to erasure or to object to any information he/she does not want to be known or disseminated on the Internet would give rise to a risk of "filtering" or "censorship," so that only "beneficial information" would be published. This, in turn, would undermine the credibility and objectivity of Internet search results.

4.- THE OPINION OF THE ADVOCATE GENERAL OF THE CJEU (25.6.13) [257]: *REJECTION OF THE RIGHT TO BE FORGOTTEN IN THE CURRENT EU LEGAL SYSTEM*

On 25 June 2013, Niilo Jääskinen, Advocate General of the CJEU, delivered its Opinion on the questions referred by the Spanish AN for a preliminary ruling in Case C-131/12, Google Spain S.L. and Google Inc. v. *Agencia Española de Protección de Datos* (AEPD) and Mario Costeja González.

4.1.- A *preliminary assumption*: the development of the Internet requires reducing the scope of protection of the right to data protection

In his *introductory remarks*, the Advocate General (AG) was based on an assumption that would totally prejudged the rest of his considerations: the extraordinary relevance of the Internet in today's society is incompatible with an interpretation of current European data protection law according to its own terms. This legislation must therefore be interpreted in a limited manner, taking into account the transformation of the information and knowledge society operated by the Internet.

The AG reflects the huge impact of the Internet on today's society, and particularly regarding the dissemination of personal information: "the internet [is] a comprehensive global stock of information which is universally accessible and searchable;"[258] "the amount of digitalized content available online has exploded. It can be easily accessed, consulted and disseminated through social media, as well as downloaded to various devices, such as tablet computers, smartphones and laptop computers;"[259] "the internet magnifies and facilitates in an unprecedented manner the dissemination of information... uploading of material on to the internet enables mass access to information which earlier could perhaps only be found after painstaking searches, and at limited physical locations. Universal access to information on the internet is possible everywhere"[260]; "many, if not most, websites and files that are accessible through them include personal data, such as names of living natural persons."[261]

---

[257] http://curia.europa.eu/juris/document/document.jsf?text=&docid=138782&pageIndex=0&doclang=ES&mode=lst&dir=&occ=first&part=1&cid=1094085
[258] Paragraph 27.
[259] Paragraph 27.
[260] Paragraph 28.
[261] Paragraph 30.

However, the above remarks did not lead the AG to warn about the potential risks for some fundamental rights (such as privacy or data protection). Quite the opposite: the AG raises all type of concerns about the dangers for Internet users stemming from an allegedly undesirable application of the existing data protection legislation. In other words, Internet users may become the victims of an exaggerated application of such legislation to the current reality of the Internet.

The AG describes situations in which this restrictive approach could be reasonable: "anyone today reading a newspaper on a tablet computer or following social media on a smartphone appears to be engaged in processing of personal data with automatic means, and could potentially fall within the scope of application of the Directive to the extent this takes place outside his purely private capacity."[262] Nevertheless, it should be noted that the case brought before the CJEU does not refer to "purely personal or household" activities on the Internet, but to the actual impact of the Internet's flagship service (search engine), managed by the all-powerful leading company in the industry (Google), with regard to the dissemination of personal data of millions of private users.

To justify this *reversion* of the current European system of guarantees for personal data laid down by Directive 95/46/EC, the Advocate General invokes a purported intention to the contrary of the 1995 European legislature. The main argument is that, at that time, no one could have foreseen the extraordinary potential and effect of the Internet on the future information society: "In 1995, generalized access to the internet was a new phenomenon."[263] According to the AG, if the European legislature *had known*, Directive 95/46/EC would have never established a system of guarantees for data protection fully applicable to the Internet.
The remarks of the Advocate General reflect *clear mistrust* of the data protection legislation in force as approved by the European legislature and interpreted by the CJEU: "At the time when the Directive was adopted in 1995, it was given a wide scope of application *ratione materiae*;"[264] "the potential scope of application of the Directive in the modern world has become be surprisingly wide;"[265] "the broad definitions of personal data, processing of personal data and controller are likely to cover an unprecedent[ed]ly wide range of new factual situations due to technological development;"[266] "the wide interpretation given by the Court to the fundamental right to private life in a data protection context

---

[262] Paragraph 29.
[263] Paragraph 27.
[264] Paragraph 26.
[265] Paragraph 29.
[266] Paragraph 30.

seems to expose any human communication by electronic means to the scrutiny by reference to this right."[267]

The *wide scope* of the European system of guarantees for data protection (its regulatory provisions and the interpretation made by the CJEU) *is what it is*, regardless of the AG's preconception. It reflects a clear purpose of EU legislation and responds to the need to adapt to technological developments (the Internet being the most important expression) of which it was and is fully aware.

In fact, when it came to reviewing the European framework for data protection, 2012 regulatory initiatives (GDPR proposal) included a wide array of guarantees addressed to the Internet. In particular, they enshrined the right to be forgotten.

Basing the arguments for the inapplicability/restriction of the scope of the current data protection legislation on the alleged unawareness of the European legislature in 1995 would only make sense if it had been inactive over the last two decades. However, that is far from true: 1) many regulations have been adopted in the field of electronic communications with the general purpose of ensuring the right to data protection under Directive 95/46/EC; 2) Article 29 Working Party (Art. 29 WP) has carried out an intense and constant effort regarding the interpretation/application of Directive 95/46/EC to the Internet (search engines, social networks, etc.). Paradoxically, the AG himself acknowledges that the opinions adopted by Art. 29 WP are "very helpful" in this "complex area where law and new technology meet."[268]

The AG's insists on denying the last two decades, in which the European legislature has deliberately attempted to subject the Internet to data protection regulations. Perhaps most shocking in that effort is how unimportant the fundamental right to data protection, enshrined in Article 8 CFREU, is to him.

Indeed, the scarce references in the AG's Opinion to Article 8 CFREU are summarized in his statement that "being a restatement of the European Union and Council of Europe *acquis* in this field, [it] emphasizes the importance of protection of personal data, but it does not as such add any significant new elements to the interpretation of the Directive."[269]

---

[267] Paragraph 29.
[268] Paragraph 31.
[269] Paragraph 113.

The Advocate General considers Article 8 CFREU as a *new element of no significance*. However, it is enshrined as a fundamental right and it is part of the primary law of the Union with the same legal value as the founding Treaties. This reflects an unambiguous and conscious commitment by the European institutions to protect that right.[270] Certainly, this constitutional relevance is influenced by the impact and risks stemming from new technologies and the Internet with regard to the protection of personal data.

The Advocate General favors a *moderate approach*, based on the *principle of proportionality*, "in order to avoid unreasonable and excessive legal consequences"[271] in interpreting the Directive, and to achieve "a correct, reasonable and proportionate balance"[272] between: 1′) the protection of personal data; 2′) the coherent interpretation of the objectives of the information society; and 3′) legitimate interests of economic operators and Internet users.

Unfortunately, neither the assumption on which his preliminary remarks are based (the need to limit the scope of protection of data protection legislation to prevent hampering the development of the Internet) nor the outcome of his reasoning lead to the conclusion that the Advocate General strikes a *moderate, reasonable and proportionate* balance.

The proportionality principle seems only an excuse for the AG to subordinate the fundamental right to data protection to the interests of the information society and of economic operators.

The AG breached the interpretative function of the principle of proportionality, which requires weighing the rights and interests at stake assessing whether the intended purposes could be achieved with less restrictive means. The AG rejected all the arguments submitted by the AEPD and advised the CJEU against taking into account the particular circumstances of each case. The AG's stance prevented a coherent application of the principle of proportionality and moved away from a moderate approach purportedly aimed at avoiding unreasonable or excessive consequences.

---

[270] Article 8 CFREU, originally adopted in 2000 in Nice, was finally recognized with a legal-constitutional status in Lisbon in 2007, and acquired full legal force since 2009.
[271] Paragraph 30.
[272] Paragraph 31.

4.2.- Application of national legislation to search engines with establishments involved in selling targeted advertising to inhabitants of that Member State

The Advocate General takes a qualitative leap in interpreting the provisions of the Directive regarding the application of national legislation. He reviews the legal criteria that could be useless, under a literal reading, for the new phenomenon of the Internet and the role played, among others, by search engines.

The AG acknowledges that the references in the Directive to "establishment" or "equipment" (Article 4(1)) were included before the large-scale provision of online services on the Internet. Therefore, "its wording is not consistent and is incomplete," and it "is not very helpful."[273] This, in turn, presents complex interpretative challenges.[274]

In this regard, the AG offers a new approach by inviting the CJEU to address the territorial application of data protection legislation from the perspective of the business model of Internet search engines and its basic indicators: advertising as the source of income and the economic *raison d'être*, and the presence of the entity in charge of advertising -linked to the Internet search engine- on national markets. The business model of Internet search engines is relevant when the processing of data is linked to the sale of targeted advertising to the residents of a Member State. This criterion is clearly influenced by: 1') the position adopted by Opinion 8/2010 of the Article 29 WP; 2') the GDPR Proposal, which provided for its application to the processing of data of EU residents by a controller not established in the Union where the processing activities are related to "the offering of goods or services to such data subjects;" 3') recent EU case law.

The AG concludes that *the subsidiaries established by Google in many Member States clearly constitute establishments* (within the meaning of Article 4(1)(a) of the Directive): Google has also registered national domains, which proves that the activity of the search engine takes national diversification into account in the display of the search results. The AG states that: "an economic operator must be considered as a single

---

[273] Paragraph 63.
[274] Google is a prime example of these difficulties: registered office in California; subsidiaries in various EU Member States coordinated by its Irish subsidiary; data centers in Belgium and Finland; lack of information on the exact geographical location of its functions; subsidiaries that allegedly do not process data and which act as commercial representatives for advertising functions; several establishments on EU territory.

unit."[275] As with national subsidiaries selling advertising, "processing of personal data takes place within the context of a controller's establishment if that establishment acts as the bridge for the referencing service to the advertising market of that Member State, even if the technical data processing operations are situated in other Member States or third countries."[276]

Ultimately, there is an "establishment" when the undertaking providing the search engine sets up in a Member State an office or subsidiary for the purpose of promoting and selling advertising space to the residents of that State.

The AG goes beyond the literal wording of Article 4(1) of Directive 95/46/EC to extend the scope of national legislation. For that purpose, he puts forward an *economistic interpretation* that refers to the impact of the "business model" of search engines. By doing so, he rejects a *protective interpretation* of the fundamental right to data protection based on new Article 8 CFREU to ensure the *effective legal consideration* of such right against search engines.

This case raised the question as to whether Article 8 CFREU required the application of the Directive in the Member States where the *center of gravity of the conflict* is located and more effective protection of the rights of European Union citizens is possible. This would allow citizens of a Member State to bring actions against the search engines before their national courts, instead of having to seize the courts of California or other States. The AG denied such possibility.

According to the AG, the *geographical center of gravity of the dispute was not sufficient to render the Directive applicable:*[277] Article 51(2) CFREU does not extend the scope of EU law beyond the Union's powers, nor does it establish any new power or task for the Union, and it does not

---

[275] Paragraph 66.

[276] Paragraph 67.

[277] The AG ignores the case law of the CJEU on *Date Advertising v. Olivier and Martínez* (Case C-509/09 and C-161/10, 25 October 2011). According to this doctrine, claims for breach of fundamental rights on the Internet can be brought before the courts of the State where the affected party has its *center of interests*. The case of *Date Advertising v. Olivier and Martínez* addressed the issue of the applicable national jurisdiction in disputes relating to the Internet. The connecting factor of the place where the damage occurs was hardly applicable to the Internet, so the CJEU concluded that the huge potential impact that content placed online can have on the *personality rights* of an individual "might best be assessed by the court of the place where the alleged victim has his *center of interests*" (i.e., his *habitual residence*).

modify the powers and tasks as defined by the Treaties. the interpretation of Directive 95/46/EC in accordance with the CFREU cannot add any new elements that might give rise to the territorial applicability of the national legislation implementing the Directive to a *targeted public*: "Nationality or place of habitual residence of data subjects, or the physical location of the personal data is not decisive."[278] Also the fact that Google's website specifically addresses a national public is not decisive to trigger the applicability of the national legislation to the search engine.

4.3.- The search engine "processes" personal data, but it is not the "controller" due to its *unawareness* of their nature as personal data

The AG acknowledges that Internet search engines process personal data in their typical functions: crawling, indexing, storing and displaying personal data contained on source web pages.

However, the AG considers that these activities do not make the search engine a "controller," since it works without human interaction with the data collected, indexed and displayed for such purposes. This conclusion is reinforced by the fact that the controller is *unaware* that it is processing data that technically qualify as personal data. That is the core argument underlying Google's lack of responsibility for search engine activities.[279]

The AG first considers a *literal and teleological* interpretation of Article 2(d) of Directive 95/46/EC ("'controller' is the natural or legal person [...] which alone or jointly with others determines the purposes and means of the processing of personal data"). This would lead to the "logical conclusion"[280] that Internet search engines should fall within the concept of "controller." In fact, all parties to the case (Spain, Italy, Austria, Poland, and the European Commission), except for Google and Greece, proposed that approach (i.e., to regard Google as a controller).

---

[278] Paragraph 55.
[279] The AG departs from the case law of the CJEU in *Google France v. Louis Vuitton* (Cases C-236/08 to C-238/08, 23 February 2010), in which the Court had found that Internet Search engines are not liable unless they play an *active* role not just technical, automatic and passive. In *Google France v. Louis Vuitton*, the CJEU recalled that exemptions from liability apply to Internet search engines when their activity is "of a mere technical, automatic and passive nature," which implies that it "has neither knowledge of nor control over the information which is transmitted or stored." In that specific case, Google processed data and determined the display of the advertising links according to the price paid by the advertiser: its liability would stem from the drafting of the commercial message accompanying the promotional link or the selection of the keywords.
[280] Paragraph 77.

The AG -even acknowledging that a teleological interpretation would be in line with the broad concepts conceived precisely to cover new technological developments- rejects this option and puts forward a line of argument to adapt the Directive's interpretation to new technological phenomena such as search engines: the *principle of proportionality*, i.e. weighing the purposes of the Directive and the means for enforcement provided thereby, this principle would require striking a *fair and reasonable balance*.

According to the AG, Directive 95/46/EC intends to allocate *responsibilities* on the basis of the following assumption: "the controller knows what he is doing in relation to the personal data concerned, in the sense that he is aware of what kind of personal data he is processing and why. In other words, the data processing must appear to him as processing of personal data, that is 'information relating to an identified or identifiable natural person' in some semantically relevant way and not a mere computer code."[281]

This conclusion can have unexpected implications regarding the reversion of data protection guarantees against the Internet and many other new technological developments: the blind activity of search engines based on mathematical algorithms without human intervention would never give rise to liability, given the unawareness of the processing and the "randomness" of personal data for crawlers or robots. Following the AG, this can be summarized as follows:

1) Internet search engines merely locate information without any control over the personal data included on third-party web pages.

2) Search engines are not aware of the existence of personal data (only of the "possibility" that web pages include them).

3) Crawled and indexed source web pages do not specifically "identify" personal data.

4) Search engines have no relation with the content of source web pages of third parties, nor does it have any means of changing the information in host servers.

5) Search engines, as tools for locating information, have no control whatsoever over the content, nor can it distinguish between personal data ("relating to an identifiable individual") and other data.

---

[281] Paragraph 83.

6) If search engines do not control and are not aware of the processing of personal data, they cannot be considered as a controller or responsible for compliance with the controller's obligations.

The AG draws important conclusions from this line of argument: search engines cannot in law or in fact fulfil the obligations of controller. Therefore, according to a reasonable interpretation of the Directive, they should not be considered as "controllers" in order to avoid the "absurd" conclusion[282] that Internet search engines are incompatible with EU law.

This approach is hardly moderate. Far from achieving a "balanced and reasonable outcome" in the application of the principle of proportionality, it excludes any accountability for search engines and the processing of personal data on the basis of an alleged legal and factual impossibility of enforcement.

Only two circumstances would trigger the liability of search engines: a) failure to comply with the exclusion codes on a source web page; and b) failure to update the cache memory of search engines.

Two considerations can be made: 1) the AG admits the liability of search engines when the exclusion codes are ignored or when the search results are not updated. This, in turn, seems to prove that search engines are "aware" and "decide" or "control" the processing of personal data. Since the data (personal or otherwise) would still be processed through an algorithm, without human interaction, and in a discriminate manner, there would be no "awareness" either in these cases -which undermines the original argument of the AG; 2) the AG insistently seeks to exclude the liability of search engines based on the Opinions of the Article 29 WP and, in particular its Opinion 1/2008: "the principle of proportionality requires that to the extent that a search engine provider acts purely as an intermediary, it should not be considered as the principal controller with regard to the content related processing of personal data that is taking place. In this case the principal controllers of personal data are the information providers."[283]

However, the AG's reading of Opinion 1/2008 is rather limited regarding the "primary" liability as opposed to the "secondary" liability, which requires distinguishing between the position of controller of a source web page and the search engines acting only as intermediaries. The AG

---

[282] Paragraph 90.
[283] Paragraph 88.

ignores an essential part of that Opinion: "The formal, legal and practical control the search engine has over the personal data involved is usually limited to the possibility of removing data from its servers. With regard to the removal of personal data from their index and search results, search engines have sufficient control to consider them as controllers (either alone or jointly with others)[284]."

Consequently, the Opinion is unambiguous in considering the source web page as *principal controller* regarding the content of search queries, but it does not exclude that search engines may be held secondarily liable: rather, it expressly states that they have *sufficient control* that should be ensured by 1´) removing data from their servers; 2´) removing data from their indexes and search results when so required by national legislation. In fact, Opinion 1/2008 recalls that, in some EU Member States (like Spain), data protection authorities have specifically regulated the obligation of search engine providers to remove data from the content of search indexes on the basis of the right to object enshrined in Article 14 of the Data Protection Directive. As can be seen, the AG relied only partly on the well-balanced and weighed criteria set forth in the Opinions of the Article 29 Working Party.

4.4.- The Directive does not provide for a general right to be forgotten based on *subjective preferences*

The Advocate General confirms an obvious truth: the Data Protection Directive does not establish a right to be forgotten. The right to be forgotten is a new expression coined in the context of the current development of the Internet. It refers to the need to adopt measures preventing the undesired retention of personal data on the Internet, but its theoretical boundaries are far from established. There is still no legal basis for this concept.

Other than a journalistic reference to the term "right to be forgotten," the questions referred for a preliminary ruling asked whether the right to erasure and blocking [Article 12(b)] and the right to object [Article 14(a)] enabled the data subject to prevent indexing of potentially harmful information relating to him/her personally. Under the latter right, the data subject is entitled to object at any time on compelling legitimate grounds relating to his/her personal situation to the processing of data relating to him/her.

---

[284] http://ec.europa.eu/justice/data-protection/article-29/documentation/opinion-recommendation/index_en.htm

According to the AG, the right to object requires weighing the interests of search engines or third parties against those of the data subject. His assessment is quite clear: 1') "A subjective preference alone does not amount to a compelling legitimate ground"[285] justifying the exercise of the right to object under Article 14(a) of Directive 95/46/EC; 2') Internet search engines serve legitimate purposes: making information more easily accessible for Internet users, rendering dissemination of the information uploaded on the Internet more effective, and providing advertising services linked to the search queries. These purposes have legal basis, since they relate to three fundamental rights enshrined in the Carter: freedom of information, freedom of expression, and freedom to conduct a business.

The AG clearly reappraises the interests of search engines, including them within the scope of protection of the European system of fundamental rights. At the same time, he devalues the interests of individuals by equating them to "subjective preferences" -which do not amount to a compelling legitimate ground that could justify the exercise of the right to object. Furthermore, he does not grant any practical value to the fundamental right to data protection enshrined in the CFREU. The AG's weighing would not be so unbalanced if he had defined the limits between the "compelling legitimate grounds relating to his/her situation" and mere "subjective preferences."

In view of the above, it is rather immaterial whether the AG rejects (as he does) the recognition of a general right to be forgotten on the Internet under the Directive.

However, the AG went even further and stated his position against the prevalence of a general right to be forgotten over other fundamental rights like the following: 1) The internet users' right to seek and receive information made available on the internet -by source web pages and search engines- as a manifestation of the freedom of expression and information under Article 11 CFREU. Web page publishers are protected by the freedom of expression when they make content available on the Internet, particularly when such activity is not limited to indexing and seeks to achieve wide dissemination; 2) A newspaper publisher's freedom of information protects the publication of the printed version of newspapers on the Internet, and censuring it "would amount to falsification of history."[286]

---

[285] Paragraph 108.
[286] Paragraph 129.

The AG praised the role of Internet search engines in the information society, considering them holders of fundamental rights: 1) Search engines provide their services in the framework of a business activity protected by the freedom to conduct a business under Article 16 CFREU, and they exercise their freedom of expression when they make available Internet information location tools;[287] 2) In today's society, search engines are one of the most important ways to exercise the right to information, which covers the right to seek information relating to other individuals.[288] 3) Internet users' right to information would be

---

[287] The AG extends to search engines the protection granted to freedom of expression in terms identical to those used in the USA by EUGENE VOLOKH and DONALD M. FALK: "Google, Microsoft's Bing, and Yahoo! Search exercise editorial judgment about what constitutes useful information and convey that information—which is to say, they speak—to their users. In this respect, they are analogous to newspapers and book publishers that convey a wide range of information from news stories and selected columns by outside contributors to stock listings, movie listings, bestseller lists, and restaurant guides. And all of these speakers are shielded by the First Amendment" (*First Amendment Protection for Search Engine Search Results*, Paper Commissioned by Google, April, 2012, UCLA School of Law, http://www.volokh.com/wp-content/uploads/2012/05/SearchEngineFirstAmendment.pdf). However, it is worth recalling the very critical opinion of JEFFREY ROSEN: "this dramatic First Amendment claim is unfortunate and should be challenged" ("Free speech, privacy and the web that never forgets," *Telecommunications and High Technology Law*, vol. 9, 2011, p. 346).

[288] The increasing importance of Internet search engines has given rise to proposals for a public regulation of the Internet, against the traditional advocacy for a "free and open" Internet. See, in this regard, VIVA R. MOFFAT: "Regulating Search," *Harvard Journal of Law & Technology*, vol. 22-2, Spring, 2009, pp. 475-513; JAMES GRIMMELMANN: "The Structure of Search Engine Law," *Iowa Law Review*, vol. 93, 2007-2008, pp. 1-64; and EMILY B. LAIDLAW: "Private Power, Public Interest: An Examination of Search Engine Accountability," *International Journal of Law and Information Technology*, vol. 17-1, 2008, pp. 113-145.

compromised if the search about an individual did not generate truthful results reflecting the relevant web pages.[289]

It is objectionable that the AG's opinion on Internet search engines is not accompanied by an equivalent description of the risks stemming from this service for the fundamental rights to privacy and data protection is questionable.

The AG rejects any possibility of finding a balanced compromise for the protection of the rights at stake. Surprisingly, he advises the CJEU against weighing the relevant interests to solve this conflict between fundamental rights: "I would also discourage the Court from concluding that these conflicting interests could satisfactorily be balanced in individual cases on a case-by-case basis, with the judgment to be left to the internet search engine service provider."[290] The AG intended to avoid any temptation on the CJEU's part to admit the Spanish model of protection of the right to be forgotten: a case-by-case assessment of the adequacy of the right to object, based on individual circumstances, regarding the removal of links from search results.

The AG shows an unjustified fear when it comes to entitling search engines to remove content from their indexes: "the automatic withdrawal of links to any objected contents or to an unmanageable number of requests handled by the most popular and important internet search engine service providers."[291] It is telling that the AG warns about an underlying risk: "Internet search engine service providers should not be saddled with such an obligation."[292]

---

[289] The authorized opinion of FR. LA RUE reminds us that "intermediaries play a fundamental role in enabling Internet users to enjoy their right to freedom of expression and access to information. Given their unprecedented influence over how and what is circulated on the Internet, States have increasingly sought to exert control over them and to hold them legally liable for failing to prevent access to content deemed to be illegal ... intermediaries should not be held liable for refusing to take action that infringes individuals' human rights. Any requests submitted to intermediaries to prevent access to certain content, or to disclose private information for strictly limited purposes such as administration of criminal justice, should be done through an order issued by a court or a competent body which is independent of any political, commercial or other unwarranted influences." (*Report of the Special Rapporteur on the promotion and protection of the right to freedom of opinion and expression*, United Nations General Assembly, 16 May 2011, p. 20).
[290] Paragraph 133.
[291] Paragraph 133.
[292] Paragraph 134.

Ultimately, the AG's position is biased, from the beginning to the end of his Opinion, due to his assumption that recognizing the "right to be forgotten" could hamper the development of search engines as the leading service on the Internet and in the information society.

In conclusion, the AG ignores the core elements of the balanced model of the right to be forgotten put forward by the AEPD:[293] reactive (rather than preventive) and individual (rather than general) recognition of the right to object based on compelling legitimate grounds relating to the subject's particular situation (very different, then from mere personal whim).

5.- THE JUDGMENT OF THE CJEU (*CASE C-131/12*, 13 MAY 2014, *GOOGLE SPAIN v. AEPD*): THE UNQUESTIONABLE EFFECTIVE PROTECTION OF THE RIGHT TO BE FORGOTTEN AGAINST INTERNET SEARCH ENGINES

Against all odds -given the radical Opinion of Advocate General Mr. Jääskinen, and taking into account that the CJEU usually follows the Advocate General's Opinion- the judgment of the CJEU of 13 May 2014 (*Case C-131/12, Google Spain v. AEPD*) settled the matter recognizing the right to be forgotten against Internet search engines.[294]

The CJEU upheld every aspect of the AEPD's resolution and fully confirmed all its legal arguments. The brief operative part shows that this judgment marks a turning point in the history of the Internet. It does not only affect the protection of fundamental rights of users (privacy and protection of personal data), but also requires redesigning some of the most popular Internet services (search engines, social networks, etc.).[295]

---

[293] The balance advocated by the Spanish model of the right to be forgotten aimed at fulfilling the first of the five principles (*balance*) which, according to FRED CATE, should guide regulatory action regarding the protection of privacy on the Internet ("Principles of Internet Privacy," *Connecticut Law Review*, vol. 32, 2000, p. 879).

[294] MÓNICA VILASAU SOLANA: "El caso Google Spain: la afirmación del buscador como responsable del tratamiento y el reconocimiento del derecho al olvido (análisis de la STJUE de 13 de mayo de 2014)," *Revista de Internet, Derecho y Política*, vol. 18, June, 2014, pp. 16-32; ANDRÉS BOIX PALOP: "El equilibrio entre los derechos del artículo 18 de la Constitución. El `derecho al olvido´ y las libertades informativas tras la sentencia Google," *Revista General de Derecho Administrativo*, vol. 38, January, 2015, pp. 1-40.

[295] For a good example of this, see the Opinion of the Article 29 Working Party on *Update of Opinion 8/2010 on applicable law in light of the CJEU judgement in Google Spain*, adopted on 16 December 2015 (http://ec.europa.eu/justice/data-protection/article-29/documentation/opinion-recommendation/files/2015/wp179_en_update.pdf).

5.1.- The *constitutional* protection of the right to data protection as a general principle of EU law enshrined in the Charter of Fundamental Rights of the European Union (CFREU)

In *Google Spain v. AEPD*, the CJEU assumed its position as guarantor of rights. It confirmed the legal relevance recently attributed to the right to protection of personal data both by the case law and the European "constitutional" framework:

1′) The CJEU departed from a *high level of protection* of this right in Recital 10 of Directive 95/46/EC: "the object of the national laws on the processing of personal data is to protect fundamental rights and freedoms, notably the right to privacy, which is recognized both in Article 8 of the European Convention for the Protection of Human Rights and Fundamental Freedoms and in the general principles of Community law; whereas, for that reason , the approximation of those laws must not result in any lessening of the protection they afford but must, on the contrary, seek to ensure a high level of protection in the Community."[296]

2′) The CJEU has not addressed the implementation of this right as an isolated right legally recognized by Directive 95/46/EC. Rather, the CJEU set forth an interpretation consistent with the *protection of fundamental rights as general principles of EU law* which it must ensure. Articles 7 and 8 of the CFREU enshrine the right to respect for private and family life (privacy) and the right to protection of personal data, respectively. In fact, Article 8(2) and 8(3) require that such data must be processed fairly for specified purposes and on the basis of the consent of the person concerned or some other legitimate basis laid down by law. Everyone has the right of access to data which has been collected concerning him or her, and the right to have it rectified. Compliance with these rules shall be subject to control by an independent authority.[297]

5.2.- An impeccable understanding of the function of Internet search engines in today's information society and of their impact on privacy

This outcome can only be explained on the basis of a specific position taken by the CJEU regarding the effects of the Internet on today's society.

Far from passing a general judgment on the global impact of the Internet (its advantages, social and economic relevance, etc.), the CJEU limited its

---

[296] Paragraph 66.
[297] Paragraphs 68 and 69.

assessment to the particular function of search engines and its effect on data protection. Its conclusion in this regard, which was in turn the starting point for its legal reasoning, was that "the organization and aggregation of information published on the internet that are effected by search engines with the aim of facilitating their users' access to that information may, when users carry out their search on the basis of an individual's name, result in them obtaining through the list of results a structured overview of the information relating to that individual that can be found on the internet enabling them to establish a more or less detailed profile of the data subject."[298]

This activity carried out by search engine providers, broadly outlined by the CJEU, is not neutral. Quite the contrary, it affects the rights of citizens, as the Court superbly puts it: "Inasmuch as the activity of a search engine is therefore liable to affect significantly, and additionally compared with that of the publishers of websites, the fundamental rights to privacy and to the protection of personal data, the operator of the search engine as the person determining the purposes and means of that activity must ensure, within the framework of its responsibilities, powers and capabilities, that the activity meets the requirements of Directive 95/46 in order that the guarantees laid down by the directive may have full effect and that effective and complete protection of data subjects, in particular of their right to privacy, may actually be achieved."[299]

5.3.- The activity of search engines constitutes "processing" of "personal data"

Faced with Google's claim that the activity of search engines cannot be regarded as processing of data, all other participants in the proceedings (Mr. Costeja, the Spanish, Italian, Austrian, Greek, and Polish Governments, the European Commission, and the Advocate General) considered that such activity clearly constituted "processing of personal data" within the meaning of Directive 95/46/EC.

Following its own case law doctrine, first issued in *Lindqvist*, the CJEU confirmed the applicability and full force of Article 2(b) of Directive 95/46/EC: "in exploring the internet automatically, constantly and systematically in search of the information which is published there, the operator of a search engine 'collects' such data which it subsequently 'retrieves', 'records' and 'organizes' within the framework of its indexing programs, 'stores' on its servers and, as the case may be, 'discloses' and 'makes available' to its users in the form of lists of search results. As

---

[298] Paragraph 37.
[299] Paragraph 38.

those operations are referred to expressly and unconditionally in Article 2(b) of Directive 95/46, they must be classified as 'processing'."[300]

The CJEU rejected that the automatic nature of search engines made them neutral intermediaries outside the scope of the obligations stemming from processing of data: 1´) "Regardless of the fact that the operator of the search engine also carries out the same operations in respect of other types of information and does not distinguish between the latter and the personal data;"[301] 2´) "Nor is the foregoing finding affected by the fact that those data have already been published on the internet and are not altered by the search engine;"[302] 3´) "it follows from the definition contained in Article 2(b) of Directive 95/46 that, whilst the alteration of personal data indeed constitutes processing within the meaning of the directive, the other operations which are mentioned there do not, on the other hand, in any way require that the personal data be altered."[303]

5.4.- National subsidiaries intended to sell advertising space offered by the search engine are "establishments" subject to national legislation

The CJEU confirmed that Google Spain constitutes a stable arrangement in Spain with separate legal personality, since it is a subsidiary of Google Inc. in Spain. In other words, it is an "establishment" within the meaning of Article 4(1)(a) of Directive 95/46/EC.

To reach this conclusion, the CJEU bases its interpretation on Recital 19 of the Directive, which refers to two essential elements: 1´) the effective and real exercise of activity through stable arrangements; 2´) the legal form of such an establishment, whether simply branch or a subsidiary with a legal personality, is not the determining factor in this respect.

In order to fulfil these requirements and hence to apply national legislation, the processing of data must be carried out "in the context of the activities" of such "establishment."
Google tried to divest itself of responsibility by submitting that the processing of data was exclusively carried out by Google Inc. as the operator of Google Search, without any intervention on the part of Google Spain (whose activity is limited to promoting Google's advertising activity). However, the CJEU considered that the effective

---

[300] Paragraph 28.
[301] Paragraph 28.
[302] Paragraph 29.
[303] Paragraph 31.

and complete protection required by Directive 95/46/EC prevented a restrictive interpretation of the expression "in the context of the activities," in the sense that the processing had to be carried out "by" the establishment.[304]

Taking into account Recitals 18 and 20, and Article 4 of Directive 95/46/EC, "the European Union legislature sought to prevent individuals from being deprived of the protection guaranteed by the directive and that protection from being circumvented, by prescribing a particularly broad territorial scope."[305] The CJEU concluded that the processing of data takes place "in the context of the activities" of the establishment "if the latter is intended to promote and sell, in that Member State, advertising space offered by the search engine which serves to make the service offered by that engine profitable. In such circumstances, the activities of the operator of the search engine and those of its establishment situated in the Member State concerned are inextricably linked since the activities relating to the advertising space constitute the means of rendering the search engine at issue economically profitable and that engine is, at the same time, the means enabling those activities to be performed."[306]

5.5.- Internet search engines have a primary "responsibility," separate and different from that of webmasters

The CJEU unambiguously considers the operator of the Internet search engine as the controller of the processing of data, since it "determines the purposes and means of the processing of personal data" within the meaning of Article 2(d) of Directive 95/46/EC:[307] "it would be contrary not only to the clear wording of that provision but also to its objective - which is to ensure, through a broad definition of the concept of 'controller', effective and complete protection of data subjects- to exclude the operator of a search engine from that definition on the ground that it does not exercise control over the personal data published on the web pages of third parties."[308]

---

[304] Paragraphs 52 and 53.
[305] Paragraph 54.
[306] Paragraphs 55 and 56.
[307] This was also the approach taken by Mr. Costeja, the Spanish, Italian, Austrian, and Polish Governments, as well as by the European Commission. On the other hand, both the Advocate General and the Greek Government (and, of course, Google) considered that "inasmuch as search engines serve merely as intermediaries, the undertakings which operate them cannot be regarded as 'controllers', except where they store data in an 'intermediate memory' or 'cache memory' for a period which exceeds that which is technically necessary" (Paragraph 24).
[308] Paragraph 34.

What is then the responsibility of webmasters? The CJEU lays down several defining criteria:

1′) The processing of data carried out by search engines is different from that carried out by publishers of websites.[309]

2′) Search engines have a multiplying effect on the processing of data from source websites: "it is undisputed that that activity of search engines plays a decisive role in the overall dissemination of those data in that it renders the latter accessible to any internet user making a search on the basis of the data subject's name, including to internet users who otherwise would not have found the web page on which those data are published.[310]

3′) The intrusion of Internet search engines on the privacy of personal data is significantly higher than that of source websites: "since the inclusion in the list of results, displayed following a search made on the basis of a person's name, of a web page and of the information contained on it relating to that person makes access to that information appreciably easier for any internet user making a search in respect of the person concerned and may play a decisive role in the dissemination of that information, it is liable to constitute a more significant interference with the data subject's fundamental right to privacy than the publication on the web page."[311]

3′) The fact that publishers of websites do not use exclusion protocols such as "robot.txt" or "*Noindex*" or "*Noarchive*" tags does not mean that the operator of a search engine "search engine is released from its responsibility,"[312] since Article 2(d) of Directive 95/46/EC expressly provides that the purposes and means of processing can be determined "alone or jointly with others."

4′) Given the ease with which information published online can be replicated on other sites, data users would not be effectively protected if they were required to obtain the erasure of the relevant information from the publishers of websites first or in parallel to the request for removal from the list of search results.[313]

---

[309] Paragraph 35.
[310] Paragraph 36.
[311] Paragraph 87.
[312] Paragraph 39
[313] Paragraph 84.

Therefore, regardless of the citizens' exercise of rights vis-à-vis webmasters, Internet search engines must comply with such requests when they are directly addressed to them within the specific context of their activity.

5.6.- The right to data protection prevails over the "mere economic interest" of search engines, which are not covered by the "journalistic exemption"

Article 7(f) of Directive 95/46/EC provides in principle for the processing of data by search engines, as it is necessary for their legitimate economic and commercial interests, except when such interests are overridden by the data subject's fundamental rights and freedoms, in particular the protection of his/her personal data.

It is in this regard that we find one of the most important conclusions of the CJEU: *Internet search engines have no grounds for processing personal data other than* "merely the economic interest."[314] Hence, search engines cannot justify their activity on the fundamental right to information, nor can they claim to be a news organization or part of the media. In the same line, they cannot evade their responsibility on the basis of their alleged neutrality.

The CJEU admits that, sometimes, a web page may invoke the *journalistic exemption* provided by Article 9 of Directive 95/46/EC, according to which the Directive shall not apply when the processing of personal data is carried out "solely for journalistic purposes." However, "that does not appear to be so in the case of the processing carried out by the operator of a search engine":[315] it is not a news organization and its activity is not covered by the right to information (as it may happen sometimes with Internet websites).

This reconsideration of the legal status of the activity carried out by search engines will be of the utmost importance for the weighing required by the legislation. The citizens' fundamental rights will prevail over other interests -also legitimate but inferior to the fundamental rights enshrined in Articles 7 and 8 CFREU.

5.7.- The individual right to data protection prevails over a general "interest of Internet users"

The CJEU does not recognize from the outset an alleged legitimate

---

[314] Paragraph 81.
[315] Paragraph 85.

interest of "internet users" that may override the interest of data subject regarding the removal of their personal data from search results. The CJEU considers that, "inasmuch as the removal of links from the list of results could, depending on the information at issue, have effects upon the legitimate interest of internet users potentially interested in having access to that information."[316] That is why "a fair balance should be sought in particular between that interest and the data subject's fundamental rights under Articles 7 and 8 of the Charter."[317]

The CJEU identified the two opposing elements relevant for such weighing. It also limited extraordinarily the importance of the legitimate interest of internet users over third parties' personal data indexed by search engines: 1´) The data subject's rights override, as a general rule, the interest of internet users; 2´) In specific cases, the *interest of the public* may prevail depending on the nature of the information in question and its sensitivity for the data subject's private life, "according to the role played by the data subject in public life."[318]

The CJEU concludes that the interest of internet users may only override the data subject's rights in specific cases; for instance, when the personal data to be removed from search indexes concern a public figure or some information of public interest. In any case, consideration must be given to the nature and sensitivity of the information, as well as its potential impact on the data subject's private life.

5.8.- The rights to erasure and to object as a balanced tool to require the search engines to remove the data even if they were lawfully published and even if the webmaster has not erased them

The CJEU addresses the central issue of whether Articles 12(b) and 14(1)(a) of Directive 95/46/EC require search engines to remove from the list of results the personal data also when such information is not erased beforehand or simultaneously from the web pages, and even if the publication is lawful.

Google invoked the principle of proportionality to claim that the requests of data subjects had to be lodged (exclusively) with the publisher of the website. The CJEU dismissed this approach. It also rejected that imposing such obligation upon search engines could violate the fundamental rights of webmasters, of internet users, or of the search engine itself.

---

[316] Paragraph 81.
[317] Paragraph 81.
[318] Paragraph 81.

The CJEU carries out an all-encompassing assessment of all the principles and rights covered by the Directive. It focuses, in particular, on the principle of data quality as well as on the right to erasure and to object. Its conclusion is that, if these requirements are not met, the search engine must take every reasonable step to erase or rectify the data.

In the CJEU's view, the rights to erasure and to object enshrined in Articles 12(b) and 14(1)(a) of the Directive are the appropriate legal instruments to safeguard the principle of data quality and to protect a well-balanced and weighed right to be forgotten, applied on a case-by-case basis, according to the individual circumstances of the data subject. The right to object -as advocated by the AEPD- allows the data subject to object at any time on compelling legitimate grounds relating to his/her particular situation, to the processing of data relating to him/her, save where otherwise provided by national legislation, or where there are overriding interests, rights or freedoms.

The CJEU provides a succinct but wonderfully clear explanation of how the processing of personal data by Internet search engines can significantly affect the fundamental rights to privacy and data protection: "processing of personal data carried out by the operator of a search engine is liable to affect significantly the fundamental rights to privacy and to the protection of personal data when the search by means of that engine is carried out on the basis of an individual's name, since that processing enables any internet user to obtain through the list of results a structured overview of the information relating to that individual that can be found on the internet — information which potentially concerns a vast number of aspects of his private life and which, without the search engine, could not have been interconnected or could have been only with great difficulty — and thereby to establish a more or less detailed profile of him. Furthermore, the effect of the interference with those rights of the data subject is heightened on account of the important role played by the internet and search engines in modern society, which render the information contained in such a list of results ubiquitous."[319]

The *potential seriousness of that interference*[320] is sufficient grounds for the CJEU to trigger the exercise of the individual right to erasure and to object. Justifying the compelling legitimate grounds relating to the data subject's particular situation requires little additional effort: neither the mere economic interest of the search engine nor a general interest of internet users (other than the specific right to information regarding issues of public interest) can be relied on against the data subject's interest.

---

[319] Paragraph 80.
[320] Paragraph 81.

In conclusion, the CJEU considers that Internet search engines are obliged to remove from the list of results the links to web pages published by third parties, even if such information is not previously or simultaneously erased from those web pages, and even if its publication is lawful.

5.9.- The "course of time" justifies the right to be forgotten without "harm or prejudice" being required

The CJEU also addressed the last question on whether the rights to rectification, erasure, blocking and to object enshrined in Articles 12(b) and 14(1)(a) of Directive 95/46/EC enabled the data subject, after a certain period of time, to request the search engine to erase the data collected from websites lawfully published by third parties and containing true information, when such information may be prejudicial to him/her.

The CJEU referred to the *principles of data quality* set forth in Article 6 of the Directive: personal data must be processed "fairly and lawfully;" "for specified, explicit and legitimate purposes;" and such personal data must be "adequate, relevant and not excessive in relation to the purposes for which they are collected and/or further processed;" they must also be "accurate and kept up to date," and "kept in a form which permits identification of data subjects for no longer than is necessary for the purposes for which the data were collected or for which they are further processed [with] appropriate safeguards for personal data stored for longer periods for historical, statistical or scientific use."

The CJEU draws some very interesting conclusions regarding the impact of the "course of time" on the information society: 1') "even initially lawful processing of accurate data may, in the course of time, become incompatible with the directive where those data are no longer necessary in the light of the purposes for which they were collected or processed;"[321] 2') search engines must erase the personal data published lawfully by third parties because their inclusion in the list of results is, "at this point in time," incompatible with Article 6 of the Directive, having regard to all the circumstances of the case, to be inadequate, irrelevant or no longer relevant, or excessive;[322] 3') the affirmation of the right to erasure or the right to object does not depend on harm or prejudice being caused to the data subject: "it is not necessary in order to find such a right that the inclusion of the information in question in the list of results

---

[321] Paragraph 93.
[322] Paragraph 94.

causes prejudice to the data subject."[323]

Ultimately, the CJEU concluded that "the course of time" affects "data quality;" adequate, relevant and not excessive data can cease to be so only due to the effect of passing of time. In particular, data relevance is affected by the course of time once the purposes for which they were collected are no longer valid. This justifies the erasure of such information. In this regard, no damage has to be proved as part of the requirement to justify compelling legitimate grounds relating to the data subject's personal situation (in order to exercise the right to object).

Finally, the CJEU sums up its underlying reasoning in *Google v. AEPD*: "the display, in the list of results [...], of links to pages of the on-line archives of a daily newspaper that contain announcements mentioning the data subject's name and relating to a real-estate auction connected with attachment proceedings for the recovery of social security debts, it should be held that, having regard to the sensitivity for the data subject's private life of the information contained in those announcements and to the fact that its initial publication had taken place 16 years earlier, the data subject establishes a right that that information should no longer be linked to his name by means of such a list."[324] Mr. Costeja was entitled to have those links removed from Google's list of results.

5.10.- Limits of the right to be forgotten: data concerning "public figures" or "information of public interest"

There are several relevant CJEU's decisions regarding the limits of the right to be forgotten when the data subject is a public figure, when they concern information of public interest or when the processing is carried out for journalistic purposes.

Processing of data "solely for journalistic purposes" is covered by the exemption under Article 9 of Directive 95/46/EC, and it prevents the application of data protection legislation even if such processing is carried out by *online media* or other website publishers. In these cases, the CJEU rejects the exercise of the right to be forgotten against the webmaster.

According to the CJEU, Internet search engines are neither online media nor are they covered by the journalistic exemption, and they cannot invoke the right to information. Data subjects are not entitled to exercise the right to be forgotten against websites that process data "for purposes

---

[323] Paragraph 96.
[324] Paragraph 98.

of journalism." However, they can assert such right vis-à-vis the operator of the search engine in certain circumstances through the exercise of the rights to erasure and to object enshrined in Articles 12(b) and 14(1)(a) of Directive 95/46/EC.[325] Search engines process data within the meaning of Article 2(b) of Directive 95/46/EC, even if the information in question has already been published by the media. Any other interpretation (i.e., not considering the indexing of information contained on online media websites as processing of data) would imply, as the CJEU warns, "a general derogation from the application of Directive 95/46," which "would largely deprive the directive of its effect."[326]

The expansive force of the right to be forgotten vis-à-vis search engines is extraordinary, and only very specific interests and rights can be balanced against it.

Neither the mere economic interest of search engines nor the interest of internet users are sufficient to override the right to be forgotten but in very particular cases, according to the nature of the information and its sensitivity for the data subject's private life, always taking into account the role played by the data subject in public life.[327]

The public interest of personal data must be assessed and weighed against the impact on the data subject's private life in order to determine whether the interest of publishing the information or its erasure/oblivion must prevail. The data subject will not be entitled to request the removal of personal data from the list of results if it is concluded, "for particular reasons, such as the role played by the data subject in public life, that the interference with his fundamental rights is justified by the preponderant interest of the general public in having, on account of inclusion in the list of results, access to the information in question."[328]

---

[325] Paragraph 85.
[326] Paragraph 30.
[327] Paragraph 81.
[328] Paragraph 97.

CHAPTER V

THE IMPLEMENTATION OF THE CJEU JUDGMENT (*CASE GOOGLE V. SPAIN*)

1.- GOOGLE COMPLIES WITH THE CJEU JUDGMENT: AN UNNECESSARY ADVISORY COUNCIL

The legal grounds provided by the CJEU in its legal reasoning were irreproachable. However, some concerns could arise regarding its effectiveness and implementation in the face of potential technological difficulties.

The challenged AEPD resolutions ordered Google to erase personal data from its search indexes, in addition to preventing any potential crawling of personal data already removed by the search engine, given the current technological development.

The CJEU's Judgment had to be construed in broad terms. The right to be forgotten would thus mean the right to de-list search results, as well as the right to have search engines prevent any potential crawling and indexation of erased results. Nevertheless, as the AEPD had already pointed out in response to the questions posed by the technology industry (particularly Google), there still were concerns about the effectiveness of the CJEU's Judgment regarding the purported limitations of the technology available to fulfill the right to be forgotten.

However, in a rather surprising move, a few days after the CJEU's Judgment, a Google representative reported to the Hamburg Data Protection Authority its intention to quickly implement a technology that could fulfill the right to be forgotten.[329]

First, Google set up an Advisory Council on "the right to be forgotten" made up of prestigious experts. Its purpose was to advise Google on how to strike a fair balance between the right to privacy and access to information of public interest in compliance with the CJEU's Judgment in *Google v. Spain*. This Advisory Council launched an image campaign to restore Google's battered reputation. It held six public sessions with experts from various European countries between September and November 2014.

---

[329] "Google prepara una herramienta para borrar 'links' en Europa" ("Google is preparing a tool to erase 'links' in Europe"), 16 May 2014, *http://tecnologia.elpais.com.*

The *Report of the Advisory Council to Google on the Right to be Forgotten*[330] was released on 6 February 2015. Although this Report barely adds anything to the criteria laid down by the CJEU's ruling, it somehow tried to narrow its scope.

1.- The Report downgrades the notion of the "right to be forgotten" by using the term "de-listing."[331]

2.- The Report narrows the right to de-list to the exercise of the right to object, whether the processing causes harm or is prejudicial in some way to the data subject. Actually, the judgment allowed for exercising the right to be forgotten through the right to object and the right to erasure, "with no need to justify any prejudice." Therefore, the Report conflicts with the CJEU Judgment when it makes the following claim: "the question of whether the data subject experiences harm from such accessibility to the information is in our view relevant to this balancing test (...). Assessing harm to the data subject must be done on an ethical, legal, and practical basis (...) well analyzed and developed in case law outside the data protection context, particularly law concerning defamation and privacy claims. The animating values in those cases often concern personal honor, dignity, and reputation as well as the protection of sensitive or intimate personal information."[332] This intentional confusion of rights can only be construed as an attempt to narrow the meaning awarded by the CJEU to the right to be forgotten as a right that can be invoked when the data quality principle is breached due to the "course of the time."

3.- The Report identified four criteria to evaluate de-listing requests from individual data subjects (without hierarchy and subject to the relevant evolution according to technical changes): a) data subject's role in public life;[333] b) nature of the information;[334] c) source of the information;[335] d)

---

[330] https://buermeyer.de/wp/wp-content/uploads/2012/02/Report-of-the-Advisory-Committee-to-Google-on-the-Right-to-be-Forgotten.pdf
[331] *Report of the Advisory Council to Google on the Right to be Forgotten*, 6 February 2015, p. 5.
[332] *Report of the Advisory Council to Google on the Right to be Forgotten...*, p. 6.
[333] The Report provides three categories of persons according to the role played by individuals in public life: "1) Individuals with clear roles in public life (for example, politicians, CEOs, celebrities, religious leaders, sports stars, performing artists): de-listing requests from such individuals are less likely to justify de-listing, since the public will generally have an overriding interest in finding information about them via a name-based search. 2) Individuals with no discernable role in public life: de-listing requests for such individuals are more likely to justify de-listing. 3) Individuals with a limited or context-specific role in

the course of the time.[336] The Report makes a reasonable effort to provide practical examples. However, there are endless possible cases that cannot be reasonably covered by any list of examples. The assessment of the Advisory Council is often questionable, but we must keep in mind that

---

public life (for example, school directors, some kinds of public employees, persons thrust into the public eye because of events beyond their control, or individuals who may play a public role within a specific community because of their profession): de-listing requests from such individuals are neither less nor more likely to justify de-listing, as the specific content of the information being listed is probably going to weigh more heavily on the de-listing decision" (*Report of the Advisory Council to Google on the Right to be Forgotten...*, pp. 7-8).

[334] The Report lists the following types of information that bias toward an individual's strong privacy interest: 1. Information related to an individual's intimate or sex life; 2) Personal financial information; 3) Private contact or identification information; 4) Information deemed sensitive under EU Data Protection law; 5) Private information about minors; 6) Information that is false, makes an inaccurate association or puts the data subject at risk of harm; 7) Information that may heighten the data subject's privacy interests because it appears in image or video form. Conversely, the Report provides information that bias toward a public interest: 1) Information relevant to political discourse, citizen engagement, or governance; 2) Information relevant to religious or philosophical discourse; 3) Information that relates to public health and consumer protection; 4) Information related to criminal activity; 5) Information that contributes to a debate on a matter of general interest; 6) Information that is factual and true; 7) Information integral to the historical record; 8) Information integral to scientific inquiry or artistic expression (*Report of the Advisory Council to Google on the Right to be Forgotten...*, pp. 9-13).

[335] According to the Report, the following are valuable sources of information triggering public interest: "a journalistic entity operating under journalistic norms and best practices (...) Government publications (...) recognized bloggers or individual authors of good reputation with substantial credibility and/or readership." Conversely, the Report denies the right to de-list when "information is published by or with the consent of the data subject. This is especially true in cases where the data subject can remove the information with relative ease directly from the original source webpage, for example by deleting his or her own post on a social network" (*Report of the Advisory Council to Google on the Right to be Forgotten...*, pp. 9-13).

[336] The Report provides examples where the course of the time would cover the right to be forgotten: "if the data subject's role in public life is limited or has changed (...). The severity of a crime and the time passed may together favor de-listing, such as in the case of a minor crime committed many years in the past (...). A politician may leave public office and seek out a private life (...), [t]he data subject's childhood". On the other hand, "[i]t could also suggest an ongoing public interest in the information if a data subject has committed fraud and may potentially be in new positions of trust, or if a data subject has committed a crime of sexual violence and could possibly seek a job as a teacher or a profession of public trust that involves entering private homes" (*Report of the Advisory Council to Google on the Right to be Forgotten*, 6 February 2015, p. 14).

---

the Data Protection Authority and, where appropriate, domestic courts, may review the application of these criteria on a case-by-case basis.

4.- The Report advises Google on the de-listing procedure, and, at the request of media representatives, recommends as good practice that the search engine should notify the webmasters a de-listing decision to the extent allowed by law: "in complex cases, it may be appropriate for the search engine to notify the webmaster prior to reaching an actual de-listing decision." Nevertheless, at the consultation stage, some experts argued that "notifying webmasters may adversely impact the data subject's privacy rights if the webmaster is able to discern either from the notice itself or indirectly who the requesting data subject is."[337]

5.- Google's de-listing decisions are subject to appeal. First, they can be challenged before the national Data Protection Authority and, where appropriate, any party concerned can bring a claim before the courts of justice. At the consultation stage, the question whether webmasters were entitled to challenge Google's decisions before data protection authorities (DPAs) and courts was also on the table. The Report sided with the webmasters: "publishers should have means to challenge improper delistings before a DPA or a similar public authority."[338]

6.- One of the most challenging issues tackled by the Report was the geographic scope for de-listing. Once again, in spite of its reputation and independence, the Advisory Board supported Google's stance to limit the territorial scope of the right to de-list to European domains (*www.google.es, www.google.it, www.google.fr...*), thereby excluding non-EU domains (such as *www.google.com*).

The Report considered that the CJEU's ruling was not sufficiently precise regarding the search engine versions to which the right to de-list had to be applied, and refused to extend it to *www.google.com* using various arguments: a) Google's statistical argument: "Google has told us that over 95% of all queries originating in Europe are on local versions of the search engine. Given this background, we believe that delistings applied to the European versions of search will, as a general rule, protect the rights of the data subject adequately in the current state of affairs and technology;"[339] b) The competing interests outside of Europe: "there is a competing interest on the part of users outside of Europe to access

[337] *Report of the Advisory Council to Google on the Right to be Forgotten...*, p. 17.
[338] *Report of the Advisory Council to Google on the Right to be Forgotten...*, p. 18.
[339] *Report of the Advisory Council to Google on the Right to be Forgotten...*, p. 19

information via a name-based search in accordance with the laws of their country, which may be in conflict with the delistings afforded by the Ruling;"[340] c) The competing interests within Europe: "There is also a competing interest on the part of users within Europe to access versions of search other than their own;"[341] d) The repressive political regimes: "(...) if repressive regimes point to such a precedent in an effort to 'lock' their users into heavily censored versions of search results;"[342] e) The ineffectiveness of de-listing www.google.com: "It is unclear whether such measures would be meaningfully more effective than Google's existing model, given the widespread availability of tools to circumvent such blocks."[343]

Nevertheless, the insistence of the Advisory Council to uphold Google's refusal to extend the right to www.google.com did not prevent it from acknowledging a piece of irrefutable evidence: "In considering whether to apply a de-listing to versions of search targeted at users outside of Europe, including globally, we acknowledge that doing so may ensure more absolute protection of a data subject's rights."[344]

Finally, the Report suggested that Google should ensure the utmost transparency within the legal limits and the protection of the data subjects' privacy through anonymized and aggregated statistics, references to adopted policies, and the process and criteria used to evaluate de-listing requests.

Google's *Transparency Report*[345] expressly states the established policies and procedures to ensure the right to be forgotten. The data provided by Google (mere statistics) on the acknowledgment of the right to be forgotten are of little interest. From 29 May 2014 to 10 November 2016, Google received 579,480 requests *(assessing 1,766,675 URLs). Out of the URLs assessed overall, 644,537 (43.2 %) were removed, whereas 847,074 (56.8%) were not de-listed. If the figures are broken down by EU countries, it is worth noting the number of requests received from France (148,671), United Kingdom (98,460), Germany (85,491), Spain (49,753) or Italy (38,431).*

---

[340] *Report of the Advisory Council to Google on the Right to be Forgotten...*, p. 20
[341] *Report of the Advisory Council to Google on the Right to be Forgotten...*, p. 20
[342] *Report of the Advisory Council to Google on the Right to be Forgotten...*, p. 20
[343] *Report of the Advisory Council to Google on the Right to be Forgotten...*, p. 20
[344] *Report of the Advisory Council to Google on the Right to be Forgotten...*, p. 19
[345] https://www.google.com/transparencyreport/removals/europeprivacy/?hl=en

*Google's unsatisfactory transparency policy regarding the implementation of the right to be forgotten was exposed by the "Open Letter to Google: Release RTBF compliance data"[346] published by Internet scholars on 13 May 2015. According to this significant number of scholars, t*he "implementation of the ruling should be much more transparent for at least two reasons: (1) the public should be able to find out how digital platforms exercise their tremendous power over readily accessible information; and (2) implementation of the ruling will affect the future of the RTBF in Europe and elsewhere, and will more generally inform global efforts to accommodate privacy rights with other interests in data flows."[347]

The importance of transparency in handling requests involving the right to be forgotten is self-evident and it is perfectly illustrated by the Letter: "only about 1% of requesters denied de-listing are appealing those decisions to national Data Protection Authorities. Webmasters are notified in more than a quarter of de-listing cases. They can appeal the decision to Google, and there is evidence that Google may revise its decision. In the remainder of cases, the entire process is silent and opaque, with very little public process or understanding of de-listing."[348] There is no excuse for Google's lack of transparency. Effectively guaranteeing compliance with

---

[346] https://medium.com/@ellgood/open-letter-to-google-from-80-internet-scholars-release-rtbf-compliance-data-cbfc6d59f1bd#.ov0xsocwg

[347] The Letter established minimum parameters that Google had to publish as to ensure the right to be forgotten: categories of RTBF requests/requesters that are excluded or presumptively excluded and how those categories are defined and assessed; 2) categories of RTBF requests/requesters that are accepted or presumptively accepted and how those categories are defined and assessed; 3) proportion of requests and successful delistings that concern categories including: (a) victims of crime or tragedy; (b) health information; (c) address or telephone number; (d) intimate information or photos; (e) people incidentally mentioned in a news story; (f) information about subjects who are minors; (g) accusations for which the claimant was subsequently exonerated, acquitted, or not charged; and (h) political opinions no longer held. 4) breakdown of overall requests according to the Article 29 WP Guidelines categories; 5) reasons for denial of de-listing; 6) reasons for grant of de-listing; 7) categories of public figures denied de-listing; 8) source of material for de-listed; 9) proportion of overall requests and successful delistings concerning information first made available by the requestor; 10) proportion of searches for de-listed pages that actually involve the requester's name; 11) proportion of delistings for which the original publisher or the relevant data protection authority participated in the decision; 12) specification of (a) types of webmasters that are not notified by default; (b) proportion of delistings where the webmaster additionally removes information or applies robots.txt at source; and (c) proportion of delistings where the webmaster lodges an objection.

[348] https://medium.com/@ellgood/open-letter-to-google-from-80-internet-scholars-release-rtbf-compliance-data-cbfc6d59f1bd#.ov0xsocwg

the CJEU's ruling requires comprehensive public information by all search engines, and particularly from Google.

2.- THE EFFECTIVENESS OF THE ARTICLE 29 WORKING PARTY GUIDELINES ON THE IMPLEMENTATION OF THE CJEU'S JUDGMENT

On 26 November, 2014, Article 29 Working Party (WP) issued a document on the implementation of the CJEU's ruling: *Guidelines on the implementation of the Court of Justice of the European Union judgment on "Google Spain and Inc. v. Agencia Española de Protección de Datos (AEPD) and Mario Costeja González" C-131/121.* [349]

The Article 29 WP examined the CJEU's legal reasoning and laid down the common interpretative criteria to be followed by the national Data Protection Authorities regarding the implementation of the CJEU's ruling:

1) Search engines process personal data. Therefore, search engine providers must assume their responsibilities stemming from EU law; particularly, they must guarantee the rights to erasure and to object.

2) Search engine activities have a significant impact on the rights to privacy and data protection, since they enable a massive access to data as well as profiling. Data subject rights prevail over the economic interest of search engines, as well as over the interest of Internet users. However, we must weigh each situation on a case-by-case basis, in order to strike a fair balance between the rights and legal interests at stake: having regard to the type of information and the sensitivity of the data. The public interest of data will largely depend on the role played by the data subject in public life.

3) The rights to erasure and to object only affect the search results of name-based searches, but they do not require removing either search engine indexes or source website indexes. Personal information remains untouched on the original website, and it will be accessible by the search engine through keywords other than the data subject's name.

4) Freedom of information remains unaffected when personal information of public interest is involved, due to the very nature of the information or because it affects a public figure, since in this case the "right to be

---

[349]http://ec.europa.eu/justice/data-protection/article-29/documentation/opinion-recommendation/files/2014/wp225_en.pdf

forgotten" is not acknowledged. The impact of these rights on Internet editors' and users' freedoms of expression and information is very little.

5) Citizens may invoke the right to be forgotten vis-à-vis the search engine, with no need for a prior request to the original website. Search engine providers and webmasters process data in two very distinct ways, which differ in terms of lawfulness and impact on individuals' privacy.

6) Even if the source website's content is legal, the universal dissemination of a search engine, along with the additional information it provides following a name-based search, may unreasonably or disproportionately impact on individuals' privacy with the course of time.

7) Internal search engines of different sites or media web pages are unaffected by the CJEU's ruling, since they provide information from specific websites and do not allow to establish a complete profile of the affected individual.

8) Limiting the effectiveness of the CJEU's ruling to EU domains does not satisfactorily guarantee the rights of data subjects, and it implies circumventing EU law. The right to be forgotten should also be effective on all relevant domains accessible from the EU, including ".com".

9) The practice of informing users that the list of results to their queries is incomplete as per EU law is based on no legal requirement, unless users cannot conclude that one particular individual has invoked the right to be forgotten.

10) Informing the webmasters that some web pages cannot be accessed from the search engine in response to a specific name-based query has no legal basis, since webmasters do not have a right to be indexed.

11) Search engines should disclose the de-listing criteria they use, as well as detailed and anonymized statistics regarding the type of data whose oblivion has been accepted or rejected.

Furthermore, the Article 29 WP came up with a list of common criteria to assess the requests and complaints filed by individuals when their right to be forgotten is rejected, with the aim of achieving a harmonized implementation in the EU as a whole.

On 29 June 2015, the Article 29 Working Party began to assess the practice of national Data Protection Authorities, and it concluded that the right to be forgotten was effectively protected: a) each decision was adopted seeking a fair balance between the right to data protection and the public interest of information; b) all the criteria laid down in the Article 29 WP guidelines were relevant and effective, particularly those relating to whether the data subject was a "public figure" or whether he or she plays "a role in public life." However, DPAs considered necessary to carry out a more comprehensive evaluation of the requests, and it further specified when a given piece of personal information must be de-listed because it is not "up to date." Search engines justified the cases where the right to be forgotten was rejected, mostly based on the connection of personal data with professional activities or with current events.

3.- THE FRENCH DATA PROTECTION AUTHORITY (CNIL) SANCTIONS GOOGLE: GOOGLE'S MISLEADING ANNOUNCEMENT EXTENDING THE RIGHT TO BE FORGOTTEN TO THE ".COM" DOMAIN

The French Data Protection Authority (CNIL) has played a key role in the implementation of the CJEU's ruling in connection with the broadening of its territorial scope to the domain "www.google.com." In fact, on 24 March 2016, the CNIL imposed a EUR 100,000 fine on Google for its refusal to comply with the CNIL Chair's injunction to extend de-listing to all of its search engine's domain name extensions.

After the CJEU's ruling, the CNIL asked Google to de-list results regardless of the domain name's geographic extension (".fr," ".com," etc.). Google accepted to de-list only on the search engine's European geographic extensions. In May 2015, the CNIL Chair issued a formal injunction to extend de-listing to all of the "Google Search" extensions. Given Google's failure to comply with the injunction, the CNIL decided to fine Google: "The right to be de-listed is derived from the right to privacy, which is a universally recognized fundamental right laid down in international human rights law. Only de-listing on all of the search engine's extensions, regardless of the extension used, or the geographic origin of the person performing the search, can effectively uphold this right."[350]

The CNIL's decision was based on the following legal reasoning: 1) Google search engine service represents a single processing operation and the different geographic extensions (".fr," ".es," ".com," etc.) cannot be considered separate processing operations. 2) For people residing in France to effectively exercise their right to be de-listed, the de-listing must be applied to the entire processing operation. 3) Applying de-listing to all of the extensions does not curtail freedom of expression insofar as it

---

[350] https://www.cnil.fr/en/right-be-de-listed-cnil-restricted-committee-imposes-eu100000-fine-google

does not entail any deletion of content from the Internet because these pages can still be accessed when the search is performed using words other than the name and last name.[351]

On 11 February 2016, Google had announced its intention to extend the right to be forgotten to all its domains accessed in the EU: "Search results removals will now be applied to domains beyond Europe, including google.com, if the browser is located within the European Union."[352] However, Google's announcement was tricky, as evidenced by the response to one of its Frequently Asked Questions (FAQs) included in the Transparency Report: "We de-list URLs from all European Google Search domains (google.fr, google.de, google.es, etc.) and use geolocation signals to restrict access to the URL from the country of the person requesting the removal. For example, let's say we de-list a URL as a result of a request from John Smith in the United Kingdom. Users in the UK would not see the URL in search results for queries containing [john smith] when searching on any Google Search domain, including google.com. Users outside of the UK could see the URL in search results when they search for [john smith] on any non-European Google Search domain."[353]

Ultimately, as had already reported to the CNIL, Google simply prevented that any person located in Europe could access the ".com" domain. However, any user from outside the EU could still access such content under an EU domain using "google.com."

4.- THE INCONSISTENT CASE LAW OF THE SPANISH SUPREME COURT. THE AEPD SANCTIONS GOOGLE FOR NOTIFYING THE WEBMASTER

Following the CJEU's ruling, the Spanish National High Court (*Audiencia Nacional*) decided to apply the CJEU's doctrine to all pending and future cases involving the right to be forgotten. Obviously, upon examining the circumstances of each specific case, Spain's High Court

---

[351] Google appealed to the *Conseil d'État* against the CNIL decision to apply search results ruling to all its domains ("Google takes right to be forgotten battle to France's highest court", 19 May 2016, https://www.theguardian.com/technology/2016/may/19/google-right-to-be-forgotten-fight-france-highest-court).

[352] "Google to extend 'right to be forgotten' to all its domains accessed in EU," *The Guardian*, 11 February 2016 (https://www.theguardian.com/technology/2016/feb/11/google-extend-right-to-be-forgotten-googlecom).

[353] 10.11.16, https://www.google.com/transparencyreport/removals/europeprivacy/faq/?hl=en

either upheld or dismissed the requests for de-listing.

Many High Court decisions were appealed to the Supreme Court, which surprisingly applied blatantly contradictory doctrines depending on the Chamber hearing the appeal: the Civil Chamber strictly abided by the CJEU's legal reasoning; nonetheless, the Contentious-Administrative Chamber inexplicably disregarded the CJEU's arguments and reviewed core aspects of the right to be forgotten regarding the differing degree of responsibility of Google Spain and Google Inc.

Supreme Court Judgment (STS) no. 1280/2016 of 5 April 2016, delivered by the Civil Chamber, confirmed that Google Spain could be the defendant in a fundamental rights protection procedure, since it is held accountable in Spain for any data processing activities carried out by Google Search. This accountability must be construed in broad terms, in line with the purpose of the Directive.

As regards evidence, STS no. 1280/2016 stated the following: Google Inc. has designated Google Spain as the entity responsible in Spain for processing two files registered by Google in the Spanish Data Protection Agency (AEPD); as soon as the AEPD has urged Google Spain to stop the processing of data of a given individual, such processing has been cancelled. Google Spain has accepted to be a party to prior proceedings regarding the effects in Spain of Google's search engine activity. Such data processing is performed within the scope of the Spanish parent company's and subsidiary's joint activities: "The *effet utile* of EU law would be largely diminished if data subjects had to find out the specific functions of each company comprising a large corporation that owns a search engine. In fact, this information is sometimes a business secret, and in any case not publicly accessible. The Directive's *effet utile* would also be undermined if the data controller's specific legal form in each Member State became a significant aspect, as intended by Google Spain. Actually, this would force data subjects to bring claims against companies established abroad. Even if data subjects were to bring an action in Spain, it would be complicated for most individuals to file a fundamental rights protection claim against a company with registered office in the United States; seeking an effective legal remedy within a reasonable time period would also be difficult, because it is expensive to translate the claim and any related documents into English, as well as because of the delays attached to summoning the defendant (since international legal assistance would have to be sought). In light of the foregoing, the fundamental rights at stake could be further breached due to the said delays and drawbacks)." The foregoing arguments are conclusive and consistent with the CJEU's Judgment.

Notwithstanding the foregoing, STS no. 964/2016, of 14 April 2016, takes an unexpected turn -with unforeseeable consequences. In this ruling, Google Spain was deemed as the data controller (and thus responsible for the processing of data) and the entity responsible for guaranteeing the right to be forgotten.

STS no. 964/2016 denies that Google Spain's and Google Inc.'s joint responsibility could only arise from the fact that both companies make up a business unit. According to the Spanish Supreme Court, joint or shared liability can only be established if it has not been proven that Google Spain carries out data indexation activities. In order for Google Spain to be held liable, its involvement in the purposes and means of processing must be determined on a case-by-case basis, "which has not occurred in this case with respect to Google Spain." Google Spain's liability cannot be based on its business or corporate ties with Google Inc.: "Google Inc. actually operates the search engine -Google Search, and there is no evidence whatsoever of any involvement of Google Spain, S.L., whose activities are in line with those of an establishment (either a subsidiary or a branch) of Google Inc. Accordingly, Google Spain, S.L. is a company intended to sell search engine advertising space, and thus its activities are economically connected with its parent company's, yet essentially different from the determination of purposes and means of processing. There must be no confusion between determining the purposes and means of processing, which define a data controller, and any other supporting activities aimed at achieving the aims pursued." In sum, STS no. 964/2016 runs counter to the binding doctrine set out in the CJEU's ruling, and it ends up excluding Google Spain's liability.[354] This inconsistency[355] within the Spanish Supreme Court and with respect to

---

[354] It is surprising that STS no. 964/2016 is based on the following argument from authority to allocate liability between Google Inc. and Google Spain: "the foregoing conclusion is ratified by Google Inc.'s actions. In the light of the CJEU's Judgment, of 13 May 2014, Google Inc. has decided to set up an Advisory Council made up of experts in EU law and headed by Google Inc.'s CEO. The purpose of this council is to comply with the so-called 'right to be forgotten' online acknowledged in the abovementioned ruling. In order to effectively implement this right with regards to potential users of its search engine, it has made available to all potential users a form to request the deletion of personal data, and such request would have to be assessed by the Advisory Council. Google Inc.'s decision evidences that it is the sole responsible for the data processing of its search engine, and not Google Spain, S.L.".

[355] JOSÉ LÓPEZ CALVO: "*Sobre la aparente discrepancia entre la Salas Contencioso y Civil del TS sobre derecho al olvido. Un problema de diferente visión sobre la congruencia entre pretensiones de las partes y fallo. Google Sp, al menos, como establecimiento de Google Inc.*", ed. Sepín, April 2016 (http://www.sepin.es/revistas-digitales/revista.asp?cde=50&id=31443).

the CJEU will inevitably trigger legal claims that will have to be settled by the CJEU.

In addition, the implementation of the CJEU's ruling, as well as of the criteria laid down by the Article 29 WP Guidelines, led the AEPD to impose a EUR 150,000 fine on Google Inc. on 14 September 2016, for communicating to the webmasters the "URLs" that had been removed based on the right to be forgotten.

On 26 March 2015, various complaints were filed for the notices provided by Google to two Spanish media announcing the removal of results with content published by those media, as well as for Google's warning on its website, which stated the following: "we submit a copy of all legal notices we receive to the Chilling Effects project for publication and recording purposes. Chilling Effects (...) provides a database of requests for content removal from the Internet." In fact, on 9 December 2015 and 23 February 2016, additional complaints were filed regarding web addresses from the domain *lumendatabase.org*,[356] where complaints for content removal on the Internet are accessible by Spanish citizens. In other words, the subject-matter of the complaints included the policy of notices submitted to users on incomplete results and the reporting to third parties of the results that were de-listed by the search engine.

The AEPD concluded that such notice to webmasters is neither compatible with the de-listing search results, nor justified by a search engine's legitimate interest or by webmasters' freedom of expression. EU data protection law does not require search engines to report to

---

[356] "Lumen is a project of the Berkman Klein Center for Internet & Society at Harvard University. Lumen is an independent 3rd party research project studying cease and desist letters concerning online content. We collect and analyze complaints about online activity, especially requests to remove content from online. Our goals are to educate the public, to facilitate research about the different kinds of complaints and requests for removal -both legitimate and questionable- that are being sent to Internet publishers and service providers, and to provide as much transparency as possible about the 'ecology' of such notices, in terms of who is sending them and why, and to what effect. Our database contains millions of notices, some of them with valid legal basis, some of them without, and some on the murky border. Our posting of a notice does not indicate a judgment among these possibilities, nor are we authenticating the provenance of notices or making any judgment on the validity of the claims they raise. Lumen is a unique collaboration among law school clinics and the Electronic Frontier Foundation. Conceived and developed at the Berkman Klein Center for Internet & Society by Berkman Fellow Wendy Seltzer, Lumen was nurtured with help from law clinics at Harvard, Berkeley, Stanford, University of San Francisco, University of Maine, George Washington School of Law, and Santa Clara University School of Law" (https://www.lumendatabase.org/pages/about).

webmasters that certain content results published thereby have been removed. The AEPD established that the said notice constitutes data processing: "when Google notifies an editor that a given URL has been blocked pursuant to a request based on data protection legislation, editors are being notified that one of the identified individuals included on the website to which that URL directs has requested blocking. Sometimes, the data subject can be identified straight away, when there is only a first name on the website. However, some other times there will be several first names, which does not preclude that personal data are being transmitted, which may affect every data subject, some of them, or just one" (Resolution no. 2232/2016). This processing of data requires a legal basis that cannot be found in Directive 95/46/EC. Therefore, search engines should not notify webmasters that some websites will not appear in name-based search results.[357]

---

[357] Indeed, in the allegations made in these sanctioning proceedings, Google reported that it was preparing a list of web categories for which it would be inappropriate to submit such notices: "for instance, Google has adopted a policy of not submitting notices to webmasters of pornographic sites. Google is increasing the categories of malicious websites whose webmasters will not receive any notices (...). Google's intention is to ensure that the approach is balanced and proportionate."

ANNEX

*GUIDELINES ON THE IMPLEMENTATION OF THE COURT OF
JUSTICE OF THE EUROPEAN UNION JUDGMENT ON "GOOGLE
SPAIN AND INC V.* AGENCIA ESPAÑOLA DE PROTECCIÓN DE
DATOS (AEPD) AND MARIO COSTEJA GONZÁLEZ" C-131/12.

ARTICLE 29 DATA PROTECTION

Adopted on 26 November 2014

EXECUTIVE SUMMARY

1. Search engines as data controllers

The ruling recognises that search engine operators process personal data
and qualify as data controllers within the meaning of Article 2 of
Directive 95/46/EC. The processing of personal data carried out in the
context of the activity of the search engine must be distinguished from,
and is additional to that carried out by publishers of third-party websites.

2. A fair balance between fundamental rights and interests

In the terms of the Court, "in the light of the potential seriousness of the
impact of this processing on the fundamental rights to privacy and data
protection, the rights of the data subject prevail, as a general rule, over the
economic interest of the search engine and that of internet users to have
access to the personal information through the search engine". However,
a balance of the relevant rights and interests has to be made and the
outcome may depend on the nature and sensitivity of the processed data
and on the interest of the public in having access to that particular
information. The interest of the public will be significantly greater if the
data subject plays a role in public life.

3. Limited impact of de-listing on the access to information

In practice, the impact of the de-listing on individuals' rights to freedom
of expression and access to information will prove to be very limited.
When assessing the relevant circumstances, DPAs will systematically
take into account the interest of the public in having access to the

information. If the interest of the public overrides the rights of the data subject, de-listing will not be appropriate.

4. No information is deleted from the original source

The judgment states that the right only affects the results obtained from searches made on the basis of a person's name and does not require deletion of the link from the indexes of the search engine altogether. That is, the original information will still be accessible using other search terms, or by direct access to the publisher's original source.

5. No obligation on data subjects to contact the original website

Individuals are not obliged to contact the original website in order to exercise their rights towards the search engines. Data protection law applies to the activity of a search engine acting as a controller. Therefore, data subjects shall be able to exercise their rights in accordance with the provisions of Directive 95/46/EC and, more specifically, of the national laws that implement it. 3.

6. Data subjects' entitlement to request delisting

Under EU law, everyone has a right to data protection. In practice, DPAs will focus on claims where there is a clear link between the data subject and the EU, for instance where the data subject is a citizen or resident of an EU Member State.

7. Territorial effect of a de-listing decision

In order to give full effect to the data subject's rights as defined in the Court's ruling, de-listing decisions must be implemented in such a way that they guarantee the effective and complete protection of data subjects' rights and that EU law cannot be circumvented. In that sense, limiting de-listing to EU domains on the grounds that users tend to access search engines via their national domains cannot be considered a sufficient means to satisfactorily guarantee the rights of data subjects according to the ruling. In practice, this means that in any case de-listing should also be effective on all relevant domains, including .com.

8. Information to the public on the delisting of specific links

The practice of informing the users of search engines that the list of results to their queries is not complete as a consequence of the application of European data protection law based on any no legal requirement under data protection rules. Such a practice would only be acceptable if the information is presented in such a way that users cannot, in any case, conclude that one particular individual has asked for the removal of results concerning him or her.

9. Communication to website editors on the delisting of specific links

Search engines should not as a general practice inform the webmasters of the pages affected by removals of the fact that some web pages cannot be acceded from the search engine in response to a specific name-based query. There is no legal basis for such routine communication under EU data protection law.

In some cases, search engines may want to contact the original editor in relation to particular request prior to any delisting decision, in order to obtain additional information for the assessment of the circumstances surrounding that request.

Taking into account the important role that search engines play in the dissemination and accessibility of information posted on the Internet and the legitimate expectations that webmasters may have with regard to the indexing and presentation of information in response to users' queries, the Working Party 29 (hereinafter: the Working Party) strongly encourages the search engines to provide the delisting criteria they use, and to make more detailed statistics available.

TABLE OF CONTENTS

PART I: Interpretation of the CJEU Judgment

PART II: List of common criteria for the handling of complaints by European data protection authorities

PART I: Interpretation of the CJEU Judgment

This document is designed to provide information as to how the European Data Protection Authorities ("DPAs") assembled in the Article 29 Working Party intend to implement the judgment of the Court of Justice of the European Union (hereinafter: CJEU) in the case of "Google Spain SL and Google Inc. v Agencia Española de Protección de Datos (AEPD) and Mario Costeja González" (C-131/12). It also contains the list of common criteria which the DPAs will apply to handle the complaints, on a case-by-case basis, filed with their national offices following refusals of de-listing by search engines. The list of criteria should be seen as a flexible working tool which aims at helping DPAs during the decision-making processes. The criteria will be applied in accordance with the relevant national legislations. No single criterion is, in itself, determinative. The list of criteria is non-exhaustive and will evolve over time, building on the experience of DPAs.

A. Search engines as controllers and legal ground

1. The ruling recognizes that search engine operators process personal data and do it as controllers in the meaning of articles 2 of Directive 95/46 (Paragraphs 27, 28 and 33).

2. The processing of personal data carried out in the context of the activity of the search engine can be distinguished from and is additional to that carried out by publishers of websites, which consists in loading the

data on an internet page (Paragraph 35).

3. The legal ground for that processing under the EU Directive is to be found in Article 7(f), the necessity for the legitimate interest of the controller or of the third parties to which data are disclosed (Paragraph 73).

4. The processing carried out by the operator of a search engine is liable to affect significantly the fundamental rights to privacy and to the protection of personal data when the search by means of that engine is carried out on the basis of an individual's name, since that processing enables any internet user to obtain through the list of results a structured overview of the information relating to that individual that can be found on the internet — information which potentially concerns a vast number of aspects of his private life and which, without the search engine, could not have been interconnected or could have been only with great difficulty — and thereby to establish a more or less detailed profile of him. Furthermore, the effect of the interference with those rights of the data subject is heightened on account of the important role played by the internet and search engines in modern society, which render the information contained in such a list of results ubiquitous (Paragraph 80).

5. In relation to the balance of interests that may legitimate the processing carried out by the search engine, according to the ruling, the rights of the data subject prevail as a general rule, over the economic interest of the search engine, in light of the of the potential seriousness of the impact of this processing on the fundamental rights to privacy and data protection. These rights also generally prevail over the rights of internet users to have access to the personal information through the search engine in a search on the basis of the data subject's name. However, a balance has to be struck between the different rights and interests and the outcome may depend on the nature and sensitivity of the processed data and on the interest of the public to have access to that particular information on the other, an interest which may vary, in particular, by the role played by the data subject in public life (Paragraph 81).

6. Data subjects have the right to request and, if the conditions laid down by articles 12 and 14 of Directive 95/46 are met, to obtain the removal of links to web pages published by third parties containing information relating to them from the list of results displayed following a search made on the basis of a person's name.

7. The respective legal grounds of original publishers and search engines are different. The search engine should carry out the assessment of the different elements (public interest, public relevance, nature of the data,

actual relevance...) on the basis of its own legal ground, which derives from its own economic interest and that of the users to have access to the information via the search engines and using a name as terms of search. Even when (continued) publication by the original publishers is lawful, the universal diffusion and accessibility of that information by a search engine, together with other data related to the same individual, can be unlawful due to the disproportionate impact on privacy.

The ruling does not oblige search engines to permanently carry out that assessment in relation to all the information they process, but only when they have to respond to data subjects' requests for the exercise of their rights.

8. The interest of search engines in processing personal data is economic. But there is also an interest of internet users in receiving the information using the search engines. In that sense, the fundamental right of freedom of expression, understood as "the freedom to receive and impart information and ideas" in article 11 of the European Charter of Fundamental Rights, has to be taken into consideration when assessing data subjects' requests.

9. The impact of the exercise of individuals' rights on the freedom of expression of original publishers and users will generally be very limited. Search engines must take the interest of the public into account in having access to the information in their assessment of the circumstances surrounding each request. Results should not be delisted if the interest of the public in having access to that information prevails. But even when a particular search result is delisted, the content on the source website is still available and the information may still be accessible through a search engine using other search terms.

B. Exercise of rights

10. Data Protection law applies to the activity of a search engine acting as a controller. Therefore, data subjects should be able to exercise their rights in accordance with the provisions of Directive 95/46 and, more specifically, of the national laws that implement it.

11. Individuals are not obliged to contact the original site, either previously or simultaneously, in order to exercise their rights towards the search engines. There are two different processing operations, with differentiated legitimacy grounds and also with different impacts on the individual's rights and interests. The individual may consider that it is better, given the circumstances of the case, to first contact the original webmaster to request the deletion of information or the application of "no

index" protocols to it, but the judgment does not require this.

12. By the same reason, an individual may choose how to exercise his or her rights in relation to search engines by selecting one or several of them. By making a request to one or several search engines the individual is making an assessment of the impact of the appearance of the controverted information in one or several of the search engines and, consequently, makes a decision on the remedies that may be sufficient to diminish or eliminate that impact.

13. While Directive 95/46 does not contain specific provisions on the means for the exercise of rights, most national data protection laws provide for great flexibility in that regard and offer data subjects the possibility of lodging their requests in a variety of ways, irrespective of the fact that the controller may have established "ad hoc" procedures.

Consequently, and as a best practice that would be in line with all possible legal requirements in all EU Member States, data subjects should be able to exercise their rights with search engine operators using any adequate means. Although the use of specific mechanisms that may be developed by search engines, namely online procedures and electronic forms, may have advantages and would be advisable because of its convenience, it should not be the exclusive way for data subjects to exercise their rights.

14. For the same reasons, search engines must follow national data protection laws with regard to the requirements for making a request and for the timeframes and contents of the answers. In particular, when a data subject requests delisting of some links, some form of identification may be demanded by the data controller, but, again, in line with what national laws consider necessary and proportionate in order to verify the identity of the applicant in the context of the request. When the controller collects identification information, adequate safeguards should be in place.

In order for the search engine to be able to make the required assessment of all the circumstances of the case, data subjects must sufficiently explain the reasons why they request delisting, identify the specific URLs and indicate whether they fulfill a role in public life, or not.

15 When a search engine refuses a delisting request, it should provide sufficient explanation to the data subject about the reasons for the refusal. It should also inform data subjects that they can turn to the data protection authority or to court if they are not satisfied with the answer. Such explanations should also be provided by data subjects to the DPA, in case they decide to refer to it.

16. The ruling considers that Google's national subsidiaries in the EU are establishments of the company and that Google's personal data processing in the search engine is carried out in the context of activities of these establishments which makes EU data protection rules applicable.

Directive 95/46 does not contain any specific provision with regard to the responsibility of establishments of the controller located in the territory of Member States. The only reference is in article 4.1.a, that states that "when the same controller is established on the territory of several Member States, he must take the necessary measures to ensure that each of these establishments complies with the obligations laid down by the national law applicable". This provision is to some extent clarified by Recital 19: "when a single controller is established on the territory of several Member States, particularly by means of subsidiaries, he must ensure, in order to avoid any circumvention of national rules, that each of the establishments fulfils the obligations imposed by the national law applicable to its activities;"

The effective application of the ruling and of data protection law requires that data subjects may exercise their rights with the national subsidiaries of search engines in their respective Member States of residence, and also that DPAs may contact their respective national subsidiaries in relation to requests or complaints lodged by data subjects.

These subsidiaries are of course free to follow internal procedures to deal with the requests, either directly or by forwarding the requests to other establishments of the company. It might also be reasonable to expect that as a first reaction they advise data subjects to use the "ad hoc" procedures developed by the company and the corresponding electronic forms. But if the data subject insists in contacting the national subsidiary they should not reject the request.

C. Scope

17. The ruling is specifically addressed to generalist search engines, but that does not mean that it cannot be applied to other intermediaries. The rights may be exercised whenever the conditions established in the ruling are met.

18. Search engines included in web pages do not produce the same effects as "external" search engines. On the one hand, they only recover the information contained on specific web pages. On the other, and even if a user looks for the same person in a number of web pages, internal search engines will not establish a complete profile of the affected individual

and the results will not have a serious impact on him, Therefore, as a rule the right to de-listing should not apply to search engines with a restricted field of action, particularly in the case of search tools of websites of newspapers.

19. Article 8 of the EU Charter, to which the ruling explicitly refers in a number of paragraphs, to, recognizes the right to data protection to "everyone". In practice, DPAs will focus on claims where there is a clear link between the data subject and the EU, for instance where the data subject is a citizen or resident of an EU Member State.

20. As stated by the Court, EU law applies, and the ruling must be implemented with regard to the processing operation that consists in "finding information published or placed on the internet by third parties, indexing it automatically, storing it temporarily and, finally, making it available to internet users according to a particular order of preference".

The CJEU maintains that "Article 12(b) and subparagraph (a) of the first paragraph of Article 14 of Directive 95/46 are to be interpreted as meaning that, in order to comply with the rights laid down in those provisions and in so far as the conditions laid down by those provisions are in fact satisfied, the operator of a search engine is obliged to remove from the list of results displayed following a search made on the basis of a person's name links to web pages, published by third parties and containing information relating to that person".

Finally, the Court also states that "the operator of the search engine as the person determining the purposes and means of that activity must ensure, within the framework of its responsibilities, powers and capabilities, that the activity meets the requirements of Directive 95/46 in order that the guarantees laid down by the directive may have full effect and that effective and complete protection of data subjects, in particular of their right to privacy, may actually be achieved."

The ruling sets thus an obligation of results which affects the whole processing operation carried out by the search engine. The adequate implementation of the ruling must be made in such a way that data subjects are effectively protected against the impact of the universal dissemination and accessibility of personal information offered by search engines when searches are made on the basis of the name of individuals.

Although concrete solutions may vary depending on the internal organization and structure of search engines, de-listing decisions must be implemented in a way that guarantees the effective and complete protection of these rights and that EU law cannot be easily circumvented.

In that sense, limiting de-listing to EU domains on the grounds that users tend to access search engines via their national domains cannot be considered a sufficient means to satisfactorily guarantee the rights of data subjects according to the judgment. In practice, this means that in any case de-listing should also be effective on all relevant domains, including .com.

21. From the material point of view, and as it's been already mentioned, the ruling expressly states that the right only affects the results obtained on searches made by the name of the individual and never suggests that the complete deletion of the page from the indexes of the search engine is needed. The page should still be accessible using any other terms of search. It is worth mentioning that the ruling uses the term "name", without further specification. It may be thus concluded that the right applies to possible different versions of the name, including also family names or different spellings

D. Communication to third parties

22. It appears that some search engines have developed the practice of systematically informing the users of search engines of the fact that some results to their queries have been delisted in response to requests of an individual. If such information would only be visible in search results where hyperlinks were actually delisted, this would strongly undermine the purpose of the ruling. Such a practice can only be acceptable if the information is offered in such a way that users cannot in any case come to the conclusion that a specific individual has asked for the delisting of results concerning him or her.

The use of notices or statements should be made in a consistent way in order to prevent users from coming to wrong or incorrect assumptions. Given the difficulties that managing these statements on the basis of a specific type of search terms (i.e. whenever names are used) entails, it is advisable that this information is provided via a general statement permanently inserted on search engines' web pages.

23. Search engine managers should not as a general practice inform the webmasters of the pages affected by removals of the fact that some webpages cannot be acceded from the search engine in response to specific queries. Such a communication has no legal basis under EU data protection law.

As stated before, there is a crucial difference between the legal ground for the processing by search engines, and the legal ground for the processing by the original publisher. Article 7.f serves as the legal ground for processing operations which are necessary for the purposes of the legitimate interests pursued by the controller or by the third party or parties to whom the data are disclosed, except where such interests are overridden by the interests for fundamental rights and freedoms of the data subject. The interest of the original webmasters in receiving the communication is questionable for a number of reasons. On the one hand, the delisting of a hyperlink in a search result in a search for a person's name only has limited impact, as described before. On the other hand, original webmasters cannot make an effective use of the communication received, as it affects a processing operation carried out by the controller over which they have no control or influence. As a matter of fact, search engines do not recognize a legal right of publishers to have their contents indexed and displayed, or displayed in a particular order.

In any case, that interest should be balanced with the rights, freedoms and interests of the affected data subject.

No provision in EU data protection law obliges search engines to communicate to original webmasters that results relating to their content have been delisted. Such a communication is in many cases a processing of personal data and, as such, requires a proper legal ground in order to be legitimate. No legal ground can be found in article 7 of Directive 95/46 to routinely communicate de-listing decisions to primary controllers.

On the other hand, it may be legitimate for search engines to contact original publishers prior to any decision about a delisting request, in particularly difficult cases, when it is necessary to get a fuller understanding about the circumstances of the case. In those cases, search engines should take all necessary measures to properly safeguard the rights of the affected data subject.

Taking into account the important role that search engines play in the dissemination and accessibility of information posted on the Internet and the legitimate expectations that webmasters may have with regard to the indexation of information and display in response to users' queries, the Working Party strongly encourages the search engines to publish their own delisting criteria, and make more detailed statistics available.

E. Role of the DPAs

24. Despite the novel elements of the CJEU judgment, deciding whether a particular search result should be delisted involves – in essence - a routine assessment of whether the processing of personal data done by the search engine complies with the data protection principles. Therefore the Article 29 Working Group considers that complaints submitted by data subjects

to DPAs in respect of refusals or partial refusals by search engines are to be treated – as far as is possible - as formal claims as envisaged by Article 28(4) of the Directive. Accordingly, such appeals should normally be treated by DPAs under their national legislation in the same manner as all other claims/complaints/requests for mediation.

25. The Chair of the Working Party will contact search engines in order to clarify which EU establishment should be contacted by the competent DPA and will make the results of the consultation public if necessary.

Part II: List of common criteria for the handling of complaints by European data protection authorities

In its decision on 13 May 2014, the CJEU clarified the application of data protection law of to search engines. It concluded that users can request search engines, under certain conditions, to delist certain links to information affecting their privacy from the results for searches made against their name. Where a search engine refuses such a request, the data subject may bring the matter before the DPAs, or the relevant judicial authority, so that they carry out the necessary checks and take a decision in accordance with their power in national law.

It follows from the CJEU judgment that a data subject may "request [from a search engine] that the information [relating to him personally] no longer be made available to the general public on account of its inclusion in […] a list of results". The Court also ruled that "those rights override, as a rule, not only the economic interest of the operator of the search engine but also the interest of the general public in having access to that information upon a search relating to the data subject's name". This right is recognised by the CJEU in the light of the fundamental rights granted under Articles 7 and 8 of the European Charter of Fundamental Rights and in application of Article 12(b) and subparagraph (a) of the first paragraph of Article 14 of Directive 95/46/EC ("the Directive").

The Court also recognised the existence of an exception to this general rule when "for particular reasons, such as the role played by the data subject in public life […], the interference with [the] fundamental rights [of the data subject] is justified by the preponderant interest of the general public in having, on account of [the] inclusion [of the information] in the list of results, access to the information in question".
A first analysis of the complaints so far received from data subjects whose delisting requests were refused by the search engines, has enabled DPAs to establish a list of common criteria to be used by them to evaluate

whether data protection law has been complied with. DPAs will assess complaints on a case-by-case basis, using the criteria below.

The list of criteria should be seen as a flexible working tool which will help DPAs during their decision-making process. The criteria will be applied in accordance with the relevant national legislation.

In most cases, it appears that more than one criterion will need to be taken into account in order to reach a decision. In other words, no single criterion is, in itself, determinative.

Each criterion has to be applied in the light of the principles established by the CJEU and in particular in the light of the "the interest of the general public in having access to [the] information".

1. Does the search result relate to a natural person – i.e. an individual? And does the search result come up against a search on the data subject's name?

The Google judgment recognised the particular impact that an internet search, based on an individual's name, can have on his or her right to respect for private life.

DPA's will also consider pseudonyms and nicknames as relevant search terms when the individual can establish that they are linked to his/her real identity.

2. Does the data subject play a role in public life? Is the data subject a public figure?

The CJEU has made an exception for delisting requests from data subjects that play a role in public life, where there is an interest of the public in having access to information about them. This criterion is broader than the 'public figures' criterion.

What constitutes "a role in public life"?

It is not possible to establish with certainty the type of role in public life an individual must have to justify public access to information about them via a search result.

However, by way of illustration, politicians, senior public officials, business-people and members of the (regulated) professions can usually be considered to fulfill a role in public life. There is an argument in favour of the public being able to search for information relevant to their public roles and activities.

A good rule of thumb is to try to decide where the public having access to the particular information – made available through a search on the data subject's name – would protect them against improper public or professional conduct.

It is equally difficult to define the subgroup of 'public figures'. In general, it can be said that public figures are individuals who, due to their functions/commitments, have a degree of media exposure.

The Resolution 1165 (1998) of the Parliamentary Assembly of the Council of Europe on the right to privacy provides a possible definition of "public figures". It states that "Public figures are persons holding public office and/or using public resources and, more broadly speaking, all those who play a role in public life, whether in politics, the economy, the arts, the social sphere, sport or in any other domain."

There may be information about public figures that is genuinely private and that should not normally appear in search results, for example information about their health or family members. But as a rule of thumb, if applicants are public figures, and the information in question does not constitute genuinely private information, there will be a stronger argument against de-listing search results relating to them. In determining the balance, the Jurisprudence of the European Court on Human Rights (hereinafter: ECHR) is especially relevant.

ECHR, van Hannover v. Germany, 2012: "The role or function of the person concerned and the nature of the activities that are the subject of the report and/or photo constitute another important criterion, related to the preceding one. In that connection a distinction has to be made between private individuals and persons acting in a public context, as political figures or public figures. Accordingly, whilst a private individual unknown to the public may claim particular protection of his or her right to private life, the same is not true of public figures (see Minelli v. Switzerland (dec.), no. 14991/02, 14 June 2005, and Petrenco, cited above, § 55). A fundamental distinction needs to be made between reporting facts capable of contributing to a debate in a democratic society, relating to politicians in the exercise of their official functions for example, and reporting details of the private life of an individual who does not exercise such functions (see Von Hannover, cited above, § 63, and Standard Verlags GmbH, cited above, § 47)."[1]

---

[1] *See also ECHR, Axel Springer v. Germany, 2012*

3. Is the data subject a minor?

As a general rule, if a data subject is legally under age – e.g. is he or she is not yet 18 years old at the time of the publication of the information – DPAs are more likely to require de-listing of the relevant results.

The concept of "best interests of the child" has to be taken into account by DPAs. This concept can be found, *inter alia*, in article 24 of Charter of fundamental rights of the EU: "In all actions relating to children, whether taken by public authorities or private institutions, the child's best interests must be a primary consideration".

4. Is the data accurate?

In general, 'accurate' means accurate as to a matter of fact. There is a difference between a search result that clearly relates to one person's opinion of another person and one that appears to contain factual information.

In data protection law the concepts of accuracy, adequacy and incompleteness are closely related. DPAs will be more likely to consider that de-listing of a search result is appropriate where there is inaccuracy as to a matter of fact and where this presents an inaccurate, inadequate or misleading impression of an individual. When a data subject objects to a search result on the grounds that it is inaccurate, the DPAs can deal with such a request if the complainant provides all the information needed to establish the data are evidently inaccurate.

In cases where a dispute about the accuracy of information is still ongoing, for example in court or when there is on on-going police investigation, DPAs may choose not to intervene until the process is complete.

5. Is the data relevant and not excessive? a. Does the data relate to the working life of the data subject? b. Does the search result link to information which is allegedly constitutes hate speech/slander/libel or similar offences in the area of expression against the complainant? c. Is it clear that the data reflect an individual's personal opinion or does it appear to be verified fact?

The overall purpose of these criteria is to assess whether the information contained in a search result is relevant or not according to the interest of the general public in having access to the information.

Relevance is also closely related to the data's age. Depending on the facts of the case, information that was published a long time ago, e.g. 15 years ago, might be less relevant that information that was published 1 year ago.

The DPA's will assess relevance in accordance with the factors set out below.

a. Does the data relate to the working life of the data subject?

An initial distinction between private and professional life has to be made by DPAs when they examine de-listing request.

Data protection - and privacy law more widely - are primarily concerned with ensuring respect for the individual's fundamental right to privacy (and to data protection). Although all data relating to a person is personal data, not all data about a person is private. There is a basic distinction between a person's private life and their public or professional persona. The availability of information in a search result becomes more acceptable the less it reveals about a person's private life.

As a general rule, information relating to the private life of a data subject who does not play a role in public life should be considered irrelevant. However, public figures also have a right to privacy, albeit in a limited or modified form.

Information is more likely to be relevant if it relates to the current working life of the data subject but much will depend on the nature of the data subject's work and the legitimate interest of the public in having access to this information through a search on his or her name.

Two additional questions are relevant here:

- Is data about a person's work related activity excessive?
- Is the data subject still engaged in the same professional activity?

b. Does the search result link to information which is excessive or allegedly constitutes hate speech/slander/libel or similar offences in the area of expression against the complainant?

DPAs are generally not empowered and not qualified to deal with information that is likely to constitute a civil or criminal 'speech' offence against the complainant, such as hate speech, slander or libel. In such cases, DPAs will likely refer the data subject to the police and/or to court if a delisting request is refused. The situation would be different if a court had ordered that the publication of the information is indeed a criminal offence, or in violation of other laws.

Nevertheless, DPAs remain competent to assess whether data protection law has been complied with.

c. Is it clear that the data reflect an individual's personal opinion or does it appear to be verified fact?

The status of the information contained in a search result mays also be relevant, in particular the difference between personal opinion and verified fact. DPAs recognise that some search results will contain links to content that may be part of a personal campaign against someone, consisting of 'rants' and perhaps unpleasant personal comments. Although the availability of such information may be hurtful and unpleasant, this does not necessarily mean that DPAs will consider it necessary to have the relevant search result delisted. However, DPAs will be more likely to consider the de-listing of search results containing data that appears to be verified fact but that is factually inaccurate.

6. Is the information sensitive in the meaning of Article 8 of the Directive?

As a general rule, sensitive data (defined in Article 8 of the Data Protection Directive as 'special categories of data') has a greater impact on the data subject's private life than 'ordinary' personal data. A good example would be information about a person's health, sexuality or religious beliefs. DPAs are more likely to intervene when delisting requests are refused in respect of search results that reveal such information to the public.

7. Is the data up to date? Is the data being made available for longer than is necessary for the purpose of the processing?

As a general rule, DPAs will approach this factor with the objective of ensuring that information that is not reasonably current and that has become inaccurate because it is out-of-date is de-listed. Such an assessment will be dependent on the purpose of the original processing.

8. Is the data processing causing prejudice to the data subject? Does the data have a disproportionately negative privacy impact on the data subject?

There is no obligation for the data subject to demonstrate prejudice in order to request de-listing, in other words prejudice is not a condition for exercising the right recognised by the CJEU. However, where there is evidence that the availability of a search result is causing prejudice to the data subject, this would be a strong factor in favour of de-lilisting.[2]

The Directive allows the data subject to object to processing where there are compelling legitimate grounds for doing so. Where there is a justified objection, the data controller must cease processing the personal data.

The data might have a disproportionately negative impact on the data subject where a search result relates to a trivial or foolish misdemeanor which is no longer – or may never have been – the subject of public debate and where there is no wider public interest in the availability of the information.

9. Does the search result link to information that puts the data subject at risk?

DPAs will recognise that the availability of certain information through internet searches can leave data subjects open to risks such as identity theft or stalking, for example. In such cases, where the risk is substantive, DPAs are likely to consider that the de-listing of a search result is appropriate.

10. In what context was the information published? a. Was the content voluntarily made public by the data subject? b. Was the content intended to be made public? Could the data subject have reasonably known that the content would be made public?

If the only legal basis for personal data being available on the internet is consent, but the individual then revokes his or her consent, then the processing activity – i.e. the publishing – will lack a legal basis and must therefore cease.

When assessing requests, the DPA will consider whether the link should be delisted even when the name or information is not erased beforehand or simultaneously from the original source.

In particular, if the data subject consented to the original publication, but later on, is unable to revoke his or her consent, and a delisting request is

---

[2] CJUE, Google Spain SL, Google Inc. v Agencia Española de Protección de Datos (AEPD), Mario Costeja González, 13 May 2014, para. 96, **"it must be pointed out that it is not necessary in order to find such a right that the inclusion of the information in question in the list of results causes prejudice to the data subject."**

refused, the DPAs will generally consider that de-listing of the search result is appropriate.

11. Was the original content published in the context of journalistic purposes?

DPAs recognise that depending on the context, it may be relevant to consider whether the information was published for a journalistic purpose. The fact that information is published by a journalist whose job is to inform the public is a factor to weigh in the balance. However, this criterion alone does not provide a sufficient basis for refusing a request, since the ruling clearly distinguishes between the legal basis for publication by the media, and the legal basis for search engines to organise search results based on a person's name.

12. Does the publisher of the data have a legal power – or a legal obligation – to make the personal data publicly available?

Some public authorities are under a legal duty to make certain information about individuals publicly available – for example for electoral registration purposes. This varies according to Member State law and custom. Where this is the case, DPAs may not consider that de-listing is appropriate whilst the requirement on the public authority to make the information publicly available persists. However, this will have to be assessed on a case-by-case basis, together with the criteria of 'outdatedness' and irrelevance.

DPAs may consider that de-listing is appropriate even if there is a legal obligation to make the content available on the original website.

13. Does the data relate to a criminal offence?

EU Member States may have different approaches as to the public availability of information about offenders and their offences. Specific legal provisions may exist which have an impact on the availability of such information over time. DPAs will handle such cases in accordance with the relevant national principles and approaches. As a rule, DPAs are more likely to consider the de-listing of search results relating to relatively minor offences that happened a long time ago, whilst being less likely to consider the de-listing of results relating to more serious ones that happened more recently. However, these issues call for careful consideration and will be handled on a case-by-case basis.

BIBLIOGRAPHY

ABRAMS, M.: "Data origin and the proposed regulation", *Hacia un nuevo derecho europeo de protección de datos*. *Towards a new European Data Protection Regime* (eds) A. Rallo & R. García, Tirant lo Blanch, Valencia, 2015, p. 101

AKDENIZ, Y.: "To block or not to block: European approaches to content regulation, and implications for freedom of expression", *Computer Law & Security Review*, vol. 26, 2010, pp. 260-272.

ALLEN, A. & ROTENBERG: M. *Privacy Law and Society* 1517-1552, West Academic, St. Paul, 2016.

ARENAS RAMIRO, M.:

- "El derecho a la protección de datos personales: de la Jurisprudencia del ECtHR a la del TJCE", *Constitución y Democracia. 25 años de Constitución democrática en España*, vol. I, Universidad del País Vasco, 2006, pp. 575-589.
- "El derecho a la protección de datos personales en la jurisprudencia del TJCE", *Revista Aranzadi de Derecho y Nuevas Tecnologías*, vol. 4, 2006, pp. 95-119.

AUSLOOS, J.: "The 'Right to be Forgotten' - Worth remembering?", *Computer Law & Security Review*, vol. 28, 2012, pp. 143 a 152.

BENYEKHLEF, K.: "Minors, social network sites and le droit à l'oubli", Rapport rédigé pour la Fundacion Solventia, Madrid, Espagne, Mars 2010, 40 pages (avec Philippe-Antoine Couture-Ménard et Emmanuelle Paquette-Bélanger).

BERNAL, P.A.: "A right to delete?", *European Journal of Law and Technology*, vol. 2-2, 2011, pp. 1 a 18.

BOIX PALOP, A.: "El equilibrio entre los derechos del artículo 18 de la Constitución. El `derecho al olvido´ y las libertades informativas tras la sentencia Google", *Revista General de Derecho Administrativo*, vol. 38, enero, 2015, pp. 1-40.

BROCK, G.: THE RIGHT TO BE FORGOTTEN: PRIVACY AND THE MEDIA IN THE DIGITAL AGE, I.B.Tauris & Reuters Institute for the Study of Journalism, University of Oxford, London-New York, 2016.

BURGSTALLER, P.: "Search engines and the extra-territorial dimension of the EC Data Protection Law", *Computer and Telecomunications Law Review*, vol. 15-5, 2009, pp. 104-113.

CARRILLO, M.: "El derecho al olvido en Internet", *El País*, 23 de octubre de 2009.

CASTELLS, M.: *La galaxia Internet*, Areté, Barcelona, 2011.

CATE, F.H.: "Principles of Internet Privacy", *Connecticut Law Review*, vol. 32, 2000, pp. 877-896.

CERNADA BADÍA, R.: "El derecho al olvido judicial en la red", *Libertad de expresión e información en la Red. Amenazas y protección de los derechos personales*, CEPC, Madrid, 2013, p. 521.

COLLINGWOOD, L.: "Privacy in Cyberworld: Why Lock the Gate After the Horse Has Bolted?", *European Journal of Law and Technology*, vol. 3-1, 2012, pp. 1-11.

CONLEY, Ch.: "The Right to Delete", AAAI Spring Symposium Series, North America, 2010, pp. 53-58 (http://www.aaai.org/ocs/index.php/SSS/SSS10/paper/view/1158/1482).

CORTÉS, C.: "Derecho al olvido: entre la protección de datos, la memoria y la vida personal en la era digital" (http://www.palermo.edu/cele/pdf/DerechoalolvidoiLEI.pdf).

CURRIE, R.J. and SCASSA, T.: "New first principles? Assessing the Internet's challenges to jurisdiction" *Georgetown Journal of International Law*, Summer, 2011, pp. 1017.

CHÉRON, A.: "Affaire MOSLEY/GOOGLE : liberté d'expression, atteinte à la vie privée et droit à l'oubli numérique», 12 février 2014, http://www.dalloz-actualite.fr/chronique/affaire-mosleygoogle-liberte-d-expression-atteinte-vie-privee-et-droit-l-oubli-numerique#.UvuYB_GYb4g.

CHEUNG, A.S.Y.: "Rethinking Public Privacy in the Internet Era: A Study of Virtual Persecution by the Internet Crowd', *The Journal of Media Law*, vol. 1, vol. 2, December, 2009, pp. 191-217.

CHURCH, P. and KON, G.: "Google at the heart of a data protection storm", *Computer Law & Security Report*, vol. 23, 2007, pp. 461-465.

DE HERT, P. Y PAPACONSTANTINOU, V.: "The proposed data protection Regulation replacing Directive 95/46/EC: A sound system for the protection of individuals", COMPUTER LAW & SECURITY REVIEW, VOL. 28-2, APRIL, 2012, PP. 130-142.

DE TERWANGE, C.: "Privacidad en Internet y el derecho a ser olvidado/derecho al olvido", *IDP Revista de Derecho, Internet y Política*, vol. 13, 2012, pp. 53-66.

DIAZ REVORIO, F.J.: *Los Derechos Humanos ante los nuevos avances Científicos y Tecnológicos: Genética e Internet ante la Constitución*, Tirant lo Blanch, Valencia, 2009.

DUASO CALES, R.: *La protection des données personnelles contenues dans les documents publics accessibles sur Internet: le cas des données judiciaires*, Mémoire présenté à la Faculté des études supérieures de l'Université de Montréal, Décembre, 2002.

DWYER, C.: "Privacy in the Age of Google and Facebook", *IEEE Technology and Society Magazine*, Fall, 2011, pp. 58-63.

ENISA: *The right to be forgotten – between expectations and practice*, European Network and Information Security Agency, 20 de noviembre de 2012, pp. 1-22 (http://www.enisa.europa.eu/activities/identity-and-trust/library/deliverables/the-right-to-be-forgotten).

EPIC: "The Right to Be Forgotten (Google v. Spain)," https://epic.org/privacy/right-to-be-forgotten/

FAZLIOGLU, M.: "Forget me not: the clash of the right to be forgotten and freedom of expression on the Internet", *International Data Privacy Law*, vol. 3-3, 2013, pp. 149-157.

FINOCCHIARO, G.:

- *Diritto all'anonimato: anonimato, nome e identitá personale* (ed.), Cedam, Padua, 2008.
- "La memoria della rete e il diritto all'oblio", *Il diritto dell'informazione e dell'informática*, vol. 3, 2010, pp. 391-404.

FLEISCHER, P.:

- "Foggy Thinking about the Right to Oblivion", 9 de Marzo de 2011, (http://peterfleischer.blogspot.com/2011/03/foggy-thinking-about-right-to-oblivion.html).

-   "'The Right to be Forgotten', seen from Spain", 5 de septiembre de 2011, (http://peterfleischer.blogspot.com/2011/09/right-to-be-forgotten-seen-from-spain.html).
-   "The right to be forgotten, or how to edit your history", 29 de enero de 2012, (http://peterfleischer.blogspot.co.uk/2012/01/right-to-be-forgotten-or-how-to-edit.html).

GARCIA SANZ, R.M.: "Redes sociales online: fuentes de acceso público o ficheros de datos personales privados (Aplicación de las Directivas de protección de datos y privacidad en las comunicaciones electrónicas)", *Revista de Derecho Político*, vol. 81, 2011, pp. 101-154.

GOLDBERG M.A.: "The googling of online privacy: gmail, search-engine histories and the new frontier of protecting private information on the web", *Lewis and Clark Law Review*, vol. 9-1, 2005, pp. 249-272.

GOMES DE ANDRADE, R.N.: "El olvido: El derecho a ser diferente... de uno mismo. Una reconsideración del derecho a ser olvidado", *IDP Revista de Derecho, Internet y Política*, vol. 13, 2012, pp. 67-83.

GREGORIO, C. y ORNELAS, L.: *Protección de datos personales en las redes sociales digitales: en particular de niños y adolescentes*, IFAI-IFI, México, 2011.

GRIMMELMANN, J.: "The Structure of Search Engine Law", *Iowa Law Review*, vol. 93, 2007-2008, pp. 1- 64.

GUERRERO PICO, M.C.:

-   "El derecho fundamental a la protección de los datos de carácter personal en la Constitución Europea", *Revista de Derecho Constitucional Europeo*, vol. 4, 2005, pp. 293-334.
-   *El impacto de Internet en el Derecho Fundamental a la Protección de Datos de Carácter Personal*, Thomson-Civitas, Pamplona, 2006.

HALLINAN, D., FRIEDEWALD, M. Y McCARTHY, P.: "Citizens' perceptions of data protection and privacy in Europe", *Computer Law & Security Review*, vol. 28, 2012, pp. 263-272.

HEISSL, G.: "Jurisdiction for Human Rights Violations on the Internet', *European Journal of Law and Technology*, vol. 2-1, 2011, pág. 1-15.

HENDEL, J.:

-   "Why Journalists Shouldn't Fear Europe's 'Right to be Forgotten'",

25 de enero de 2012 (http://www.theatlantic.com/technology/archive/2012/01/why-journalists-shouldnt-fear-europes-right-to-be-forgotten/251955/).
- "The West's Coming Internet War", 7 de junio de 2011 (http://www.theatlantic.com/technology/archive/2011/06/the-wests-coming-internet-war/240044/).

HIRSCH, D.D.: "The Law and Policy of Online Privacy: Regulation, Self-Regulation, or Co-Regulation?", *Seattle University Law Review*, vol.34, 2011, pp. 439-480.

HOFFMAN, D., BRUENING, P. & CARTER, S.: "The riht to obscurity: how we can implement the Google Spain", *North Carolina Journal of Law & Technology*, volume 17, Issue 3, march, 2016, pp. 437-482

KANG, J-M, SONG, Y-J, CHA, J-S Y LEE, S-H.: "A Study for Security Scheme and the Right to Be Forgotten Based on Social Network Service for Smart-Phone Environment", Kim et al. (eds.) ISA 2011, CCIS 200, Springer-Verlag Berlin Heidelberg , pp. 326-332.

KEELE, B.J.: "Privacy by deletion: the need for a global data deletion principle", *Indiana Journal of Global Legal Studies*, winter, vol. 16-1, 2009, pp. 363-384.

KOSTA, E., KALLONIATIS, Ch., MITROU, L. Y KAVAKLI, E.: "The ''Panopticon'' of search engines: the response of the European data protection framework", *Digital Privacy*, Springer, vol. 16, 2010, pp. 47-54.

KRANENBORG, H.: "Google and the Right to Be Forgotten (Case C-131/12, Google Spain)", *European Data Protection Law Review*, vol. 1-1, 2015, pp. 70-79.

KUMAYAMA, K.D.: "A right to pseudonymity", *Arizona Law Review*, summer, vol. 51, 2009, pp. 427-464.

KUNER, CH.:

- *European Data Protection Law. Corporate Compliance and Regulation*, Oxford University Press, Oxford, 2007.
- "Data Protection Law and International Jurisdiction on the Internet (Part 1)", *International Journal of Law and Information Technology,* vol. 18-2, 2010, pp. 176-193.

- "Data Protection Law and International Jurisdiction on the Internet (Part 2)", *International Journal of Law and Information Technology,* vol. 18-3, 2010, pp. 227-247.

LAIDLAW, E.B.: "Private Power, Public Interest: An Examination of Search Engine Accountability", *International Journal of Law and Information Technology,* vol. 17-1, 2008, pp. 113-145.

LA RUE, FR.: *Report of the Special Rapporteur on the promotion and protection of the right to freedom of opinion and expression,* Asamblea General de Naciones Unidas, 16 mayo 2011, pág. 1-22.

LEENHEER ZIMMERMAN, D.: "The 'New' Privacy and the 'Old': Is Applying the Tort Law of Privacy Like Putting High-Button Shoes on the Internet?", *Communication Law and Policy,* vol. 17-2, 2012, pp. 107-132.

LETA AMBROSE, M.: "It's About Time: Privacy, Information Life Cycles, and the Right to be Forgotten", *Stanford Technology Law Review,* vol. 16-2, 2013, pp. 101-154.

LEVIN, A. y SANCHEZ ABRIL, P.: "Two Notions of Privacy Online", *Vanderbilt Journal of Entertainment & Technology Law,* vol. 11-4, 2009, pp. 1001-1051.

LÓPEZ AGUILAR, J.F.: "Data protection package y Parlamento Europeo", *Hacia un nuevo derecho europeo de protección de datos. Towards a new European Data Protection Regime* (eds.) A. Rallo y R. García, Tirant lo Blanch, Valencia, 2015, pp. 29-81.

LÓPEZ CALVO, J.: *"Sobre la aparente discrepancia entre la Salas Contencioso y Civil del TS sobre derecho al olvido. Un problema de diferente visión sobre la congruencia entre pretensiones de las partes y fallo. Google Sp, al menos, como establecimiento de Google Inc.",* ed. Sepin, abril, 2016 (http://www.sepin.es/revistas-digitales/revista.asp?cde=50&id=31443).

LLANEZA GONZÁLEZ, P.: *Internet y comunicaciones digitales: régimen legal de las tecnologías de la información y de la comunicación,* Bosh, Barcelona, 2000.

MALLET, "Du droit à l'oubli numérique", *Recherche Droit et Justice,* vol. 37, novembre, 2011, pág. 9.

MARSOOF, A.: "Online Social Networking and the Right to Privacy: The Conflicting Rights of Privacy and Expression", *International Journal of Law and Information Technology*, vol. 19-2, 2011, pp. 110-132.

MARTINEZ, R.:

- *Una aproximación crítica a la autodeterminación informativa*, Civitas, Pamplona, 2004.
- "Protección de datos personales y redes sociales: un cambio de paradigma", *Derecho y Redes Sociales*, A. Rallo y R. Martínez (Eds.), 2ª edición, Civitas-Thomson Reuters, Pamplona, 2013, pp. 85-118.

MAYER-SCHÖNBERGER, V.:

- "Useful Void: The Art of Forgetting in the Age of Ubiquitous Computing", Harvard University, April 2007, pp. 1-24 (http://www.vmsweb.net/attachments/pdf/Useful_Void.pdf).
- *Delete: The Virtue of Forgetting in the Digital Age*, Princeton University Press, Oxford, 2009.

MILLIER, S.L.: "The Facebook Frontier: Responding to the Changing Face of Privacy on the Internet", *Kentucky Law Journal*, vol. 97, 2008-2009, pp. 541a 564.

MOEREL, L.: "The long arm of EU data protection law: Does the Data Protection Directive apply to processing of personal data of EU citizens by websites worldwide?", *International Data Privacy Law*, vol. 1, no. 1, 2011, pp. 28-46.

MOFFAT, V.R.: "Regulating Search", *Harvard Journal of Law & Technology*, vol. 22-2, Spring, 2009, pp. 475-513.

MOREHAM, N.: "The right to respect for private life in the European Convention on Human Rights: a re-examination", *European Human Rights Law Review*, vol. 1, 2008, pp. 44-79.

MOROZOV, E.: "¿Un seguro para Internet?", *El País*, 15 de marzo de 2012.

MUTH, K.T.: "Googlestroika: Privatizing Privacy", *Duquesne Law Review*, vol. 47, 2009, pp. 337-353.

NIGER, S.: "Il diritto all'oblio", *Diritto all'anonimato: anonimato, nome e identitá personale*, G. Finocchiaro (ed.), Cedam, Padua, 2008, pp. 59-73.

NYS, H.: "Towards a Human Right 'to Be Forgotten Online'?", *European Journal of Health Law,* vol. 18, 2011, pp. 469-475.

OHM, P: "Broken promises of privacy: responding to the surprising failure of anonymization", *UCLA Law Review,* 2010, vol 57, pp. 1701 1777.

O'REILLY C.: "Finding jurisdiction to regulate Google and the Internet", *European Journal of Law and Technology,* vol. 2-1, 2011, pp. 1-13.

ORTEGA JIMÉNEZ, A.: "Derecho Internacional Privado, protección de datos, responsabilidad extracontractual y redes sociales de Internet", *Derecho y Redes Sociales,* A. Rallo y R. Martínez (Eds.), 2ª edición, Civitas-Thomson Reuters, Pamplona, 2013, pp. 335-356.

PINO, C: "El derecho al olvido", *UNO d + i Llorente & Cuenca,* vol. 13, septiembre 2013, http://www.revista-uno.com/numero-13/el-derecho-al-olvido/

POST, R.: *Google Spain, the Right to Be Forgotten, and Personal Data,* draft 2, Yale Law School, 2016 (manuscript).

POULLET, Y.: "Flujos de datos transfronterizos y extraterritorialidad: la postura europea", *Revista Española de Protección de Datos,* vol. 1, julio-diciembre, 2006, pp. 93-113.

RALLO, A.:

- "La garantía del derecho constitucional a la protección de datos personales en los órganos judiciales", *Nuevas Políticas Públicas: Anuario multidisciplinar para la modernización de las Administraciones Públicas,* vol. 5, 2009, pp. 97-116.
- "A partir de la protección de Datos. El derecho al olvido y su protección", *TELOS. Cuadernos de Comunicación e Innovación (Los derechos fundamentales en Internet),* 2010, pp. 104 a108.
- "Hacia un nuevo sistema europeo de protección de datos: las claves de la reforma", *Revista de Derecho* Político, vol. 85, septiembre-diciembre, 2012, pp. 13-56.
- "Data Protection, Social Networks, and Online Mass Media" (with R. Martínez), *European Data Protection: Coming of Age,* Serge Gutwirth, Ronald Leenes, Paul De Hert and Yves Poullet Editors, ed. Springer, London-New York, 2013, pp. 407-430.
- "La protección de la privacidad en las redes sociales de Internet: la experiencia canadiense con facebook, google y otros", *Derecho y Redes Sociales,* A. Rallo Lombarte y R. Martínez

Martínez (Editores), 2ª edición, Civitas-Thomson Reuters, Pamplona, 2013, pp. 257-284.
- "El derecho al olvido en el tiempo de Internet: la experiencia española" (*Libertà in Internet. Percorsi Costituzionali*, vol. 1 2014, pp.159-192.
- "La garantía del 'derecho al olvido' en Internet", *Actualidad Jurídica Aranzadi*, vol. 886, 5 de junio de 2014, p. 5.
- "'Right to be forgotten' ruling is an Internet privacy watershed", *International Report. Privacy & Business*, núm. 129, june, 2014, págs.. 1 a 4
- *El derecho al olvido en Internet. Google versus Spain*, CEPC, Madrid, 2014.
- "El debate europeo sobre el derecho al olvido en Internet", *Hacia un nuevo derecho europeo de protección de datos. Towards a new European Data Protection Regime* (eds) A. Rallo & R. García, Tirant lo Blanch, Valencia, 2015, pp. 703-737.

RALLO, A. y MARTINEZ, R. (Eds.): *Derecho y redes sociales*, Civitas-Thomson Reuters, 2ª ed., Pamplona, 2013.

RALLO, A. & GARCÍA, R. (eds.): *Hacia un nuevo derecho europeo de protección de datos. Towards a new European Data Protection Regime*, Tirant lo Blanch, Valencia, 2015

REDING, VIVIANE:

- "Why the EU needs new personal data protection rules?", *The European Data Protection and Privacy Conference*, Brussels, 30 de Noviembre de 2010, (http://europa.eu/rapid/press-release_SPEECH-10-700_en.htm).
- "Building Trust in Europe's Online Single Market", Speech at the American Chamber of Commerce to the EU, Brussels, 22 June 2010 (http://europa.eu/rapid/press-release_SPEECH-10-327_en.htm?locale=en).
- "The EU Data Protection Reform 2012: Making Europe the Standard Setter for Modern Data Protection Rules in the Digital Age", Innovation Conference Digital, Life, Design, Munich, 22 January 2012 (http://europa.eu/rapid/press-release_SPEECH-12-26_en.htm).
- "The European data protection framework for the twenty-first century", *International Data Privacy Law*, 2012, Vol. 2, No. 3, pág. 125.
- "Justice for Growth makes headway at today's Justice Council", Informal Justice Council, Dublin, 18 January 2013

(http://europa.eu/rapid/press-release_SPEECH-13-29_en.htm).

REIDENBERG, J.R.:

- *Lex Informatica: The Formulation of Information Policy Rules Through Technology*, Texas Law Review, vol. 76-3, 1998, pp. 553-593.
- "Yahoo and Democracy on the Internet", *Jurimetrics*, 2002, vol. 42, pp. 261-280.
- "Technology and Internet Jurisdiction", *University of Pennsylvania Law Review*, vol. 153, 2005, pp. 1951-1974.

ROSEN, J.:

- "Free speech, privacy and the web that never forgets", *Telecommunications and High Technology Law*, vol. 9, 2011, pp. 346-356.
- "The right to be forgotten", *Stanford Law Review Online*, vol. 64, 2012, pp. 88-92.
- "'The Deciders: The Future of Privacy and Free Speech in the Age of Facebook and Google'", *Fordham Law Review*, vol. 80-4, 2012, pp. 1525-1538.

ROTENBERG, M.: "The Right to Privacy is Global," *US News and World Report*, Dec. 5, 2014, https://www.usnews.com/debate-club/should-there-be-a-right-to-be-forgotten-on-the-internet/the-right-to-privacy-is-global (on global implementation of Google v. Spain).

ROTH, P.: "Data Protection Meets Web 2.0: Two Ships Passing in the Night", *UNSW Law Journal Forum*, vol. 16-1, 2011, pp. 66-83.

ROUVROY, A.: "Réinventer l'art d'oublier et de se faire oublier dans la société de l'information", abril 2008 (http://works.bepress.com/antoinette_rouvroy/5).

RUIZ MIGUEL, C.: "El derecho a la protección de datos personales en la Carta de Derechos Fundamentales de la Unión Europea: análisis crítico", *Revista de Derecho Comunitario Europeo*, vol. 14, 2003, pp. 7-43

SARTOR, G. Y VIOLA DE AZAVEDO CUNHA, M.: "The Italian Google-Case: Privacy, Freedom of Speech and Responsibility of Providers for User-Generated Contents", *International Journal of Law and Information Technology*, vol. 18-4, 2010, pp. 356-378.

SIMÓN CASTELLANO, P.:

- "The right to be forgotten under European Law: a Constitutional Debate", *Lex Electronica*, vol. 16.1 (Hiver/Winter 2012), pp. 1-30.
- *El régimen constitucional del derecho al olvido digital*, Tirant lo Blanch, Valencia, 2012.
- "El carácter relativo del derecho al olvido en la red y su relación con otros derechos, garantías e intereses legítimos", *Libertad de expresión e información en la Red. Amenazas y protección de los derechos personales*, CEPC, Madrid, 2013, pp. 451 y ss.

SOLOVE, D.J.:

- *The future of reputation: gossip, rumor, and privacy on the Internet*, New Haven and London, Yale University Press, 2007.
- "I've Got Nothing to Hide" and Other Misunderstandings of Privacy", *San Diego Law Review*, vol. 44, 2007, pp. 745-772.

SZEKELY, I.: "The Right to Forget, the Right to be Forgotten. Personal Reflections on the Fate of Personal Data in the Information Society", S. Gutwirth et al. (eds.), *European Data Protection: In Good Health?*, Springer, 2012, pp. 347-363.

TENE, O.:

- "What Google knows: privacy and Internet search engines", *Utah Law Review*, vol. 4, 2008, pp. 1433-1492.
- "Privacy: The new generations", *International Data Privacy Law*, 2011, vol. 1-1, pp. 15-27.
- "Reforming data protection in Europe and beyond: a critical assessment of the second wave of global privacy laws", *Hacia un nuevo derecho europeo de protección de datos. Towards a new European Data Protection Regime* (eds) A. Rallo & R. García, Tirant lo Blanch, Valencia, 2015, pp. 143-206.

TRUDEL, P.:

- "L'oubli en tant que droit et obligation dans les systèmes juridiques civilistes", (http://www.chairelrwilson.ca/cours/drt6913/Notes%20oubli380 8.pdf).
- "Moteurs de recherche et respect de la vie privée: version préliminaire", Rapport pour la Journée "L'économie et le droit des moteurs de recherche", Paris, 16 de mayo de 2008.

- «La menace du 'droit à l'oublie'», 5 de octubre de 2013 (http://blogues.journaldemontreal.com/pierretrudel/droit/la-menace-du-droit-a-loubli/).

TÜRK, A.: *La vie privée en péril*, Odile Jacob, Paris, 2011.

USTARAN, E.: *The future of privacy*, manuscript, 2013, pp. 1-51.

VALENTINE, D.A.: "Privacy on the Internet: the evolving legal landscape", *Computer High Technology Law Journal*, vol. 16, 2000, pp. 401-417.

VAN ALSENOY, B. & KOEKKOEK, M-: *Internet and jurisdiction after Google Spain: the extraterritorial reach of the EU's "right to be forgotten"*, Working Paper No. 152, Leuven Centre for Global Governance Studies, March 2015.

VAN EECKE, P., CRAIG, C. Y HALPERT, J.: "The first insight into the European Commission's proposal for a new European Union Data Protection Law", *Journal of Internet Law*, February, 2012, pp. 19 y ss.

VILASAU SOLANA, M.: "El caso Google Spain: la afirmación del buscador como responsable del tratamiento y el reconocimiento del derecho al olvido (análisis de la STJUE de 13 de mayo de 2014)", *Revista de Internet, Derecho y Política*, vol. 18, junio, 2014, pp. 16-32.

VLADECK, D.: "Separated by common goals: A U.S. perspective on narrowing the U.S.-EU privacy divide", *Hacia un nuevo derecho europeo de protección de datos. Towards a new European Data Protection Regime* (eds) A. Rallo & R. García, Tirant lo Blanch, Valencia, 2015, pp. 207-243.

VOLOKH, E. and FALK, D.M.: *First Amendment Protection for Search Engine Search Results*, Paper Commissioned by Google, April, 2012, UCLA School of Law, http://www.volokh.com/wp-content/uploads/2012/05/SearchEngineFirstAmendment.pdf

WARNER, J.: "The Right to Oblivion: Data Retention from Canada to Europe in Three Backward Steps", *Law & Technology Journal*, University of Ottawa, pp. 75-104.

WEBER, R. H.: "The Right to Be Forgotten: More Than a Pandora's Box?", *Journal of Intellectual Property, Information Technology and E-Commerce Law*, vol. 2, 2011, p. 120-130 (http://www.jipitec.eu/issues/jipitec-2-2-2011/3084).

WERRO, F.: "The Right to Inform v. the Right to be Forgotten: A Transatlantic Crash", *Liability in the Third Millennium, Liber Amicorum Gert Brüggemeier*, Baden-Baden, 2009, pp. 285-300.

WONG, R.: "Data Protection: The future of privacy", *Computer Law & Security Review*, 27, 2011, pp. 53 y ss.

WOO, J.: "The right not to be identified: privacy and anonymity in the interactive media environment", *New Media Society*, vol. 8-6, 2006, pp. 949-967 (http://nms.sagepub.com/content/8/6/949).

ZITTRAIN, J.: *The future of the Internet and how to stop it*, Yale University Press, New Haven, 2008.